1 SAMUEL–ESTHER

Morning Conversations

on the Rise and Fall of Kings and Kingdoms

Days 237–436 of your
devotional journey through
the Old Testament with

JON R. ROEBUCK

© 2022

Published in the United States by Nurturing Faith, Macon, GA.
Nurturing Faith is a book imprint of Good Faith Media (goodfaithmedia.org).
Library of Congress Cataloging-in-Publication Data is available.

ISBN: 978-1-63528-174-3

All rights reserved. Printed in the United States of America.

Scripture quotations taken from the (NASB®) New American Standard Bible®, Copyright © 1960, 1971, 1977, 1995, 2020 by The Lockman Foundation. Used by permission. All rights reserved. www.lockman.org

Scripture quotations marked (NLT) are taken from the Holy Bible, New Living Translation, copyright ©1996, 2004, 2015 by Tyndale House Foundation. Used by permission of Tyndale House Publishers, Carol Stream, Illinois 60188. All rights reserved.

Scripture quotations marked (NIV) are taken from the Holy Bible, New International Version®, NIV®. Copyright © 1973, 1978, 1984, 2011 by Biblica, Inc.™ Used by permission of Zondervan. All rights reserved worldwide. www.zondervan.com The "NIV" and "New International Version" are trademarks registered in the United States Patent and Trademark Office by Biblica, Inc.™

Dedication

This volume is dedicated to Rabbi Mark Schiftan, whose friendship I value, whose insight I enjoy, and whose spirit I admire.

Contents

Preface 1

1 Samuel 2
    Days 237 through 267

2 Samuel 33
    Days 268 through 291

1 Kings 57
    Days 292 through 313

2 Kings 79
    Days 314 through 338

1 Chronicles 104
    Days 339 through 367

2 Chronicles 133
    Days 368 through 403

Ezra 169
    Days 404 through 413

Nehemiah 179
    Days 414 through 426

Esther 192
    Days 427 through 436

Preface

Welcome to Volume 2 of a 5-volume collection of devotional thoughts from the Old Testament. *Morning Conversations on The Rise and Fall of Kings and Kingdoms* takes the reader through nine books of biblical history. Once again, I invite you to join with me in a fresh devotional read through the pages of the Old Testament text. My goal in writing is not to exhaustively interpret, translate, or provide full commentary on every chapter of the Old Testament, but to help you engage with the text and perhaps draw some meaningful application for each day. I have discovered a number of fascinating ways the truth of God's Word leaps off the page and into my heart. It is my hope that some of my reflections will help you with your discovery of scripture and the role of faith in your life. I use the word "Conversations" with great intentionality. I think Bible study should happen that way. God is revealed to us through God's story, and then we reflect and offer back to God the thoughts of our hearts. It is a conversation… a back-and-forth dialogue. Conversations invite us to ponder, reflect, inquire, learn, and grow.

As you read through these volumes, my hope is that you will take the time, not to simply read what I have written, but to reflect with me on what the ancients have written. Let me challenge you each morning to take a moment to read the suggested focus chapter from a trusted translation before you dive into the words I have written. Read and reflect. As you make your way through this book, and the other volumes in the set, you will discover a lot of my life story written into these pages. But more importantly, I hope you will discover a lot about God's story… the one carefully crafted and preserved for you. For in hearing God's story, you will hear the echoing refrain of God's desire to know you, to love you, and to redeem you. Welcome to the conversation.

Morning Conversations Volumes 1-5

Morning Conversations on the Creation of a People and Place is the first volume of a set that follows the natural order of the Old Testament canon, and spans the Biblical narrative from the opening chapter of Genesis to the end of the book of Ruth.

Morning Conversations on the Rise and Fall of Kings and Kingdoms continues the orderly progression, spanning the books of 1 Samuel through Esther.

Morning Conversations on the Wisdom of the Ages covers all five books of wisdom literature from Job to the Song of Solomon.

Morning Conversations on the Prophetic Word wraps up the Old Testament with a look at the books of prophecy, covering both the Major and Minor prophets, Isaiah through Malachi.

Additionally, *Morning Conversations on the New Testament* is the final volume of this collection, offering perspective from each chapter of the New Testament.

Day 237 — 1 Samuel 1: Desperate, Honest Prayers

> "'Oh no, sir!' she replied. 'I haven't been drinking wine or anything stronger. But I am very discouraged, and I was pouring out my heart to the Lord.'" 1 Samuel 1:15 (NLT)

Observation
The book of Samuel begins with the story of Elkanah, a Jewish man with two wives, Hannah and Peninnah. The family makes an annual pilgrimage to Shiloh to worship and make sacrifices. The wives receive a portion of the meat used in the sacrifice. Hannah, who is barren and childless, receives only one portion. Peninnah, who has born several children to Elkanah, receives several portions for herself and her children. Peninnah mocks Hannah, breaking her heart. Hannah prays to God out of her distraught state of mind. She promises God that if God would give her a son, that she would dedicate him, for all his life, to serving God. Eli watches her as she prays, but not hearing any words, he assumes that she is drunk. She reveals the words of her prayer indicating that she was "pouring out her heart to the Lord." God hears her prayer, and a son, Samuel, is born. She fulfills her vow after the child is several years of age by presenting him to Eli for service in the tabernacle.

Application
Having served as a pastor for more than 32 years, I have seen my share of distraught persons, pouring out their hearts over the difficulties in their lives. Some have shared about betrayal while others have lamented broken friendships. Still others have sobbed their way through grief and others have confessed poor choices and bad mistakes. I learned through the years not to try to "fix" all their ills, but to simply listen to their brokenness. I discovered that there was a catharsis as they poured out their hearts to a listening, non-judgmental ear.

Certainly, Hannah's experience echoes the same refrain. Amid great emotional upheaval, she pours out her thoughts before the Lord in prayer, laying bare all her emotions, pain, and sorrow. She finds a gentle grace and comfort through the experience. She can return to her family, no longer sad.

This is an abusive life that we live. We are abused by sadness, disappointment, failure, shame, and injustice. Our hearts are sometimes torn, and our minds are filled with distraction and despair. Where to turn? What action to take? Difficult moments are not the time to abandon our faith, but to cling to it with even greater resolve. Like Hannah, we need to pour out our hearts before the Lord. We need to pray honest, authentic, and consistent prayers, knowing that God hears each word we utter. God listens with compassion, healing, and redemption. God promises peace as we bring our needs before Him.

Prayer
Father may we know both the joy and peace of pouring out our hearts to you. Amen.

Day 238 — 1 Samuel 2: Turning a Deaf Ear to Warning

> "But Eli's sons wouldn't listen to their father, for the Lord was already planning to put them to death." 1 Samuel 2:25b (NLT)

Observation
This chapter opens with the prayer of Hannah, praising God answering her prayer by giving her a son, Samuel. Once he is old enough, Samuel is left with Eli to begin his life of service to the Lord, according to the vow that his mother had made. He will continue to grow up in the presence of the Lord, finding favor in the eyes of God. Woven into the verses of the chapter is the story of Hophni and Phinehas, the sons of Eli who serve as priests. They are corrupt and they "have no respect for the Lord or for their duty as priests." They did not heed the warnings of their father, Eli, about their disobedient behavior. Our focus verse indicates that God will deal harshly with them because of their sinfulness.

Application
Years ago, I spent the summer between my junior and senior years of high school working in a lumber mill, just on the outskirts of my hometown of Rome, Georgia. It had to be the hottest summer of my life. It was hard work. I, along with my co-workers, labored in the hot Georgia sun from early morning until late afternoon. By the end of the summer I had a great tan and some well-toned muscles. One of the experiences that I vividly remember from that summer job was something that happened on the very first day. One of the "seasoned" employees was told to show several of us around the mill. When we got to the shed where much of the raw timber was transformed into smooth planks of wood, our guide said, "Be careful around the saws." And then he held up his hand, exposing the damage done to his hand years earlier by a saw when a blade completely removed two of his fingers. Message received. I've been afraid of saws ever since. There is wisdom in hearing a warning and responding appropriately.

The scriptures contain numerous words of warning for us to read. The most poignant deal with the problem of sin. "For all have sinned and fall short of the glory of God… For the wages of sin is death" (Romans 3:23, 6:23 NASB). We are warned about our sin problem. We are told that only through the intervention of a Savior will we find hope and salvation. In response to the warning, many of us place our faith and trust in Christ. But some don't. The warning falls on deaf ears. Part of our role as believers is to clearly sound the warning to those who are allowing sin to separate them from God. If we fail to warn our friends, we bear some of the responsibility for their destruction. Let's be fervent about our faith and deliberate in the way we share the Gospel story with others.

Prayer
Father, place in us a zeal to share the story of Jesus with others. Amen.

Day 239   1 Samuel 3: Hearing God in the Dark Night

> "The lamp of God had not yet gone out, and Samuel was sleeping in the Tabernacle near the Ark of God. Suddenly the Lord called out, 'Samuel!'"
> 1 Samuel 3:3-4a (NLT)

Observation

This chapter tells of God's calling on his life, when Samuel heard the Lord's voice for the first time. The narrative indicates that "messages from the Lord were rare, and visions were quite uncommon." And so, it is not surprising that young Samuel did not recognize nor expect a "verbal" conversation with Almighty God. Notice that Samuel is sleeping in the tabernacle where he can tend to the lampstand that was to burn throughout the night. Sleeping in the tabernacle symbolizes his nearness to God's presence and purpose as opposed to Eli and his sons who are apparently some distance away both physically and spiritually. The voice of God calls Samuel in the middle of the dark night. As Samuel learns to respond to the voice of God, God carefully reveals His message and intent to Samuel.

Application

Let's talk about the dark night for a moment. We have all had them. I'm not describing some stormy night when the power goes out and everything becomes black as pitch. Instead, I am describing those chapters in our lives when the darkness of uncertainty, despair, and defeat seems to envelop our hearts and minds. We have all experienced those moments, whether we are lying in our beds wide awake in the wee hours of the morning with our minds racing a hundred miles an hour, or whether we sit in our office cubicles staring off into space, unable to hold a coherent thought because the darkness has overcome us. I'm describing those moments when we are anxious, worried, and uncertain about our life's direction and purpose. We wonder if God has forgotten about us or abandoned us to reap the results of the poor choices we have made or the directions we have traveled that take us far from Him.

But look to the story of Samuel. It is during the dark night that God clearly spoke to him. And as he learned to recognize the voice of God, the fog of uncertainty began to lift. It happens that way to us as well. As we prayerfully and honestly seek God's direction, a sense of discernment begins to chase away the darkness. It is in the stillness of our dark nights when the voice of God can clearly be heard. It is as we arrive at that moment when self-sufficiency and human wisdom run dry, that we suddenly find ourselves able to hear the still, quiet voice of God in our lives. Though none of us want to endure the dark nights, it is amid such difficult moments that we can experience the voice of God with great clarity and great assurance. The key is quietening the voices within so that we can hear His greater voice.

Prayer

Father God, we ask that you visit us during our dark nights. May we find comfort in your presence and direction for our journey. Amen.

Day 240 — 1 Samuel 4: Excited for the Wrong Reasons

> "When all the Israelites saw the Ark of the Covenant of the Lord coming into the camp, their shout of joy was so loud it made the ground shake!"
> 1 Samuel 4:5 (NLT)

Observation
As the scene opens, the Israelites are at war with the Philistines, that powerful nation in Southwest Palestine with five large cities. In a skirmish, 4000 Israelite soldiers are killed. Perplexed by the defeat, the Israelites decide to bring the Ark of the Covenant with them into battle, believing that by doing so, they will ensure the presence of God in their midst as they fight. Seeing the Ark on the battlefield brings such hope to the army that they shout so loudly that the ground shakes! The Philistines see the Ark and think, "We must now fight harder than ever before." The next day is a horrific day for the Israelites, when 30,000 soldiers are killed, including the sons of Eli. And to make matters worse, the Ark of the Covenant is captured and hauled back to the land of the Philistines. When Eli hears the news of the battle and the loss of his sons and the Ark, he falls over backward in his chair, breaks his neck, and dies.

Application
The ancient Israelites made a horrible mistake. They treated the Ark of the Covenant as though it was a good luck charm. They reasoned that if they just invoked the name of God over their plans, that somehow that would make those plans the will of God. How could they lose if they just used a little godspeak? When the Ark showed up in their camp, they shouted for joy so loudly that the ground shook under their feet. They thought they were celebrating a certain victory, but all they were celebrating was how foolish their plans had become.

Most of us who live in the Bible belt are guilty of the same infraction. No, we don't haul around a model of the Ark of the Covenant every time we leave the house, but we have become astute at throwing around a little godspeak whenever we need for our plans to sound better than those of our neighbors. We say things like this, "God told me…" or "I know God would want me to…" or even, "I need to vote for this candidate; it's God's answer for our troubles." Do you see the problem? We think that just because we connect God's name to our opinions or plans, that somehow, they are infallible. We think that as long as we invoke God's name that God is somehow joined to our purposes. The next time you think God capitulates to your whim, ask yourself a few questions concerning authority. Our goal is to discover the will of God and seek to follow God's plan. It is never our place to make our plans and foolishly think that God will be manipulated into compliance.

Prayer
Father God, forgive the foolishness of our days whenever we think that we can force your hand. Amen.

Day 241 — 1 Samuel 5: Putting God in the Wrong Place

> "The people summoned the Philistine rulers again and begged them, 'Please send the Ark of the God of Israel back to its own country, or it will kill us all.' For the deadly plague from God had already begun, and great fear was sweeping across the town." 1 Samuel 5:11 (NLT)

Observation
As you may recall from the previous chapter, the Philistines had captured the Ark of the Covenant while defeating the Israelites in battle. They took it from the battle ground at Ebenezer to their town of Ashdod where they placed it in the temple next to the idol of their pagan god, Dagon. The next morning, they discovered that the idol had toppled over. It was returned to its usual spot, but the next morning, not only had it toppled over again, but this time it also had broken into pieces. Soon, people in the town were afflicted with tumors. The Ark was then moved to Gath but again the people in the community were afflicted with tumors. The decision was made to move it to Ekron, but the people were afraid and ordered that it be returned to Israel. Many had already perished because of its presence in their midst.

Application
Sometimes we attempt to put God in the wrong place. Let's be clear about something. God is omnipresent. God is found in every place. There is no spot on the planet where we can ever travel where God's presence cannot be found, and God's voice not heard. The problem, however, is not where God can be found, but where we try to place God. Sometimes we ask God to stand beside and coexist with the gods of our own creation. We claim that God is Lord, while placing God among a lot of things that we claim to love, some of which we elevate to a status that may rival that of our Heavenly Father's place. Also, we sometimes place God in compromising positions. Galatians 2:20 states, "I have been crucified with Christ; and it is no longer I who live, but Christ lives in me; and the life that I now live in the flesh I live by faith in the Son of God, who loved me, and delivered Himself up for me" (NASB). When we profess faith in Christ, the spirit of the living Lord indwells our lives. Our bodies, our thoughts, our actions must become those of Jesus. So, when we choose to sin, we take the body of Christ and force it to be joined to our transgressions. It's odd… the very sins we want to hide from God are committed by the body that we claim is the one belonging to God.

Let's be careful today where we choose to take God. Surely, we won't stand God next to our false gods, or force God into a compromising position, will we?

Prayer
Father God, teach us that to claim your lordship means that you are to have absolute authority over all that we are and do and say. Amen.

Day 242 — 1 Samuel 6: The Value of Self Control

> "But the Lord killed seventy men from Beth-shemesh because they looked into the Ark of the Lord. And the people mourned greatly because of what the Lord had done. 'Who is able to stand in the presence of the Lord, this holy God?'" 1 Samuel 6:19-20a (NLT)

Observation
After enduring seven months of plagues and afflictions, the Philistines decided to return the Ark of the Covenant to Israel. They placed the Ark on a wooden cart drawn by two cows. As a sin offering, a small box that contained five golden tumors and five golden rats to symbolize the pestilence and plagues brought upon the five cities of the Philistines also was loaded onto the cart. The cows and cart were placed on the road that headed to Beth-shemesh. If the cows continued straight down the road and did not turn to the right or to the left, it would be a sign that God was controlling all that had taken place. When the cows pulled the cart back to Israelite territory, the people rejoiced when they saw it. They built an altar and sacrificed the cows as a form of worship. The story ends with a twist, however. Some of the men of Beth-shemesh did not honor the sacred nature of the Ark and after looking into the Ark, they perished.

Application
When Paul lists the fruit of the spirit in Galatians 5:22-23, he includes the quality of self-control. In other words, all believers who have allowed the indwelling Spirit of God to control their lives, can see various qualities emerging in their lives like, love, joy, peace, patience… etc. We can practice self-control whenever we allow the Spirit's authority to rule our lives. We will be governed, not by human thought, but by the Spirit's leadership. That helps us to make better choices and live the kinds of lives that honor God.

But notice the sin of the men of Beth-shemesh. When the Ark was returned, they decided to peek. Surely, they knew better. They knew that the Ark represented the presence of God in their midst and yet they treated it as a curiosity and not as a sacred object. They did not practice self-control and it cost them dearly. Our lack of self-control will cost us as well. For example, if we lack self-control in our diets, we will put on the pounds. If we lack self-control in our driving habits, we will receive a ticket. If we lack self-control in our work habits, we will become lazy and unproductive. If we lack self-control in our relationships, we will discover brokenness and pain. And… if we lack self-control in our disciplines of faith, we will soon find ourselves in a position of atrophy rather than growth. So, as you maneuver your way through the challenges of another day, practice a little self-control in every facet of your life. As the Spirit guides your journey, be attentive and responsive.

Prayer
Father God, we thank you for your leadership in our lives. May we have the wisdom and strength to practice self-control. Amen.

Day 243   1 Samuel 7: Here I Raise My Ebenezer

"The Ark remained in Kiriath-jearim for a long time—twenty years in all. During that time all Israel mourned because it seemed the Lord had abandoned them." 1 Samuel 7:2 (NLT)

Observation

In this chapter, the Ark of the Covenant is moved to Kiriath-jearim where it would remain for the next 20 years. This is a very difficult and dark time for the Israelites, when they even feel abandoned by God. Samuel calls the nation together at Mizpah and tells them of the need to repent for their disobedience and idol worship. As they gather to worship, the Philistines see an opportunity to attack. But during the attack, God (who was never far away from the Israelites) intervenes with a "mighty voice of thunder." The Philistines are thrown into such confusion that they are easily defeated. Samuel raises a stone in a field as a reminder of what God had done. He named the stone, "Ebenezer," which means, "Stone of help." From that time forward until the time of his death, Samuel becomes the last great judge of Israel.

Application

On my desk at work, I keep one of those little sticky note dispensers close at hand. From time to time, I will reach for one of those sticky notes and quickly jot down something that I need to remember. You've done the same thing many times. Sometimes we need to be reminded of an important name, date, meeting, etc.

The ancient Israelites erected a stone in a field and named it Ebenezer. Every time they passed by the spot, they would be reminded how, in their dark depression and fearful moment, God offered help and sustained their lives. Maybe we need to raise a few Ebenezer stones in our lives. Ever get into one of those seasons of life when you feel a little left out spiritually? You feel as though God is far away and removed from the day-to-day events of your life. You entered a dark period where you felt abandoned by God. Maybe there have been tragic events in your life. Maybe illness has plagued you for too long. Maybe a job loss or a recent move has left you feeling a little abandoned. The truth is that all of us struggle with those thoughts from time to time. We would be less-than-honest if we claimed that we never had a moment when we didn't struggle a little with our faith. That's why the Ebenezer stone was important to Israel. In the dark moments, they could look at the rock and be reminded of God's continual presence, power, and intervention in their lives. Maybe it would help for us to have tangible reminders of our faith. I'm not suggesting that you build a huge memorial in your front yard, but you ought to figure out a way to remind yourself of an answered prayer or a special blessing in your life. Plant a tree in the yard. Put a picture on your mantle. Write a word above your doorpost. Find a way to be reminded constantly of God's work in your life.

Prayer

Heavenly Father, thank you for your constant watch care over all of us. Amen.

Day 244 — 1 Samuel 8: Be Careful What You Wish For

> "But the people refused to listen to Samuel's warning. 'Even so, we still want a king,' they said. 'We want to be like the nations around us. Our king will judge us and lead us into battle.'" 1 Samuel 8:19-20 (NLT)

Observation
As the narrative continues, Samuel is aging along with his influence. He wants to appoint his own sons as judges over Israel in his place. But they are greedy. They have taken bribes. They have perverted justice. So, the elders of Israel gather and say to Samuel, "Give us a king like all the other nations around us." Samuel is angered by their insolence. But God reminds him that they are not rejecting his leadership, but the leadership of God. Samuel warns the people about the evils that having a king will bring. Sons will be drafted into military service. Fields will be confiscated. Wives and daughters will be enslaved. Taxes will be levied. Samuel even warned them with these words, "You will beg for relief from this king you are demanding, but then the LORD will not help you" (1 Samuel 8:18 NLT). Despite all the warnings, the people continued to cry out for a king.

Application
Sometimes our judgment gets clouded and we wish for things we think we want and need, but in reality, we would be better off not having. Years ago, I owned a German sports car. And ever since I sold it, I have always wanted another German-engineered car. One day I spotted a beautiful dark-blue Volkswagen Passat on a local car lot. I pulled in and looked it over. I test drove it. I haggled with the salesman. I finally determined that my life wouldn't be complete unless I owned it. There were some red flags that I should have seen. First, it had no warranty remaining. Second, I knew nothing about the dealership from which I purchased the car. And third, I paid too much to get it. But none of that outweighed my desire to have the car. And it was a great car... at least when it was running. By the end of the first year of ownership I had already spent more than $4000 in maintenance and repairs. It really was a disaster because I refused to listen to common sense and to the little words of caution in my head.

Think about your sense of judgment. Could it be that from time to time you have considered making a decision or committed to some action without really thinking through the consequences or counting the costs? Have you wished for something so badly that you even rejected God's direction for your life? God promises in the Bible to grant us wisdom if we will just ask (James 1:5). But more than asking for God's help, we must be willing to listen to God's counsel. We must be hearers and doers. There are many voices that attempt to speak wisdom into our hearts. We need to pray for discernment and then for the courage to follow the directions, and only the directions that God outlines for our lives.

Prayer
Dear God, give us wisdom we don't possess, and courage we rarely exhibit. Amen.

Day 245 — 1 Samuel 9: Looking the Part

> "His son Saul was the most handsome man in Israel—head and shoulders taller than anyone else in the land." 1 Samuel 9:2 (NLT)

Observation

As always, God was arranging people, places, and events to further God's will. The donkeys of a rich man named Kish wandered off and so his son and a servant are sent to find them. The son's name was Saul, described in our focus verse as, "the most handsome man in Israel." After several days of searching, the servant remembers that a prophet of God lives in the area and suggests that they go to him to see if he can help. As they enter the region of Zuph, they encounter Samuel. Samuel had heard from God on the previous day, that on this very day God would send him a man from the tribe of Benjamin to anoint as the first King of Israel. Samuel invites Saul and his servant into his home and the relationship between Samuel and Saul begins.

Application

If you were going to look for a king, a leader, a president, a ruler… Saul is the man you would select. He was the best-looking guy in the whole country, and he was head and shoulders taller than all the rest. Who wouldn't choose him as the new king? He certainly looked the part. And, initially, he played the part. He had early victories against the Philistines and began to rally the people together to the point they would see themselves as a nation. But read the story to its conclusion and you will see that things didn't turn out all that well. He became ineffective. His reign was short-lived. He dealt with paranoia and disillusionment. His popularity faded as future King David emerged on the scene. He looked right for the part, but lacked the disciplines needed to be an effective leader, especially in terms of obedience to God.

When choosing the next king, God would say of David, "For God sees not as man sees for man looks at the outward appearance, but the Lord looks at the heart" (1 Samuel 16:7 NASB). Just because someone looks the part doesn't guarantee that he or she will become an effective leader. It takes more than looks. It takes compassion, obedience, faithfulness, dedication, resolve, etc. The problem is that we sometimes make our assessments of others based on appearance or first impressions. And yet, so often, our initial judgements are wrong. Some of the best people I know… some of the greatest servants of God, some of the best examples of Christ, are not the people I would have suspected based merely on outward appearances. I've made a few snap judgments, and first-impression decisions and they were wrong. My challenge for you today is to look beyond the outward appearance. Get to know people at a deeper level. Begin to see in them the special qualities that God has placed in their lives to do Kingdom work. See the worth of all people and rejoice in that perspective.

Prayer

Dear God, help us to see in others, the gifts and abilities that you have placed within them. Amen.

Day 246   1 Samuel 10: A Heart Transplant

> "As Saul turned and started to leave, God gave him a new heart, and all Samuel's signs were fulfilled that day." 1 Samuel 10:9 (NLT)

Observation
Chapter 10 begins with Samuel's anointing Saul as king over Israel in a very private ceremony. Samuel tells Saul that what God is doing in his life will be confirmed by several signs as he returns to his father's house. Along the way home, Saul even runs into a group of prophets and suddenly has the ability to prophesy with them. Later in the chapter, Samuel will gather all of Israel together at Mizpah, publicly declaring that God has set Saul aside to be the king of Israel. Samuel says of Saul, "This is the man the Lord has chosen as your king. No one in all Israel is like him!" (10:24 NLT).

Application
As soon as Samuel had privately anointed Saul, the Biblical record indicates that God gave him (Saul) a new heart. God was in the process of preparing the heart and mind of Saul for the task to which he had been called. New passions, new loyalties, and new insights entered the heart and mind of Saul.

Over the past several years I have added a new title to my life. It's "Grandfather," and I couldn't be prouder to hold that title. In fact, the granddaughters call me "Papa Jon." It melts my heart every time they do so. That title has also changed the way I view various aspects of my life. I pray more fervently. I love more compassionately. I laugh more joyfully. I dream more intentionally. Becoming a grandfather has changed me. The new title has made a difference.

In terms of our faith… in the moment we claim the title of "believer" everything changes. Our status is elevated because we now belong to Christ. We see and respond to the world in different ways. Like Saul, we are given a new heart by God. The old heart that focused selfishly on meeting our own needs suddenly becomes a new heart focused outwardly on others. The new heart beating within us causes us to seek ways to uplift the downtrodden, share with the needy, forgive the broken, and heal those who are injured. As Paul writes, "This means that anyone who belongs to Christ has become a new person. The old life is gone; a new life has begun!" (2 Corinthians 5:17 NLT). In Christ, desires change, passions emerge, thoughts are redirected, destinations are altered. Simply stated, we are not the same anymore.

The new title brings a new life. And the exciting lesson to discover is that the renewal of our hearts is a continual process. Each day God renews our hearts and makes us better. Even today… if you yield to the prompting of the Spirit, God will transform you even more.

Prayer
Dear Father, thank you for the new heart that you have placed in each of us. May the "Heart of God" within us overrule the human nature it has come to supplant. Amen.

Day 247 — 1 Samuel 11: Divide and Conquer

> "The remnant of their army was so badly scattered that no two of them were left together." 1 Samuel 11:11b (NLT)

Observation
One month into his new leadership role, Saul is tested. The king of the Ammonites gathers his army to assault the citizens of Jabesh-gilead, which is an Israelite city. The townspeople, knowing they are outnumbered, seek to strike a peace treaty with the Ammonites. In exchange for their lives, they agree to become the slaves of the Ammonites. The king agrees but with the provision that all the men will have their right eye gouged out as a sign of disgrace for all of Israel to see. The citizens are given a week to consider the conditions of the peace treaty. During that week, a message is sent forth throughout all of Israel. Saul hears of the dilemma and gathers 330,000 men to battle the Ammonites. Saul and his army prevail in a most powerful way. The nation then gathers at Gilgal where a solemn ceremony is conducted to proclaim Saul as king. Notice that in the defeat of the Ammonites, the army is so decimated that no two of them are left together.

Application
There is an adage that states, "there is strength in numbers." And that's true. Whenever people are unified against a common enemy or foe, or in support of a noble cause, their strength is increased, and their resolve is heightened. We know from experience that we are stronger together than we are as individuals. It is also true, therefore, that to defeat an enemy of many, disrupting the unity makes it much easier to defeat them.

Years ago, I led recreation time at Vacation Bible School for a bunch of fruit punch infused preschoolers. As a group, they were wild and all but unmanageable. But I soon discovered that by taking the rowdiest of the group away from the others, that he lost much of his bravado, and the group soon settled back into a more peaceful group. Divide and conquer. It works with armies and preschoolers, and even with temptations. Let me explain… Our temptations tend to be very powerful, especially when we are confronted on several fronts. Maybe temptations come to our thought life, our business ethics, our marital relationships, or our internet surfing. It is easy for us to lose our way and quickly become defeated. But what if we learned to divide and conquer? What if, instead of throwing up our hands in despair because of the overwhelming power of temptation's united front, we took on the challenge of a single aspect and then moved on to the next? Let me challenge you today to focus on one single area of your life where you are feeling vulnerable to temptation. Pray for insight, strength, and courage to defeat that foe. As you gain victory, turn your attention to the next area of your life that needs attention. One by one the enemies will fall.

Prayer
Father God, give us victory over our sins and temptations. Amen.

Day 248 — 1 Samuel 12: A Failure to Pray

> "As for me, I will certainly not sin against the Lord by ending my prayers for you. And I will continue to teach you what is good and right."
> 1 Samuel 12:23 (NLT)

Observation
Chapter 12 is somewhat a farewell speech by the aging Samuel. He speaks to all of Israel about his faithful service. No one can speak a word against him. Even God is a witness of his faithful integrity, loyalty, and leadership. Samuel reminds the people of God's mighty works. He challenges them to continue to fear and worship the Lord. He cautions them that a refusal to obey God will bring God's "heavy hand" upon them. As a demonstration of God's power, Samuel calls down thunder and rain in what is normally a dry season. Samuel reminds the people that if they continue to sin, they, along with their king, will be swept away.

Application
Do you have a prayer list? Maybe a written list, or at least a mental list of people for whom you pray each day? I keep an actual written list so that I will not fail to pray carefully. If you are like me, and if you do keep a list, let me ask you to reflect on why you feel the need to pray fervently, and faithfully each day. Why is it important to be careful to remember the key people and needs in your life each day? Let's be honest... some of us pray each day as a sort of spiritual good luck charm. We are afraid that bad things will happen to those we love if we don't pray. Such a thought demonstrates a misunderstanding of God and how much God loves us. Do we honestly believe that the only reason that God blesses and protects the people in our lives is because we pray for them, rationalizing that if we don't pray, then certainly God will fail to protect them? So, at times we pray out of a fear that bad things will happen if we don't pray. Others of us pray as a way of patting ourselves on the back for our wonderful religious piety. We like being able to say to ourselves and to others that we pray faithfully each day, knowing that our bragging will cause some to think noble thoughts about us. But be reminded that if we pray only to receive the praise of men, that is all we will receive (Matthew 6:5).

Look at our focus verse for a moment. Samuel insists that he is not going to cease praying for Israel because to do so would be a sin against God. That's an important insight into why we need to pray for some people each day. If God directs us to pray, then we must pray. If God places an individual on our hearts to remember each day, then failing to bring their needs before God is a sin against God's direction in our lives. So, don't pray out of fear, guilt, or even false piety. Pray because God has prompted you to do so.

Prayer
Dear God, make us faithful prayer warriors because you have called us to that task. Amen.

Day 249   1 Samuel 13: An Insignificant Life

> "Saul was thirty years old when he became king, and he reigned for forty-two years." 1 Samuel 13:1 (NLT)

Observation

This chapter opens with a look at Saul's leadership as king over Israel, and his character flaws begin to show. The 30-year-old leader selects 3,000 special troops, sending the remaining members of his army home. Two thousand of the troops are sent to Micmash to accompany Saul. One thousand are assigned to Saul's son, Jonathon, at Gibeah. Jonathon's group attacks a Philistine garrison, which stirs up the anger of the Philistines. The Philistines gather an army of 3000 chariots, 6000 charioteers, and countless soldiers. Saul and his army become fearful of their size and strength. After waiting impatiently for Samuel to offer sacrifices to gain the Lord's favor, Saul offers the sacrifices himself. Samuel rebukes his insolence and tells him that the Lord will not allow him to lead for very long. The army scatters with only 600 men remaining. Only two swords are found among the entire group.

Application

There is no indication in our focus verse about a long-standing controversy concerning both the age Saul when he begins to reign and the length of his reign. In the ancient manuscripts, part of the Hebrew number is missing. It simply reads, "and two" leading the reader to wonder what number proceeded that phrase. According to Acts 13:21, the number should be 40, meaning that Saul reigned a total of 42 years. But that's where the controversy begins. Some translations indicate that Saul reigned for 32 years, some only 22 years. Old Testament scholar John Tullock in his book, *The Old Testament Story* (Pearson, 2011) presents compelling evidence that he only reigned 12 years. So why bring all of this up, anyway? Here's my thought... Saul's leadership was so ineffective, so weak, and so displeasing to God, that even the number of years he reigned are all but lost to the sands of time.

I find a lesson about significance in his story... and maybe in ours. Without question, each one of us wants our life to count. We want to live meaningful lives that make a difference. We long to be remembered generations after we are gone. So, what is the key to a significant life? Is our significance found in the titles we hold, the degrees we earn, the books we write, or the businesses we lead? No. Significance is found in the lives we influence, the lives we change, and the lives in which we invest. It's all about people and nothing else. What we will one day claim as trophies in the Eternal Kingdom of God are the lives we have pointed toward the Father. We should therefore strive to live "influencing" lives claimed by kindness, generosity, and grace. The more we value only ourselves, the less value our lives will have. The more we give ourselves away, the greater legacy we will claim.

Prayer

Dear God, may we invest ourselves fully into the lives of those around us. Amen.

Day 250 — 1 Samuel 14: The Danger of Impatience

> "But while Saul was talking to the priest, the confusion in the Philistine camp grew louder and louder. So Saul said to the priest, 'Never mind; let's get going!'" 1 Samuel 14:19 (NLT)

Observation
This chapter begins with the story of Jonathon secretly taking his armor bearer with him to attack a Philistine outpost. They kill 20 Philistine soldiers. When their actions are discovered, the entire Philistine army is thrown into panic and confusion. Saul sees an opportunity for victory and summons Abijah, the high priest at the time, to inquire if the Lord will bless the effort. In our focus verse, the process takes too long and Saul rushes ahead into battle without having first discerned the Lord's plan. As it turns out, the Israelites are successful, and the battle goes well with many of the animals taken as spoils. The animals are slaughtered, sacrificed, and eaten by the hungry soldiers after Saul requires the draining of blood according to Mosaic law. The chapter ends by saying that throughout Saul's reign as king, there was constant warfare with the Philistines.

Application
The discipline of waiting is difficult. We are annoyed by a long traffic signal. If we have to wait too long in a fast-food drive-thru we get a little testy. If Amazon doesn't ship our order by the next day, we become frustrated with the wait. Even a doctor's visit can drive us crazy if we have to wait too long for the doctor to make his/her rounds. And so, when matters of faith cause us to "wait on the Lord," we feel the tension rise within us. Notice in our focus verse that Saul grows too impatient while waiting for a response from the high priest. He says, "Never mind; let's get going!" The actual Hebrew translation literally means "to withdraw your hand." It's the image of disconnecting from the priest so he can quickly get out to do battle.

Whether we like it or not, sometimes our faith requires us to wait… to wait on the Lord's answer, or on the Lord's timing. We are reminded that "For My thoughts are not your thoughts, Nor are your ways My ways, declares the Lord" (Isaiah 55:8 NASB). Because our vision is limited and because our human will is too self-centered, we often become frustrated at the seemingly slow movement of God. We want God to respond to our timetable rather than be inconvenienced by God's timetable. Our impatience often leads us to make foolish choices or head in the wrong direction. As we mature in our faith, we begin to understand that the ways of God are perfect, and God's timing is always right. Sometimes we simply need to pray for patience as we wait for God to act. Just because God's answer seems slow in coming doesn't mean that God is not at work. Just wait…

Prayer
Father God, give us patience as we wait on your carefully unfolding plan. Amen.

Day 251 — 1 Samuel 15: The Expectation of Obedience

> "But Samuel replied 'What is more pleasing to the Lord: your burnt offerings and sacrifices or your obedience to his voice? Listen! Obedience is better than sacrifice, and submission is better than offering the fat of rams.'"
> 1 Samuel 15:22 (NLT)

Observation

This chapter opens with Samuel's delivering a message to King Saul from the Lord that it is time to punish the Amalakites for their opposition to Israel when the nation came out of Egypt. God's instruction to Saul was for the destruction of the Amalakite—all the citizens and all the livestock. The message was very clear and definitive. Saul mobilized his army and destroyed the Amalakites… almost. He spared the life of the king, and he allowed his soldiers to keep the best sheep, goats, cattle, and lambs. The narrative indicates that the Lord "was sorry" to have made Saul king over Israel. God regretted the level of disobedience in Saul's heart. Samuel was sent to confront Saul. He asks, "Why do I hear the bleating of sheep and goats?" Saul attempted to explain away his foolish actions. The chapter ends with Samuel declaring God's rejection of Saul as the king of Israel.

Application

We expect obedience from the things that are ours to control. For example, we expect our children to be obedient as we attempt to raise them in a way that keeps them safe and helps them become responsible as they grow older. We expect our pets to heed our call and obey our commands. We expect our devices to obey inputs we give them. When we flip the switch, we expect the lights to turn on. When we dial the thermostat, we expect the warm air to start flowing. We understand very well the definition of obedience. We just don't always want to respond whenever we are called to be obedient.

Read the focus verse again, carefully and slowly. Notice what we are to do to please the Lord. Obedience. See what God demands more than sacrifice? Obedience. More than any other expectation that God has for us, is the expectation of obedience. God expects us to listen and then to respond to all that God demands of us. God expects fidelity to scripture. God expects appropriate behavior as ambassadors. God expects us to clothe the naked and feed the hungry. God expects us to love our enemies and to forgive those who have injured us. God expects us to care for widows and orphans. The problem is rarely one of misunderstanding the expectations of God. The problem is usually one of obedience. Are we fully compliant? Do we recognize God's authority over all of life and are we willing to yield ourselves to God's direction? Ask any believer and they will quickly tell you how much they "love" God. But can we claim a love for God if we are not willing to obey fully in all areas of our lives?

Prayer

Holy Father, may we possess both the will and the courage to be obedient. Amen.

Day 252 — 1 Samuel 16: The Role of the Spirit

> "So as David stood there among his brothers, Samuel took the flask of olive oil he had brought and anointed David with the oil. And the Spirit of the Lord came powerfully upon David from that day on. Then Samuel returned to Ramah." 1 Samuel 16:13 (NLT)

Observation
This chapter tells the story of the selection and anointing of David as the next-to-be-appointed king. God sent Samuel to Bethlehem to seek out a man named Jesse who had seven sons. God told Samuel that one of those sons would be the new king. Jesse parades out all the boys, starting with the oldest. Each one is rejected until finally the youngest son, David, is brought in from the fields. He seems an unlikely choice, but God reminds Samuel that the heart matters, not outward appearance. David is anointed by Samuel and the Spirit of the Lord comes powerfully upon him. As the chapter ends, David is brought into the court of King Saul because of his musical abilities. He is able play the harp in a way that soothes Saul's troubled mind. Soon, David becomes Saul's armor bearer.

Application
The role of the Spirit is a bit different in the Old Testament than in the New Testament. In the Old Testament, the Holy Spirit was not an indwelling Spirit poured out on all the people of God. Instead, the Spirit came upon certain individuals at certain moments to accomplish certain tasks. God empowered individuals for a season to accomplish God's work. Other Old Testament examples include the Judges of Israel or those who raised prophetic voices, like Elijah. The New Testament view of the Spirit is quite different. According to the second chapter of Acts, the Holy Spirit came upon the early disciples, indwelling and empowering their lives. As Jesus had promised, the Holy Spirit came upon them to give them boldness in their witness and the power to do extraordinary things. That same indwelling Spirit now resides in each of us who call upon the name of the Lord Jesus Christ. Unlike David, we may or may not be able to play an instrument or write poetry or lead a nation. But we are equipped to do some remarkable things. The Spirit at work in us is comforting, gives wisdom, reminds us of all that Christ taught us, speaks through us, strengthens us, and encourages us. According to Galatians, when the Spirit controls our lives, we can know love, joy, peace, patience, kindness, goodness, gentleness, faithfulness, and self-control. No, Samuel didn't come to your house and anoint your head with oil. But Christ promised the coming of the Spirit, and because of that, you can do great things.

Prayer
Holy Father, thank you for your indwelling, empowering Spirit. Amen.

Day 253   1 Samuel 17: Knowing the Enemy

"David asked the soldiers standing nearby… 'Who is this pagan Philistine anyway, that he is allowed to defy the armies of the living God?'"
1 Samuel 17:26 (NLT)

Observation

First Samuel 17 contains one of the great stories of the Old Testament and certainly one of the most defining moments in David's life. This epic standoff with Goliath lifts both David's status and notoriety, propelling him into public leadership. For 40 days the army of Israel and the army of the Philistines gathered on opposing mountains separated by the Elah Valley. For those 40 days, the great Philistine giant and warrior taunted the Israelites who were fearful of his size and strength. David, who was in the region visiting his brothers who were fighting for the army of Israel, hears Goliath's taunts. He is offended that a pagan soldier is allowed to defy the armies of the Living God. Discovering that no one else dares to face him, David seeks permission from King Saul to oppose Goliath. Armed with only a slingshot, David knocks out the giant with a single shot to the forehead. He races forward and cuts off Goliath's head with Goliath's own sword. With their leader slain, the Philistines flee from the army of Israel.

Application

"Who is this pagan Philistine anyway, that he is allowed to defy the armies of the living God?" Good question… both then and now. Recognizing the power and strength of God, David was dumbfounded that anyone would dare to battle against God. Knowing that it was his purpose to honor God, David could not stand idle while God's name and reputation were assaulted. Why do we stand idle when an assault on God's purpose and plan is carried out within our culture? Understand me clearly. This is not a devotional thought declaring that Christians are under attack in America and unless we vote a certain way, or believe in a certain political position, or patronize only certain businesses that the cause of Christ will be lost. It is true that the Gospel is under attack here in the United States, but the most vicious attackers are not those on the outside who condemn the ways of God. Those who do the most damage are the ones wearing the suits and dresses on Sunday, attending church and boasting about how much they love both God and country and will gladly defend either. You see, the greatest threat to the Christian ethic and witness comes from those who claim the name but who refuse to model the love and grace of Jesus. Whenever we stand in judgment or exclude those who don't adhere to our standards, or condemn forever those who have made mistakes, or spew prejudicial rhetoric, or marginalize those whose race or ethnic origins are different from our own… it is then we mock the Gospel and defy the purposes of God. We have seen the enemy and it is us.

Prayer

Holy Father, mold us into your image and use us as your representatives. Amen.

Day 254 — 1 Samuel 18: Brokenness' Loss

> "Saul became even more afraid of him, and he remained David's enemy for the rest of his life." 1 Samuel 18:29 (NLT)

Observation
The narrative begins with a description of the close relationship between Jonathon and David... a relationship that will prove to be closer than a blood relative. As the chapter continues, the story of David's increasing success and popularity is revealed. As David's popularity increases, so does Saul's jealousy. In fact, Saul's jealousy becomes so strong that he even attempts to stab David with a spear... twice! The narrative declares that the Lord was with David so that he enjoyed continued success. He even earns Michal's hand in marriage with the killing of 200 Philistines. (Michal was the daughter of King Saul.)

Application
There are some things that are broken and never fixed. For example, about a year ago a Bradford pear tree that was planted in my front yard split during the night and a major portion of it fell on my car. The next morning, I removed the branches as carefully as I could to avoid any further damage. Once all the foliage was removed, I could see several small dents in the roof. After an insurance evaluation, including learning the cost of my deductible, I decided not to repair the car. I drive with those dents to this day. The brokenness remains. About the same time, a small rock crashed into the windshield of my daughter's car. I was concerned about the potential danger of a broken windshield and so I immediately had it replaced. It's funny... we often make value judgments about which things in our lives are worthy of repair and which ones are not.

For me, our focus verse is a sad verse. It speaks of the brokenness of a relationship caused by Saul's jealousy. Unwilling to do the difficult work of reconciliation, Saul allowed the distance to remain between himself and David until the end of his life. King Saul died without having repaired that which was broken. Take a moment to consider you own life. You probably live with some brokenness. There may be a relationship, or maybe several, that have been severed through the years. You have a choice to make. Will you mend the tear, or will you live with the loss that the broken relationship brings? Many people refuse to do the hard work of reconciliation. It begins with sharing the responsibility for the brokenness. It ends with the deliberate choice to both forgive and forget. Nothing about mending such a hurt is easy. But once the wound has healed, a relationship is recovered and joy is reclaimed. Before this day ends, begin praying for the courage and strength to do the hard work of reconciliation.

Prayer
Dear Father, burden us today with the pain of brokenness until we are willing to mend it. Amen.

Day 255 1 Samuel 19: His Mysterious Ways

"He tore off his clothes and lay naked on the ground all day and all night, prophesying in the presence of Samuel. The people who were watching exclaimed, 'What? Is even Saul a prophet?'" 1 Samuel 19:24 (NLT)

Observation
As the story of Saul and David continues to unfold, Chapter 19 opens with Saul making plans to assassinate David. Jonathon, Saul's son, hears of the plan and carefully advises David to go into hiding. For the moment, Jonathon is able to reason with his father and David is brought back into the king's court to serve him. But quickly Saul's madness returns. He throws a spear at David, who once again flees from the presence of the king. David travels to Ramah to seek counsel with Samuel. Saul learns of David's whereabouts and sends troops to kill David. But as they arrive in the city, the troops are overwhelmed by the Spirit of God and suddenly no longer seek David's life but begin prophesying. Twice more Saul sends troops but with the same results. Eventually, Saul goes himself to find David and the Spirit of the Lord comes upon him as well. His energies are turned away from his murderous intent and he too begins to prophesy. As a result, the immediate threat is thwarted.

Application
You've heard the old expression… "The Lord works in mysterious ways." This narrative is certainly an affirmation of that thought. According to our focus verse, King Saul displays the most bizarre behavior. Acting under the power of the Spirit of God, he strips off his clothing and lays naked on the ground all day and night while proclaiming the greatness of God. Some commentators argue that what Saul actually does is remove his outer robe, which was the symbol of his authority. Others argue that he is completely naked. Either way, Saul lies in the street completely incapacitated by the power of God's Spirit. He is unable to kill David, which had been his intent.

Step back from the story to consider the theme of the Spirit's protection. Just as the Spirit of God was actively involved in the story of David, that same Spirit is actively involved in our lives. The Spirit takes on several roles in our lives, including that of protection. Although typically unrevealed to us, the Spirit of God is intimately involved and active in our lives. The Spirit watches over us, completely aware of the movements of our day. Sometimes, in the placement of people and circumstance, the Spirit protects us from danger and injury in ways we can't even know. Recently my father recounted some stories to me of how his life had been saved in mysterious ways including a cow that had wandered onto a roadway and a high school quarterback who knew how to get the water out of his lungs. (Those are stories for another day!) Here's point… even this day, God is watching over you. His Spirit protects you.

Prayer
Dear God, thank you for being the guardian of our days. Amen.

Day 256   1 Samuel 20: The Power of Friendship

> "And Jonathan made David reaffirm his vow of friendship again, for Jonathan loved David as he loved himself." 1 Samuel 20:17 (NLT)

Observation
This chapter opens with Jonathon and David debating about King Saul's feelings towards David. David insists that King Saul wants him dead. Jonathon tries to argue that his father's emotional response is not quite to that level. The New Moon Festival provides an opportunity for Jonathon to test his father's level of anger. David and Jonathon decide that David will skip the event and see how Saul responds. Saul is so angered that he even hurls a spear at his own son because he knows of David and Jonathon's close friendship. David and Jonathon are forced to meet secretly and bid one another a bitter farewell. They swear out a pledge to each other to be loyal in friendship in spite of the king's anger.

Application
Perhaps the true measure of friendship is "to love someone as you love yourself." I tend to think that those of us who can claim friendships that exist on such a level are truly "blessed beyond measure." And to be honest, if we can claim even just one or two such relationships we should rejoice and be grateful. There are certainly various levels of friendship. All of us have those people in our lives with whom we often intersect and have conversation. Maybe they are our neighbors, or work associates, or employees at local businesses that we often encounter. They are our "friends," but the relationship is not very deep. And then there are others with whom we are a bit closer to in relationship. We have shared experiences through the years. We talk often. We send Christmas cards each December. We call them our "good friends," but they are not the first call we would make in a time of need or crisis. The level of relationship is certainly deeper than most, but not life dependent. And then there are the friends we love as much as we love ourselves. We share their joys. We weep with their sadness. We lean on them in a moment of crisis. We pray for them daily. We would be lost without them. They are the kinds of friends in which our conversations last a lifetime and not just for a few moments. Even though time and distance may separate us from them, there is a closeness to which we desperately cling and often acknowledge. They are the people in our lives without whom we could not truly live.

    I am blessed to have two of them in my life. There are two men that I have trusted for years with my deepest thoughts and highest respect. I would surrender my life in a moment to save theirs and they would do the same. And although I pray such a situation would never occur, it's good to know such people exist. If you have even just one of those types of friends, before this day is done, pray for them, thank God for them, and find a way to bless them.

Prayer
Dear God, thank you for the friends we love as much as ourselves. Amen.

Day 257   1 Samuel 21: A Tangible Reminder of God

> "'I only have the sword of Goliath the Philistine, whom you killed in the valley of Elah,' the priest replied. 'It is wrapped in a cloth behind the ephod. Take that if you want it, for there is nothing else here.' 'There is nothing like it!' David replied. 'Give it to me!'" 1 Samuel 21:9 (NLT)

Observation

David is very much a fugitive, running from Saul's court. He goes to Nob, about two miles east of Jerusalem, to visit Ahimelech the priest. The city is important because the tabernacle was there, and many priests lived there in order to assist in the tabernacle duties. (In the following chapter, that fact comes into play in a tragic way. Verse 7 of this chapter offers an ominous hint at what is to follow as the king's herdsman sees David in Nob.) When David arrives to visit Ahimelech, he is not entirely truthful about the circumstances in his life. He is perhaps unsure if he can trust Ahimelech fully. David asks for bread to eat along with his companions who are traveling with him. He is given the Holy Bread, which consists of twelve loaves that were placed on the golden table in the tabernacle. This bread was considered as an offering before Lord and according to Mosaic Law, could only be consumed by the priests. (Jesus will refer to this incident in Matthew 12:1-7.) David also arrives without any weapons. The only sword at Nob is the sword of Goliath that he had once used to slay the giant. David leaves Nob and travels to Philistine territory where he pretends to be a madman so that the Philistine king will avoid him.

Application

It is not by accident that the only weapon found to give to David is the sword of Goliath. David says, "There is nothing like it!" Surely, he remembers the moment when the Lord gave Goliath into his hand. It was with this very sword that David cut off the giant's head. It is a very tangible reminder to David of the Lord's power to bring victory against great odds. As he goes forth, the sword will be a reminder in his hand of God's power.

    I think it is important for the people of faith to have reminders of God's presence, power, and grace. Sometimes we need to remember the infinite God in very tangible ways. We need things we can hold, touch, and see. We need symbols that remind us of God. For me, the Bible is one of those tangible things. Believing that it contains the word of God without any mixture of error makes it a very sacred book. Just to hold it helps me to connect with God. Some people hang a cross around their neck or hang a religious symbol on the walls of their homes. There is nothing wrong with doing such things. We need the constant reminders that God is our strength our provider, and our guardian. We don't worship such things, but they help us remember to worship the one who watches over us.

Prayer

Dear God, may we be reminded again today of your grace and love for us. Amen.

Day 258 — 1 Samuel 22: The High Price of Ministry

> "Then the king said to Doeg, 'You do it.' So Doeg the Edomite turned on them and killed them that day, eighty-five priests in all, still wearing their priestly garments." 1 Samuel 22:18 (NLT)

Observation

This chapter tells of two very distinct events. The first half speaks of David, who is on the run from King Saul, finding refuge in the cave of Adullam. This outpost is about 25 miles Southwest of Jerusalem. Others begin to gather with him... family members and men who were troubled, in debt, and discouraged. More than 400 men rally behind David. David also strikes a deal with the king of Moab to offer protection for his parents, whom David fears will come under attack by King Saul. In the second half of the chapter, King Saul learns that the priests at Nob had given counsel and provision to David. (Remember that Doeg, the chief herdsman, had seen the exchange between David and the priest named Ahimelech.) Ahimelech is brought before King Saul because of his actions. He pleads that he had no ill-intent against the king and that he had acted innocently. The king orders the slaughter of all 85 priests and their families. The scriptures state that even the wives, children, babies, and livestock are slain.

Application

Sometimes, there is a very costly price to be paid whenever we minister to the needs of people. In this chapter, the priests are slaughtered along with their families because they give provision and aid to David. As David hears the news, he is devastated. Over the course of three decades of pastoral ministry, I experienced moments when there was a costly price to be paid for meeting the needs of people. No, my preaching or counsel to others did not bring about a massacre, but there were difficult moments. I discovered that at times, when walking a family through a very difficult moment like a death or a marriage disruption, that even though I was a source of comfort and wisdom, they later associated me with that difficult chapter in their lives and I lost both friendship and contact with those people. It was not that I had failed them, but that the crisis was difficult for them to bear, and I was a reminder of that dark time. (I don't know if most of you who read this thought will understand that line of thinking, but the ministers who read this surely will.)

My point is to simply say that there is a price to be paid when doing ministry. More than just the interruption of time, or the expense of offering care, sometimes investing in others will claim a close friendship or lose a fellow church member in the process. Sometimes in the need to "start over," your personal connection to that person is lost. Their need to start fresh means casting aside the things of the past. It's okay. It's what ministry sometimes demands.

Prayer

God, may we know the joy of ministry to others as we sometimes feel the pain. Amen.

Day 259 1 Samuel 23: One-Track Mind

> "'Discover his hiding places, and come back when you are sure. Then I'll go with you. And if he is in the area at all, I'll track him down, even if I have to search every hiding place in Judah!'" 1 Samuel 23:23 (NLT)

Observation

There's a "cat and mouse game" going on between King Saul and David. David is desperately fleeing the king to save his life. As the chapter begins, David and his men are in a small town named Keilah to help the citizens escape from the Philistines who are attacking them. David wins the battle, but when Saul discovers that David is there he tries to capture him. David and his men must flee to the hill country of Ziph. Soon, Saul pursues him in that place as well. David then flees to Maon and, again, Saul chases after him. In a dramatic moment, David and his men are on one side of a mountain and Saul and his army are on the opposite side. An urgent message is sent to Saul concerning a Philistine uprising. He must abandon his pursuit of David to return home to fight the Philistines. David narrowly escapes again.

Application

You've heard of people with a "one-track mind." These are people whose minds become captivated by a single idea, maybe a pursuit, perhaps a quest of some kind. They become so narrowly focused that they seem to abandon all else going on around them to pursue whatever it is that draws their attention. We all know people like that... and to be honest, most of us have been that person at some point. I readily confess that I can become captivated by something that seemingly takes over all other conscious and rational thought. Usually, it's buying a new car that takes over my mind. I will decide that it's time for a new car, pursue the purchase of that car, scan a dozen lots, search the web, and not rest until I have conquered that foe. Some people develop a one-track mind toward other pursuits. It could be an all-consuming hobby. It could be a project at work. It could even be an addiction that pushes out all sensible thought from our minds. In the story of King Saul, his one-track mind was his pursuit of David. All he could think about was finding and killing his rival. It was a destructive and overbearing force in his heart and mind. In fact, having a one-track mind is usually a very negative thing. It causes us to lose our common sense and abandon other people and pursuits that need our attention. But there is one scenario in which having a one-track mind can be a good thing. In fact, we are called to such a laser focus. The greatest commandment of all, according to Jesus, says that we are to "Love the Lord your God with all your heart, all your soul, and all your mind" (Matthew 22:37 NLT). I hope that it will be said of all of us that we possess a relentless pursuit of God. Nothing should matter more.

Prayer

Holy God, may we offer you the best energy and focus of our lives. Amen.

Day 260   1 Samuel 24: The Triumph of Mercy

> "And he said to David, 'You are a better man than I am, for you have repaid me good for evil.'" 1 Samuel 24:17 (NLT)

Observation
Shortly after his latest battle with the Philistines, King Saul continues his pursuit of David, who has fled into the wilderness of En-gedi. David and his men were hiding deep within a cave when the king and his soldiers pass nearby. The king stops and enters that very cave in order to "relieve himself." David slips up behind him, but rather than kill him, David cuts off a small corner of Saul's robe. As Saul and his troops continue on their way, David yells from a distance and holds up the piece of Saul's robe as a proof of the mercy he has extended towards Saul. David declares that he will not harm Saul because Saul is the Lord's anointed to rule over Israel. Saul acknowledges David's kindness and realizes that David will in fact be a great king over Israel. Saul asks David to swear out an oath that when David comes to power that he will not kill Saul's family nor destroy the line of his descendants.

Application
The extending of mercy is one of those great gifts that blesses both the giver and the recipient. Certainly, Saul receives a great blessing from David's merciful act. Saul's life could have been taken from him in a moment. As David extends mercy, he receives the joy that comes when a person acts with utter kindness rather than retaliatory revenge. In his act of mercy, David has both spared the king and honored his God.

Mercy is always a choice. Whenever we are in the position of extending justifiable punishment or retribution and we choose instead to offer mercy, haven't we discovered a better way to live, to relate, and to model the love of Christ? Jesus Himself declared that we are to "be merciful, just as your Father is merciful" (Luke 6:36 NASB). In fact, he reminds us that in offering mercy we find mercy for our own lives. "Blessed are the merciful, for they shall receive mercy" (Matthew 5:7 NASB). It's a Jesus ethic and a Gospel demand. And yes… it is sometimes hard to extend because it cuts against the grain of human nature.

I find it interesting that we often plead with God to have mercy on someone's soul for the wrongs they have committed or the pain they have inflicted. And maybe at times it is a cry for God to have mercy on us, to somehow ease our suffering in the midst of great pain and anguish. But maybe there are those moments, when rather than asking God to have mercy on us, we should ask God to give us the courage to have mercy on others. Rather than yield to the pressures of normal human response, we should pray for the strength to act more like our Savior who spoke of forgiveness in the midst of persecution and grace in the midst of pain.

Prayer
Holy God, may we extend the same mercy to others today that we crave from you.

Day 261   1 Samuel 25: The Value of Good Advice

> "David replied to Abigail, 'Praise the Lord, the God of Israel, who has sent you to meet me today! Thank God for your good sense! Bless you for keeping me from murder and from carrying out vengeance with my own hands.'" 1 Samuel 25:32-33 (NLT)

Observation
Samuel, the prophet of God, has died. He is buried at his home in Ramah. This signifies the end of an era in the life of the nation. He is mourned by all of Israel. The rest of the chapter is devoted to the story of Nabal and Abigail. Nabal is described as "crude and mean in all his dealings." His wife, Abigail, is described as "sensible and beautiful." David sends 10 of his men to Nabal to ask for provisions, reminding him that David and his men had acted kindly toward Nabal's shepherds. Nabal calls David and his men a band of outlaws and refuses to help. David is offended and prepares to enact vengeance. Abigail hears about all that is to take place. She goes out to meet with David and explains the situation more fully. (Her words are the longest recorded speech by a woman in the Old Testament.) She convinces David not to act in vengeance. When she returns home to tell Nabal what she has done, he suffers a stroke and dies 10 days later. After his death, David takes Abigail as his wife. The story is significant in that future King David learns a valuable lesson in acting only on the Lord's initiative and not on his own selfish motivations.

Application
Years ago, at one of our wedding showers, my wife and I were handed a stack of index cards on which friends at the shower had written words of advice and counsel. I recall that we had to stand and read all the tidbits of wisdom to the assembled group. Some words of advice were funny, others were serious, and some were even a bit embarrassing to read. To be honest, I don't remember any of those words of advice except for the words written on one card. It read, "Don't join a record club." I got the feeling that the author of that advice was speaking from personal experience! Over the course of life, we get a lot of advice from a lot of sources. Some of it is good advice and we would do well to listen. And quite frankly, sometimes we get bad advice. The hard part is distinguishing between the two. My question for you this morning is, "What kind of advice are you offering to others, and what is the foundation for the advice you are offering?" Certainly, most of us can offer the advice of personal experience… "This is what happened to me." But hopefully we can offer wisdom that comes from a source much deeper than our own intellect. That source is the Bible. In the Bible we find wisdom, insight, and perspective. So maybe the best advice you can offer someone today is to read it.

Prayer
Dear Father, may we find our wisdom and insight from your Word. Amen.

Day 262   1 Samuel 26: The Reward of Obedience

> "The Lord gives his own reward for doing good and for being loyal, and I refused to kill you even when the Lord placed you in my power, for you are the Lord's anointed one." 1 Samuel 26:23 (NLT)

Observation
This chapter tells the story of how David once again spares the life of King Saul. David and his men have taken refuge in the arid region near the Dead Sea. Saul, along with 3,000 troops, search for him. David discovers the location of Saul's encampment, and sneaks into the camp at night. He finds Saul, who is asleep, surrounded by a circle of sleeping soldiers. Saul's spear is stuck in the ground right beside his head. David could end his life but refuses because he continues to believe that Saul is the Lord's anointed. The next day, from a safe distance, David shouts at Saul and reveals what he has done and how he could have taken Saul's life. Saul once again repents for his intent to harm David. Their shouted blessings toward each other was their final conversation.

Application
We understand reward and punishment. From the time we were very young, we were taught that system of justice. If we behaved well, we were rewarded. If we were disobedient, we were punished. Parents continue to use rewards to entice their children to play by the rules and follow proper instruction. A child may receive a trip to the ice cream store, an extra hour of TV, or maybe a new video game because of the right behavior. The converse is also true... a child might receive a spanking, time out, or be sent to his or her room for exhibiting poor behavior. Obviously, the joy is in being rewarded. In this story, David declares that he will receive a reward from God for his obedience and loyalty. He knows that God will bless him in some way.

Let's be clear... our motivation for doing the right thing and living a godly life should not be getting some blessing from God. Our motivation for living a godly life is to live like Christ. Because of our love for him, we want to please him and follow his direction to the very best of our ability. We obey him because we love him. But notice what David writes... "The Lord gives his own reward for doing good and for being loyal." Here's the takeaway from that verse... God is very much aware of our good deeds. God knows our hearts and sees all the acts of grace and kindness that we offer to others. Such things are not forgotten. The immediate reward that we claim is the joy in knowing that we have pleased God. Our spirits should be lifted with the simple knowledge that we have acted in ways that please God and represent God well. But don't forget about the great reward that all of us receive because of our faith... salvation through Christ our Lord. Can there be any greater blessing?

Prayer
Father God, thank you for your continual gifts of grace in our lives. Amen.

Day 263 — 1 Samuel 27: Finding Refuge

> "But David kept thinking to himself, 'Someday Saul is going to get me. The best thing I can do is escape to the Philistines. Then Saul will stop hunting for me in Israelite territory, and I will finally be safe.'" 1 Samuel 27:1 (NLT)

Observation

As this chapter opens, David remains fearful of Saul. His life on the run has become wearisome, especially now that wives and children have been added to the numbers of those traveling with David and his men. (Some commentators estimate that this total group was now more than 1,000 persons.) David goes to Achish, the Philistine king of Gath, to ask for asylum. David's belief is that Saul will not search for him while he lives in Philistine territory. For the next 16 months David and his band of followers live in the town of Ziglag. During this period, David and his men carry out covert operations against three groups of people, slaughtering each group and taking much in plunder. He lies to Achish when the king asks where he has been fighting. He leads Achish to think that he has fought against people in Israel, which would be acceptable to Achish. (The reader may question both the slaughter of three people groups and the deception of David. It is suggested that David was completing the work of ridding the nation of pagan people, something that the Israelites had failed to do during the time of the conquest. Perhaps this portion of the story of David is told to describe the development of his leadership and military skills.)

Application

David sought a place of refuge. He and his men, along with their families, needed a place to rest, to recover, to reassess their life purpose and direction. We need such a place of refuge as well. All of us become weary because of the constant pressures of life. We look for those places where we can find rest both physically and emotionally. As David will later write, we need "to be led beside the still waters" for a while. We sometimes just need a break from all the turmoil that swirls around daily life. So, where do we find such places of refuge and such moments of rest? It varies. Sometimes the solitude of a quiet drive to work may ease our minds. Sometimes we can relax in front of a roaring fire with a good book in our laps. Maybe the place of retreat is the shelter of your home, where you are greeted with a warm welcome and deep appreciation at the end of a long day at work. Many find a gentle grace in a long afternoon walk. We need those moments. We need to find a place of refuge in our troubling world. It is also vital to find the places of refuge that only faith can provide. Jesus says to "come unto Me, all you who are weary and heavy-laden, and I will give you rest" (Matthew 11:28). So today, amid the madness, take a moment to revel in the knowledge that your needs are known by your Father and that you are loved beyond measure.

Prayer

Father God, thank you for providing us with a place of refuge and acceptance. Amen.

Day 264   1 Samuel 28: Desperate Measures

> "'Why have you disturbed me by calling me back? Samuel asked Saul. Because I am in deep trouble,' Saul replied. 'The Philistines are at war with me, and God has left me and won't reply by prophets or dreams. So I have called for you to tell me what to do.'" 1 Samuel 28:15 (NLT)

Observation
This chapter is surely one of the strangest in all of scripture. Saul finds himself about to go into battle again with the Philistines. As the armies gather for war, Saul sees the size of the Philistine army and is understandably fearful. He prays to God for wisdom about what to do. He does not hear a response from the Lord, nor does the casting of lots reveal any answer, nor is there a prophetic word from the prophets of Israel. Saul must resort to extreme measures. Although he had banned the presence of mediums and seers from the land, he travels to Endor, disguises himself, and consults with a witch. Saul asks the witch to conjure up the spirit of Samuel so that Saul can inquire of Samuel what he should do. Suddenly the spirit of Samuel appears, surprising both Saul and the witch! Samuel has nothing good to report. He tells Saul that the kingdom of Israel has been torn from his hands and that both he and his sons will die in battle.

Application
It's a weird story, right? The fact that the spirit of Samuel rises from the dead to speak to Saul is just not the kind of thing you read about every day. It illustrates the lengths to which Saul is willing to go, vainly attempting to find favor with God. He wants God to give him good news about the battle, when in fact, Saul had already determined the course of action by his continual disobedience. You've heard the old expression, "desperate times call for desperate measures." There are those moments, presented to us by time and circumstance, in which we resort to desperate measures to solve a crisis. Maybe we make a foolish financial decision to temporarily solve a financial need. It could be that we make a foolish pledge or promise to gain someone's favor. Once, when snowed-in by a freak snowstorm, my wife and I chopped up a ping-pong table to burn in the fireplace to keep our young children warm. Desperate times and desperate measures. There are those life jarring moments when we are pushed to our wit's end. In desperation, we cry out to God and make all kinds of promises. "I will be in church every Sunday for the rest of my life!" "I will give more than a tithe this Sunday." "I will volunteer at the food bank." We think we have to beg God into acting on our behalf. What we fail to remember is that we are loved extravagantly by God, and we are already the objects of God's good grace. Desperate times should not lead us to foolish action, but to a gratitude knowing that God is always present with us, hearing and responding to our desperate cries.

Prayer
Father, remind us today, that you love us extravagantly and care for us tenderly. Amen.

Day 265 — 1 Samuel 29: The Providence of God

> "But the Philistine commanders were angry. 'Send him back to the town you've given him!' they demanded. 'He can't go into the battle with us. What if he turns against us in battle and becomes our adversary? Is there any better way for him to reconcile himself with his master than by handing our heads over to him?'" 1 Samuel 29:4 (NLT)

Observation

Chapter 29 begins with David in quite a dilemma. For the previous 16 months, David and his entourage have been guests of King Achish. Back at the start of chapter 28, Achish had told David that he and his men would be expected to fight with the Philistine army. The problem is that the Philistines are about to go to war with Israel. David and his men will have to do battle against King Saul and all their fellow Israelites. But as they head off to battle, the other leaders of Philistia are very wary of David and his men. They do not trust David to fight against his own people. Even with repeated assurances from King Achish, the other leaders will not change their minds. David and his men are sent away, unable to fight with the Philistine forces. The providence of God, right?

Application

Have you experienced the providence of God in your life? I'm sure you have, even if you didn't know it at the time or even acknowledge it now. Because of God's infinite wisdom and love for each of us, God is constantly arranging people, place, and moment. God acts in our lives in ways we can't begin to even fathom. In God's care for us, God constantly protects and provides for our needs.

My father recently reminded me of a story from his adolescent years. Not too far from his home there was a swimming hole fed by a creek. It was a treacherous place and he, who could not swim, had been told countless times by his parents not to go near. But one day, while both his mother and father were not at home, some older boys came by the house and asked him to go with them to the swimming hole. "What could possibly go wrong?" he asked himself. My father waded in the shallow water. It felt cool and inviting. He waded in a bit deeper... and then a bit deeper. He took one step too many and suddenly there was no ground beneath him. He fought and flailed in the water but was soon overcome. An older boy, the high school quarterback, saw him go under. He dove in and pulled my unconscious father to the shore. And somehow knowing instinctively what to do, he started compressing the water out of his chest. Dad started to cough up the water and clear his lungs. The older boy literally saved his life. Coincidence? Good luck? Or was it the providence of God? You may not be at risk today of drowning, but still you are in desperate need of God's watch care. Not to worry... nothing is a surprise to God... He has you covered.

Prayer

Father, thank you for your constant care in our lives. Amen.

Day 266 — 1 Samuel 30: Revived!

> "'To whom do you belong, and where do you come from?' David asked him. 'I am an Egyptian—the slave of an Amalekite,' he replied. 'My master abandoned me three days ago because I was sick.'" 1 Samuel 30:13 (NLT)

Observation
As David and his men were returning home after being told by the Philistines that their help was not needed or welcomed, they discovered that a band of Amalekites had raided and pillaged their town of Ziglag and had taken all the women and children hostage. After grieving their loss, David and his 600 men went in search of the Amalakites. Along the way, they discovered a man discarded in a field. Left to die, he had been there for three days and nights without food or water. David gave him food to revive him. It turns out he was a slave to one of the Amalakites who had destroyed Ziglag. He leads David to their camp. David and his men destroy the Amalakites and recover all that had been taken, including all the women and children.

Application
I have to wonder about this poor slave, left behind in a field to die. How horrible his life must have been. He was separated from family and homeland. He had been brutally treated as a slave. He had been discarded like a pair of worn-out shoes. And suddenly, who comes along but the future king of Israel. (Like the lesson from yesterday's devotion, the proof of God's provision is all over this story.) David gives him food and water and the promise of protection. And through the knowledge he possesses, David is able to find his wife and children again.

I also wonder what the rest of his life must have resembled. Did he ever make it home again? Did he get to hold his wife, or hug his children, or sleep in his own bed ever again? And if he lived to tell about it all, how many times did he tell the story of being left for dead, only to be brought to life again through the compassionate act of David. It makes me wonder about our life stories and if we talk about the Savior who revives us often enough. The scriptures remind us "that even though we were dead because of our sins, he gave us life when he raised Christ from the dead" (Ephesians 2:5 NLT). We have been revived from the shame and guilt of our sins and made fully alive by the grace of Jesus Christ. And the day will come… when we will rise from the deadness of human existence, to live forever with Christ in glory. So, what are we doing with THAT story? Do we speak of the saving love of Christ often enough? Do we tell of his saving death on the cross? Do we invite others to enjoy the life we now experience in Christ? Faith-sharing takes intentionality. If you are bold enough to pray for God to provide you with an opportunity to share your faith, you better be ready to start a conversation.

Prayer
Father, give us an opportunity to share our story with someone who needs to hear.

Day 267 — 1 Samuel 31: The Offer of Dignity

> "Then they took their bones and buried them beneath the tamarisk tree at Jabesh, and they fasted for seven days." 1 Samuel 31:13

Observation

This final chapter in the book of 1 Samuel tells the story of the death of Saul and the events following the discovery of his body. In a fierce battle on Mount Gilboa, the Philistines closed in on the army of Israel and killed Saul's sons. Saul was wounded severely by a Philistine arrow. As he struggled, he told his armor bearer to take his sword and kill him so that the pagan Philistines would not abuse him and torture him. The armor bearer refuses to do so and therefore, Saul falls on his own sword. When the armor bearer sees what he has done, he too takes his own life to die beside the king. The following day, the Philistines discover the body of the king. They cut off his head, strip him of his armor, and fasten his body to the city wall of Beth-shan. When the people of Jabesh-Gilead hear the news, they make their way through the treacherous night and claim Saul's body and those of his sons. They provide a proper burial by burning the bodies and burying the bones, followed by a period of mourning.

Application

Obviously, this is a terrible end to Saul's very troubled life. And even though he has not governed well, the men of Jabesh-Gilead offer him the dignity of a proper burial along with an appropriate period of grief. In other words, they did the "right thing." They honored the king and his leadership because he was the Lord's anointed. They treated his body with respect and refused to let the Philistines abuse it.

Let's talk for a moment this morning, about the offer of dignity. Yes, there is an important sense of propriety that should be extended to those who have died. In my ministry as a pastor, I always appreciated funeral directors who went about their work with compassionate care for the family and a sense of respect for the deceased person. But let me move the conversation well beyond this theme of offering dignity to the fallen. It is even more important for us to offer dignity and civility to the living… to everyone we encounter each day. We must do so because each person we meet has been created in the image of our God and is valued enormously by God. And so, every person deserves our respect, our consideration, and even our attention. We must offer every person the dignity they deserve because they are a creation of God. Such a thought has lots of ramifications. To offer dignity means that we acknowledge the worth of every person, that we respect their rights, that we refuse to cave-in to prejudicial thought or preconceived assessments of value, that we respond to needs and listen to their plight. Offering dignity means that we take on the role of being a true Christian in every sense of the word.

Prayer

Father, conform us into the image of your son, so that we will honor you. Amen.

Day 268 — 2 Samuel 1: The Tangled Web

> "'So I killed him,' the Amalekite told David, 'for I knew he couldn't live. Then I took his crown and his armband, and I have brought them here to you, my lord.'" 2 Samuel 1:10 (NLT)

Observation

This opening chapter is divided into two distinct parts. The first half tells the story of how David learns the news of the deaths of Saul and Jonathan. A man arrives from the Israelite encampment with his clothes torn and ashes on his head, obvious signs of mourning. He tells David the sad news but with a twist. He embellishes the story by telling David that he himself had slain Saul in obedience to Saul's instruction. David and his men spend the day weeping and fasting to honor the fallen king. The deceptive servant who told the falsehood is later killed by David's order for having slain the anointed king of Israel. The second half of the chapter records the words of a funeral song written by David to honor and remember Saul and Jonathan.

Application

Deception carries a high price. In this story, the servant claims credit for an action he did not perform, perhaps thinking that David would reward him in some way for his merciful act towards Saul. The result is unexpected. His lie brought about his own execution.

Remember the short verse written by Sir Walter Scott in his 1808 poem titled, "Marmion": "Oh what a tangled web we weave, when first we practice to deceive." It's an apt description of the entanglement that our deceptions create. We truly spin a web with the falsehoods we create. The problem is that, ultimately, we are the ones caught in its grip. Whenever we willfully choose the path of falsehood, we diminish who we are. Though the simple lie may free us from immediate discomfort or finger-pointing, the truth is that lying erodes both our character and reputation. As soon as we are willing to destroy the truth, we are willing to destroy ourselves. When our words are untrustworthy, our ability to influence others is lost.

How can we reclaim the trust we long to have in the hearts and minds of others that has been destroyed by our deception? It's not an easy task nor a quick fix. The road to redemption is paved with two stones… the stone of confession and the stone of consistency. Confession admits the infraction and clears the air. Confession is important to offer to the offended, and to self, and certainly unto God. Consistency is the proof provided over time that we are sincere about reclaiming our reputation. It requires the practice of honesty in both the small and great facets of our lives. Consistent, honest, and forthright behavior must be displayed as a way of life, without wavering or compromise. Reclaiming trust takes time. So, if your reputation needs a little help these days, vow this moment to begin anew. Time will tell.

Prayer

Father, may we live honest, faithful, and consistent lives. Amen.

Day 269   2 Samuel 2: The Escalation of Anger

> "Abner shouted down to Joab, 'Must we always be killing each other? Don't you realize that bitterness is the only result? When will you call off your men from chasing their Israelite brothers?'" 2 Samuel 2:26 (NLT)

Observation
This chapter tells of a very difficult and dark beginning to the reign of King David. After inquiring of God, David returns to Judah (southern region of Israel) and settles in Hebron where he will begin a 7½ year reign over Judah. The northern region, known as Israel, is governed by King Ishbosheth, who is the son of King Saul. Tensions mount, and civil war breaks out between the north and the south. This chapter records an incident at Gibeon where the armies meet. It is decided that each side will put forth 12 men to fight. There is no decisive victory as all 24 die by the sword. A fierce battle ensues, and the tension and violence continue to ramp-up. Finally, according to our focus verse, the General of the north shouts to the General of the south, calling for an end to the hostility that has already claimed 379 lives. The skirmish ends, but the civil war will continue for years.

Application
I read a story years ago about a hockey fan who became so angry when his team lost the Stanley Cup in the final seconds that he threw a bottle at the TV screen. The screen shattered. Realizing that he had ruined his TV made his anger flare even more. He grabbed the TV and threw it out of his second story window. (Although he failed to open the window first!) He looked out the window only to discover that the TV landed on his own car. Becoming even more furious, he ran downstairs, got in his car, and sped around the block. He lost control of his car and crashed into a telephone pole, which sent him to the hospital with multiple cuts and bruises and a concussion. His destructive anger escalated to the point that he almost killed himself!

Conflict and anger can have that kind of effect in our lives. At first, we become a little annoyed. Then we let things fester to the point that the annoyance builds into anger. Anger then leads to destructive behavior. And unless the anger is addressed and resolved, we lash out at others, destroying both relationships and reputation.

Here's a tough question to ask yourself this morning, "What makes me angry today?" Most of us could give a bullet-point list of several things that are really starting to get to us. We have a choice to make… get better or get bitter. Remember the words of James, "For the anger of man does not achieve the righteousness of God" (James 1:20 NASB). Whenever we allow anger to rule our lives, we destroy our better selves and thwart much of what the Spirit longs to do through our witness. Resolve today that you will not let anger win. Claim it and tame it.

Prayer
Father, remind us that the work of your Spirit in us, will result in self-control. Amen.

Day 270 2 Samuel 3: Quenching the Dangerous Thirst for Power

> "May God strike me and even kill me if I don't do everything I can to help David get what the Lord has promised him!" 2 Samuel 3:9 (NLT)

Observation
These words are spoken by a man named Abner, about whom much of this chapter is written. Abner is a powerful leader among those in Israel who remained loyal to the dynasty of Saul. But the day comes when Ishbosheth, Saul's son who is now ruling, accuses Abner of sleeping with one of his father's concubines. Abner is angered by the accusation and vows to help David rise to power over all of Israel. To prove his loyalty to David, at David's request, Abner returns David's wife Michal to him. Abner gathers support for David among other leaders in Israel and among the tribe of Benjamin. Joab, who is David's general, learns of Abner's visit to see and speak with David. He accuses Abner of being a spy and hunts him down, killing him at the city gate of Hebron. David is angered by Joab's action and prays for God to repay his evil deed.

Application
There are many twists and turns to the plot line, but a common thread holds the story together. It's the alluring temptation of power and what lengths some will go to in order to claim a stake in it. Particularly in this story, Abner, Joab, and Ishbosheth are all seeking to gain greater power and influence, and in their pursuit, they claim many lives, including their own.

These men were not the first, nor the last, to be victimized by their greed for power. Many a life has been ruined by the constant desire to control, to manipulate, and to exert influence. Those in power feed on its strong allure. Having authority over others and having the ability to command the actions of others is simply intoxicating to many. And the problem is that many will go to great lengths to obtain it. But the Gospel paints a very different view of power and influence. Jesus said that the least will become the greatest in the Kingdom and those who are now first, will one day become last. It's a very counter-cultural view of our world. Jesus insists that it is in our willingness to invest deeply in serving others, not in overpowering them, that we will find our greatest joy and our most permanent sense of fulfillment. In fact, Jesus even said to the disciples gathered around the table, "If I then, the Lord and the Teacher, washed your feet, you also ought to wash one another's feet" (John 13:14 NASB). How would it change your perspective today, if you spent your energies trying to serve others rather than trying to control them? What if today is not about feeding your ego, but all about solving the hurts, pains, and problems of someone else? What if you craved servanthood with the same intensity you direct on obtaining power? Master or servant? What's your role?

Prayer
Father, give us a servant's heart and the courage to lead not by power, but by humility. Amen.

Day 271 — 2 Samuel 4: Caring for the Children

> "(Saul's son Jonathan had a son named Mephibosheth, who was crippled as a child. He was five years old when the report came from Jezreel that Saul and Jonathan had been killed in battle. When the child's nurse heard the news, she picked him up and fled. But as she hurried away, she dropped him, and he became crippled.)" 2 Samuel 4:4 (NLT)

Observation

This chapter tells the story of the murder of Ishbosheth, the king of northern Israel. When the news of Abner's (Ishbosheth's general) death reaches the king, the entire nation is paralyzed by fear and uncertainty. Two brothers, Baanah and Recab, who had served as captains in Ishbosheth's army, seized the opportunity to gain political advantage with David. One day while the doorkeeper of the palace was sleeping, these two slipped into the napping king's bedroom and killed him. They presented Ishbosheth's head to King David at Hebron thinking that their actions would please the king. Instead, David is angered that they have slain an innocent man. The two are executed because of their actions.

Right in the middle of that narrative, the writer of 2 Samuel interjects parenthetically this brief story about Saul's grandson who is crippled when he is accidentally dropped by his nurse. He is crippled for life in both feet and will never walk again.

Application

I find it interesting that in her attempt to protect Mephiosheth, the nurse dropped him, causing a life-altering injury. This brief story illustrates one of the most difficult aspects of parenting faced by all of us who have the joy and the responsibility of raising children. Of course, the safety and well-being of our children is absolutely priority #1. As parents, we do everything within our ability to ensure that our children are nurtured meaningfully, protected mightily, and loved lavishly. We are charged with helping them survive and thrive through childhood and adolescence so that they will become responsible, well-adjusted adults. However, there is a fine balance to be struck between proper nurturing and "over-protection." Here at the university where I work, stories surface from time to time about "hover parents" who come to campus and frantically attempt to protect and control their student's environment. There have even been reports of mothers who try to stay in the dorms with their freshmen daughters! This is where parenting can be difficult. How does one protect while at the same time providing room for a child to grow and learn things independently? It's hard to fight the urge to step in when, as a parent, you see your child making a poor choice. The key is not in making all the choices for them, but to provide them with the tools needed to make good choices on their own. It's hard work. So, to all of you parents reading this devotion, my prayers are with you in this vitally important role.

Prayer

Father, bless those who parent, with wisdom, patience, and love. Amen.

Day 272 — 2 Samuel 5: The Sound of God

> "When you hear a sound like marching feet in the tops of the poplar trees, be on the alert! That will be the signal that the Lord is moving ahead of you to strike down the Philistine army." 2 Samuel 5:24 (NLT)

Observation
This chapter tells the story of David becoming king over all of Israel. All the tribal leaders gather at Hebron to anoint David as the leader of a united nation. The narrative reveals that David will reign for 40 years. (Seven years over Judah in Hebron and 33 over all of Israel in Jerusalem.) This chapter also tells the story of how David and his men captured Jerusalem from the Jebusites, how he moved the capital to that city, and how King Hiram of Tyre, sent materials and labor to build David a royal palace. The remainder of the chapter tells the story of David's huge victory over the Philistines. As David was careful to inquire of God concerning the battle, God revealed to him that he would know the time would be right to attack when he heard "a sound like marching feet in the tops of the poplar trees," indicating that God was leading the way.

Application
Sometimes we don't take the time to listen to the sounds of the world around us. We get in such a rush in the day-to-day that the only sounds that we notice are the blaring, annoying ones. We hear a siren, maybe a loud commercial, or the honking of a car horn. We miss a lot of other sounds because we don't make listening an "active pursuit." The sounds are there all the time... we just don't make hearing them a priority. One of my favorite TV shows is CBS Sunday Morning. I like the moment at the end of the show when they feature a National Park, always closing the segment with a quiet minute to enjoy the sounds of nature. In that moment, the listener hears the rush of a waterfall, the chirping of a bird, or maybe the whisper of a gentle breeze. It takes a little effort to hear the details of life that swirl all around us.

In this Bible passage, I wonder about the intensity with which David and his men listened for the sound of God in the treetops. Can't you see them, hushed, reverent, and with hands cupped to their ears, waiting to hear the distinctive sound of God passing overhead? I would hope that we would put equal effort into listening intently for the voice of God in our lives. Some may argue that God never speaks... but maybe God does all the time, we just don't pay attention. Maybe we let too many other voices drown out the words that God longs to impart. Let me invite you to listen today with a little more intentionality. Listen to what nature declares, or what scripture reveals, or even what a friend relates. It just may be God who is speaking.

Prayer
Speak, Lord, and give us the solitude and wisdom to listen. Amen.

Day 273

2 Samuel 6: Unbridled Joy

> "And David danced before the Lord with all his might, wearing a priestly garment." 2 Samuel 6:14 (NLT)

Observation
The Ark of the Covenant had been somewhat neglected during the reign of King Saul. David, in his pursuit of God, desired to move the Ark to a proper place of prominence as the center piece of the capital city of Jerusalem. The Ark was placed on a cart drawn by oxen and the procession to Jerusalem was begun. Remember however, that according to Levitical law, it was to be carried only by poles on the shoulders of the priests (Numbers 4:15). During the transport, an ox stumbled, and it seemed as though the Ark would fall. A man named Uzzah reached up to steady it and was struck dead as a result. David learns the lesson and when a second attempt is made to move it to Jerusalem, it is carried on poles as God had instructed. In fact, after only six steps, the procession is stopped for a moment of sacrifice and worship. (Some scholars suggest that a similar sacrifice was made after every six steps along the journey.) David is so excited to bring it into Jerusalem that he breaks out in a wild, exuberant dance at the head of the procession. His wife, Michal, scolds him for his actions. She will remain childless for the rest of her life for criticizing his celebration before the Lord.

Application
A lot has been written about this event in David's life. Various translators pick apart the ancient texts to discern what, in fact, David was wearing as he danced the before the Lord. Some suggest that he was naked, or scantily clad. Others say that he was wearing a priestly garment even though he was not a priest. I rather believe that the point of the story is not that David was ill-clad for the moment, but that David was willing to abandon his decorum and express his joy and celebration of the Lord. In other words, David worshipped with reckless abandonment, like a child who lets the rhythm of a song overtake him and he suddenly leaps and skips and dances to the music.

I am not suggesting that we become "out of control" when we worship. Certainly in the context of corporate worship, there are ways to appropriately express our worship and gratitude before God. But I am suggesting that we become willing to let go of our rigid and mechanical system of worship that doesn't allow us to express the joy of our hearts. No, I am not talking about dancing in the aisle, or jumping over a pew. I am talking about allowing joy to be seen in our faces, laughter in our voices, praises on our lips, and "living water" flow out of our eyes. And I don't mean in just the single hour of worship each Sunday. All of life should become as an act of worship before God and we should allow ourselves the right to express our joy and emotions before God.

Prayer
Heavenly Father, free us all to a life of authentic and joyful worship. Amen.

Day 274   **2 Samuel 7: A Proper House**

> "The king summoned Nathan the prophet. 'Look,' David said, 'I am living in a beautiful cedar palace, but the Ark of God is out there in a tent!'"
> 2 Samuel 7:2 (NLT)

Observation

As chapter 7 rolls around, David has settled into life as the king and leader of Israel. According to the scriptures, David has, "rest on every side from all his enemies." Now that his attention is no longer diverted towards fighting the battles of his nation, David becomes focused on the house of God. He is concerned that he lives in a palace of splendor while the presence of God seems to dwell in a house of canvas. He inquires of the Prophet Nathan if he should begin the construction of what will become the Temple. The Lord reveals to Nathan that David is not to build the Temple, but that one of his sons will be given that task. The second half of the chapter is devoted to an extended prayer of thanks from the heart of David.

Application

Nearly two decades ago, we moved our family to Nashville to accept the call of pastoring the Woodmont Baptist Church. One of the exciting aspects of our move as a family was the ability to plan and build a new home. I remember the joy we shared in picking out the lot and then deciding on the features. We chose the floor plan, the color of the brick, the type of carpet and hardwood, along with the kitchen appliances. Our decisions were not made quickly or lightly. We carefully anticipated the needs of our family and built accordingly. Our desire was to live in a sturdy and strong house that would provide a place of shelter and nurture throughout the years.

In 1 Corinthians 3:16, Paul reminds us, "Do you not know that you are a temple of God and that the Spirit of God dwells in you?" (NASB). Knowing that God is not contained in structures built by human hands, we must affirm that God lives in us. How well we construct and maintain God's dwelling place is important. Part of this conversation certainly could be devoted to the stewardship of our physical bodies. It should be apparent to all, that the healthier our lifestyles, the greater the length of time that God might be able to work through us. It does matter how well we care for ourselves. But another portion of this conversation must also focus on the "inner self." We must be conscious of what we allow to cohabitate with God's Spirit within us. Because we are human, it is easy for us to make all kinds of room for our human nature. We can let greed, lust, anger, and bitterness crowd out the room we should be reserving for God's Spirit. Allowing God to truly indwell our lives is a conscious and deliberate choice. It should make sense, that the more we allow God to fill our lives, the less room we leave for any unwanted thought to take root. Let's create space for God. Let's resolve that we will build God a proper house.

Prayer

Father, help us to create usable, livable, and sacred space for you in our lives. Amen.

Day 275 — 2 Samuel 8: Management vs. Leadership

> "After this, David defeated and subdued the Philistines by conquering Gath, their largest town. David also conquered the land of Moab."
> 2 Samuel 8:1-2b (NLT)

Observation

Chapter 8 instructs the reader about the expansion of the kingdom of Israel under David's leadership. The rapid growth and military victories are evidence of God's grace and favor in David's life. David is victorious in every geographical direction. He defeats the Philistines in the west, the Moabites in the east, the kingdom of Hadadezar in the north, and the Edomites in the south. The kingdom grows in such size and influence that David creates a bureaucracy to administer the functions of government. Several of his key leaders are named in this chapter.

There is a small, but important detail to highlight in this chapter. As the chapter describes the various military conquests, it is always David who leads the battle. He is clearly in charge and clearly leading every assault and conquest. Three chapters from now, the narrative will describe David's great sin with Bathsheba. Read that story closely and you will discover that David is not in his usual place leading his army, but instead, he has sent his generals in his place. He goes from leadership to management.

Application

Because I direct a leadership institute here at Belmont, I am always curious about leadership styles and initiatives. In a class that I teach with undergraduates on servant leadership, we often discuss the difference between leadership and management. Although there are many definitions of each term, there is one simple distinction that seems to rise to the surface of every discussion. Gifted and experienced leaders state it this way... "Managers manage things; leaders lead people." Managers in an organization tend to manage things like budgets, resources, time sheets, inventory, etc. Leaders, on the other hand, tend to be out front, leading co-workers by example and by instilling core values. Leaders "inspire" others. They literally take the spirit of passion and vision they have for their organization and place it into the lives of other people. King David tended to do well when he led but was not so successful when he merely managed.

So, here's my question for you today... Are you managing those entrusted to you—family, friends, co-workers—or are you leading them? Leaders inspire. They move to the front and encourage others to follow them. They lead by example. In terms of Kingdom work, you will do well as you learn to live authentically and honestly, and then lead through example. Look to the leadership example of Christ. "Follow Me, and I will make your fishers of men" (Matthew 4:19 NASB). If you want to make a significant difference in the lives of others, lead by example.

Prayer

Father, inspire us that we might in turn, inspire others. Amen.

Day 276   2 Samuel 9: Keeping Your Word

> "'Don't be afraid!' David said. 'I intend to show kindness to you because of my promise to your father, Jonathan. I will give you all the property that once belonged to your grandfather Saul, and you will eat here with me at the king's table!'" 2 Samuel 9:7 (NLT)

Observation
Chapter 9 tells the story of an extraordinary act of kindness by King David. Remembering an earlier promise that he made to Jonathan to protect and care for his family, David initiates an inquiry to see if there are any descendants of Saul's household remaining. Ziba, the caretaker of Saul's estate, reminds David that Mephibosheth is still alive. Mephibosheth was Jonathan's son, crippled for life when the nurse holding him dropped him as the news of Saul and Jonathan's deaths reached her ears. David moves Mephibosheth, along with his family, to Jerusalem. He returns all of Saul's land to him and promises that he will eat at the king's table for the rest of his life. Eating at the king's table was a privilege reserved for only the king's sons and high officials. In this act, David displays kindness to a direct descendant of King Saul, whom some may have seen as a potential threat to David.

Application
I was reading a book on leadership recently, when the following quote caught my attention: "In a 2009 international study, the majority of people said they trust a stranger more than they trust their own boss" (James Kouzess & Barry Posner, *The Truth About Leadership*, San Francisco: Jossey-Bass, 2010, 75.) I found that shocking. All of us who serve as leaders would like to think we have established such a sense of truth and authenticity in our various roles that such a quote would not apply to us. We want people to trust our words, our actions, and our motivations. The same hope should apply to any person, especially to those who are of the household of faith. We all realize that a lack of credibility can ruin our reputation and damage the effectiveness of our witness. We must be persons of integrity, honesty, and consistency. Let me invite you this morning to do a little soul-searching by asking this question, "Am I trustworthy?" Are you? Are you reliable? Do you keep your promises? Can the people around you trust what you are saying? Jesus once said that those who were faithful in the little things, could be trusted to be faithful in the greater things (Luke 16:10). At the end of the day, the measure of our credibility may not be measured by the lifelong promises that we make, but in the small day-to-day commitments that we keep. Have you kept today's promises? Have you fulfilled the small commitments made to those around you this week? Have you valued others by honoring the pledges you have made to them? May God help us all to be faithful in both the large and small commitments we make.

Prayer
Father, forge in us the integrity needed to be trusted. Amen.

Day 277 — 2 Samuel 10: Listening to Bad Advice

> "The Ammonite commanders said to Hanun, their master, 'Do you really think these men are coming here to honor your father? No! David has sent them to spy out the city so they can come in and conquer it!'"
> 2 Samuel 10:3 (NLT)

Observation

This chapter continues the story of David's rise to power and reign of influence. As the chapter begins, David desires to show kindness to Hanun, whose recently deceased father was king of Ammon. David sends an envoy of ambassadors to express his grief. Hanun begins to listen to the voices of his advisors who insist that the gesture is insincere and that the Israelites are spies. The ambassadors are mistreated. The Ammonites shave off half of their beards and cut their robes exposing their buttocks. Both are acts of great insult and shame. To shame the ambassadors of the king is to bring shame to the king himself. The action of the Ammonites becomes a call to war. Realizing the power of the Israelite army, Hanun hires mercenary soldiers to bolster his army. The result is not good. David leads the Israelites into battle. Seven-hundred charioteers and 40,000 foot-soldiers from Ammon lose their lives as David's power continues to build.

Application

It's interesting where we seek advice these days. With more of us making purchases on-line, we tend to look at the "ratings and reviews" offered by each website. For example, recently I wanted to buy a pair of shoes from Amazon. So naturally, I read through the various reviews that people offered about their experience with a particular brand of shoes. Some had very positive things to say, while others gave the shoes a poor rating. I looked at a different pair which had only superior on-line ratings. I bought that pair of shoes based solely on the advice given by other on-line shoppers.

Where can we get consistent, valuable, and dependable advice these days on life-long, destiny-determining choices? Where do we get advice for the really big decisions? I would challenge you to stay in the Word of God. With every major life decision, we should ask, "What wisdom does God's Word bring to this moment?" Joined to that is the need to pray for the Spirit's direction and wisdom in our lives. Let me also challenge you to pay attention to the "advisors" that you allow in your life. In today's text, Hanun's downfall was caused by listening to men who offered bad advice and counsel. Consider for a moment who is in your circle of counsel. Are there trusted voices who have the wisdom of both age and experience? Are there friends who will tell you the truth and not just what you want to hear? Choose your advisors carefully and listen closely.

Prayer

Father, may we have the common sense to surround ourselves with wise counsel. Amen.

Day 278   2 Samuel 11: The Place of Failure

> "In the spring of the year, when kings normally go out to war, David sent Joab and the Israelite army to fight the Ammonites. They destroyed the Ammonite army and laid siege to the city of Rabbah. However, David stayed behind in Jerusalem." 2 Samuel 11:1 (NLT)

Observation
Chapter 11 tells the sordid tale of David's great sin. He falters. He stumbles. He disappoints himself and most importantly, he displeases God. It all begins, as our focus verse indicates, when David chooses not to go out with his army to lead his soldiers in battle. He finds himself in the wrong place. On a late afternoon stroll across the roof of his palace, he spots Bathsheba while she bathes. He takes a long and lingering look. He inquires about her and then sends for her. The result of his indiscretion is a pregnancy. His sin with Bathsheba will not be hidden for long. Wanting to cover up his sin, David orders her husband, Uriah, home from the war and encourages him to sleep with his wife. When this tactic fails, he has Uriah placed at the forefront of the next battle where he is killed. Now a grieving widow, Bathsheba is taken into David's household and becomes one of his wives.

Application
Obviously, there are many facets to this story. It is one of the defining moments in David's life. (Psalm 51 is a reflection of his deep grief and shame.) I want you to notice where the story gets off track. It all starts with the first verse when David is not where he is supposed to be. Rather than lead his troops, he remains at the palace. He is in the place of failure. He made the choice to live for the moment in a place where he should not have been. Had he been on the battlefield, the lure of temptation would not have reached his heart. A couple of thoughts… first, sometimes we sin because we allow ourselves to be in the wrong place physically. You may have heard the old expression that parents sometimes offer their teenage kids when imposing a curfew… "Nothing good happens after midnight." It is true that often we are undone by temptation because we go to the wrong place and engage in the wrong activities. We set ourselves up for failure because we step into the wrong setting. It could be a bar, a co-worker's office, an on-line chat room, or a room filled with the wrong influence. Second, sometimes we sin because we allow ourselves to be in the wrong place emotionally. We allow ourselves to be in the wrong relationships. At other moments, we enter into dark places because we have let the key relationships of our lives slip into angry periods of resentment and neglect. We let our frustrations and disappointments talk us into betraying our best thoughts and relationships. So be careful. Make sure that today you are not standing in the place of failure.

Prayer
Father, teach us to guard our hearts, our eyes, our thoughts, and our lives. Amen.

Day 279 — 2 Samuel 12: The Scars of Forgiveness

> "Then David confessed to Nathan, 'I have sinned against the Lord.' Nathan replied, 'Yes, but the Lord has forgiven you, and you won't die for this sin. Nevertheless, because you have shown utter contempt for the Lord by doing this, your child will die.'" 2 Samuel 12:13-14 (NLT)

Observation
God sends a prophet named Nathan to David to confront David about his sin with Bathsheba and the taking of Uriah's life. Nathan tells a parable about a rich man who owns many sheep and cattle, and a poor man who owns only one beloved lamb. When the rich man needs to provide a meal for a guest, he takes the poor man's lamb, slaughters it, and serves it to his guest. When David hears the story, he is furious. Nathan declares, "You are the man!" He confronts David with the horrific nature of what he has done. Nathan declares that David will "live by the sword," meaning that there will be little rest from conflict during his rule. (Three of David's sons will die violent deaths.) David confesses his sin before the Lord. Nathan declares that the Lord has forgiven David but that the child born as a result, will die.

Application
Do you remember the episode of *The Andy Griffith Show* when Opie gets a wood burning tool and he burns the house number into the wooden door frame? Andy corrects the behavior and certainly forgives him, but... the mistake is going to last for a while, or at least until the damage can be repaired. I'm reminded of the same message in this story of David. Our sins can be forgiven, but the consequences of our actions are not so quickly erased. What a great God we serve and what great assurances we hold from God's Word! God works constantly at our redemption. God longs to heal our brokenness and forgive our transgressions. God separates us from our sins "as far as the east is from the west" (Psalm 103:12a NASB). In fact, we are promised that "If we will confess our sins, He is faithful and just to forgive our sins and cleanse us from all unrighteousness" (1 John 1:9 NASB). God does not hold a grudge against us because of our failures. The whole point of the atoning death of Christ is so that our sins do not have to define us nor condemn us. Grace fills the heart of God. But please understand that though we might revel in the joy of our redemption, we may still have to work hard at cleaning up the mess that our mistakes have created. Our sins can damage relationships and reputations. Our sins can cause harm and inflict pain. Though our sins are erased in the heart and mind of God, the scars of our actions can linger among those we have injured. So, what to do? Accept God's grace. Forgive yourself. Start the long and slow process of healing the brokenness your actions have caused. Regret your actions forever, or work toward redemption... Your choice.

Prayer
God, may we find healing in your forgiveness and grace among those we have hurt.

Day 280 — 2 Samuel 13: Temptation's Power

> "Then suddenly Amnon's love turned to hate, and he hated her even more than he had loved her. 'Get out of here!' he snarled at her."
> 2 Samuel 13:15 (NLT)

Observation
Chapter 13 is a bit complicated and crazy. It tells a shameful family story of lust, power, rape, and revenge. Remember as you read the story that David has multiple wives and many children. Absalom and Tamar are full brother and sister, having both the same father (King David) and mother. They share a very close bond. Amnon is David's firstborn son (born to a different mother) who falls in love with his half-sister Tamar. His love/lust for her is both overwhelming and forbidden according to Mosaic law (Leviticus 18:11). Jonadab, a cousin of Amnon, creates a plan for Amnon that will allow him to be alone with Tamar. The plan works, and while alone Amnon overpowers and rapes Tamar. As soon as the deed is done, Amnon's emotions completely reverse. Where he had once felt great passion for Tamar, he now feels great hatred. The shame of his deeds has made him hate both himself and the victim of his deeds. Absalom discovers what has happened, and two years later, when an opportunity arises, he has several of his servants kill Amnon in revenge for what he has done to his beloved sister.

Application
Perhaps you recall the iconic Christmas movie played endlessly each year on Christmas day, simply titled, *A Christmas Story*. One of the story lines features Ralphie, who has been waiting with almost unbearable anticipation to receive his Little Orphan Annie decoder in the mail so that he can decipher a secret message. With great excitement, he decodes the hidden message, "Be sure to drink your Ovaltine." "A crummy commercial?" asks Ralphie with great disgust. The great anticipation had turned to great disappointment. That's the way temptation works. When the serpent lured Adam and Eve with the forbidden fruit, the promise was of great power and wisdom. As soon as they gave in to the temptation, they discovered shame, remorse, and brokenness. They hated what they suddenly saw in themselves. I can't begin to know what tempts you today. You may feel the lure of power, revenge, or sexual fulfillment. You may feel tempted to act on your greed, your anger, or your lust. Don't think for a moment you are immune or strong enough in your own power to defeat whatever temptation brings your way. To listen to temptation's siren voice will surely draw you into ruin. What to do? Christ gave us an answer… honest prayer in the face of our weak resolve. "And lead us not into temptation, but deliver us from evil." There is a powerful force attempting to claim you as its next victim. Pray fervently and stand strong.

Prayer
God, give us strength today to say no to the soul-threatening influences of temptation. Amen

Day 281 — 2 Samuel 14: Restoration

> "All of us must die eventually. Our lives are like water spilled out on the ground, which cannot be gathered up again. But God does not just sweep life away; instead, he devises ways to bring us back when we have been separated from him." 2 Samuel 14:14 (NLT)

Observation
Chapter 14 opens with a deep divide in David's family due to Absalom's vengeful murder of Amnon. (Both are sons of David.) Joab, the king's general, perceives that David's heart has been pierced by three years of separation from his third son, Absalom. Joab longs to bring reconciliation. He devises a plan that involves using a woman from Tekoa to present a fabricated judicial case before the king. Her story involves a widow whose two sons had been in conflict, resulting in the death of one of those sons. She tells the king that her extended family wants to execute the remaining son for his crime. David insists that such action is wrong and that he would provide protection. The woman then tells David that her story is really about his own household. He is convicted about the brokenness within his family and moves Absalom to Jerusalem where they will eventually be reconciled.

Application
About a year ago, a tree fell on my car, leaving a few scratches and dents. I decided to save the $500 deductible and live with the imperfections. I was able to buff away the scratches and "pop out" a few of the dents. Most who look at my car never notice the little dings and dents that remain, but I notice. It's difficult to enjoy the beauty of the car because I tend to see only the imperfections. If I had been willing to pay the cost of restoration, I would know the joy of driving my car again. You get the point. Restoration costs... but taking the effort to erase the brokenness is well worth the pain and expense. We know that "God demonstrates His own love toward us, in that while we were yet sinners, Christ died for us" (Romans 5:8 NASB). God's refusal to accept brokenness forced payment of a heavy restoration price. God offered the gift of Jesus so that we would know redemption and grace. So, let me ask, are we willing to pay the price of restoration that the brokenness in our lives forces us to pay? Not all the relationships in our lives are as we would want them to be. There are strained relationships with family members, neighbors, co-workers, and former friends. For whatever reason, we are often content to "write-off" the relationship. But what we fail to see is that with each severed relationship, we lose a little of ourselves. We lose the potential to grow, to gain perspective, to know joy, to contribute to someone's life. We must pray to become more like God We must long for restoration. It is a difficult task, this job of mending fences and healing hurt. I pray we will never become satisfied with the imperfections of our broken lives.

Prayer
Father God, may we take on the hard task of reconciliation and restoration. Amen.

Day 282

2 Samuel 15: A Smooth Talker

> "When people tried to bow before him, Absalom wouldn't let them. Instead, he took them by the hand and kissed them. Absalom did this with everyone who came to the king for judgment, and so he stole the hearts of all the people of Israel." 2 Samuel 15:5-6 (NLT)

Observation

Let's remember a couple things about Absalom. First, he was the third oldest son of David, and because of the deaths of the two oldest sons, he was first in the line of succession to become king. Second, he was an impressive figure. Second Samuel 14:25 says, "Now Absalom was praised as the most handsome man in all Israel. He was flawless from head to foot" (NLT). Not content to be just the prince of Israel, Absalom begins to undermine the authority and influence of his father, David. He would position himself at the city gate each morning and greet travelers who entered the city in hopes to have the king rule in whatever judicial case they brought to him. With his smooth talk and crafty words, he "stole the hearts of all the people." As the narrative progresses, Absalom travels away from Jerusalem under the guise of going to Hebron to offer a sacrifice. While there he continues to galvanize support for himself against the king. His very successful manipulations rally the tribes of Israel in his support. As they march on Jerusalem to overthrow the king, David has to flee the city. He leaves the Ark of the Covenant in the city as a sign of the Lord's presence, telling the people that if it is the will of the Lord, he will return.

Application

Absalom is a politician of the first order. He's the kind of man who would hug all the women and kiss all the babies. His good looks, along with his persuasive language, made him absolutely irresistible to most. With great precision and well-timed remarks, he quickly turned the people away from King David. He's not the first smooth talker we encounter in scripture. Back in Genesis 3 we read of the ways that satan began to spin a web of deceit and doubt. Soon Eve and Adam were talked into doing things they knew were against God's decrees. Move ahead to the days of Jesus. Remember how satan tempted Jesus in the wilderness? And then remember how the scriptures indicate that satan left him "until an opportune time" (Luke 4:13 NASB). That same voice of evil continues to seek disruption in our relationship with God. With smooth words, or deliciously lustful thoughts, or bitter feelings of revenge, or selfish motivations, his words can penetrate both hearts and minds until we no longer stand strong in the face of temptation. We are swayed by his allure and the false promises that he makes. So, pay attention today at who greets you at the city gate of your life. Beware that someone already has a plan to destroy your life and your relationship with God. Be strong. Be courageous. Be smart.

Prayer

God, give us the wisdom needed today to see the influence of evil and resist. Amen.

Day 283 — 2 Samuel 16: When Life Catches Up with Us

> "The king and all who were with him grew weary along the way, so they rested when they reached the Jordan River." 2 Samuel 16:14 (NLT)

Observation
This chapter continues the narrative of Absalom's rebellion. As the story begins, David and his entourage are fleeing Jerusalem. Ziba, who is a servant to Mephibosheth—grandson of King Saul—offers provisions of bread, raisins, and wine for David and his men. Ziba tells David that Mephisbosheth has stayed in Jerusalem hoping to reclaim the kingdom of his grandfather. David believes Ziba's story and promises that Ziba will claim all of Mephibosheth's possessions. (It is later discovered that Ziba is more of an opportunist and has not been forthright in all that he has said to David.) As David and his men continue to flee, he is taunted by a man named Shimei, who is also part of Saul's clan. David and his men travel all the way to the Jordan river before resting. In the meantime, Absalom has entered Jerusalem, and under the advice of a man named Hushai, sleeps with all of David's palace concubines who had been left behind. His actions have both moral and political ramifications.

Application
Admittedly, this chapter has a lot of plot twists and various characters are introduced. It's a little hard to follow all the action as it quickly unfolds. Part of the intention of the writer is to show the chaos surrounding David. Most commentators point to God's continual punishment and correction of David for his great sin with Bathsheba and the killing of her husband. It is readily apparent that David knows little rest and peace. His life is in turmoil. He questions the loyalty of those around him. He is both mentally and physically exhausted. He finally arrives at a safe spot where he and his men can rest in the midst of the turmoil. David and his men are not the only ones who could use a little rest. Most of us feel the constant tension of a hectic, over-scheduled life. We get pulled in all directions. We resemble the old circus act of a man spinning a bunch of plates. Most of us rush around just trying to keep it all going. You know all too well what I am describing. There are work demands, family schedules, unplanned interruptions, emergencies, crisis moments, etc. There are days we can't run fast enough to get ahead of it all. So where do we find our rest? How can we carve out a little space to catch our breath and rest for a moment? I remember the wise counsel of a seminary professor who once told me, "Recess daily, relax weekly, and retreat monthly." It's good advice that we need to hear. So, try this… somewhere during this day, take just 15 minutes to be alone and without distraction. Turn off the phone. Turn off the television. Turn away from the crowd. Take a little recess. It won't solve all the problems, but it's a start. Attempt to make it a daily habit.

Prayer
God, teach us to find the quiet moments within our hectic days. Amen.

Day 284   2 Samuel 17: When Things Don't Go Your Way

> "When Ahithophel realized that his advice had not been followed, he saddled his donkey, went to his hometown, set his affairs in order, and hanged himself. He died there and was buried in the family tomb."
> 2 Samuel 17:23 (NLT)

Observation
Chapter 17 opens with Ahithophel offering words of counsel to Absalom. He advises Absalom that he should attack David with a mighty force of 12,000 soldiers. When King David is killed, the kingdom will belong to Absalom. Absalom also seeks the counsel of Hushai, who unbeknownst to Absalom is a friend, supporter, and spy of King David. He rejects the counsel of Ahithophel telling Absalom that his plan could backfire and that Absalom himself should lead the attack against David. When it becomes apparent that Absalom prefers the plans of Hushai, Hushai secretly sends word to David to warn him and to instruct him to flee beyond the Jordan River. When Ahithophel learns that his counsel has not been accepted, he realizes that Absalom's coup d'état is doomed to failure and that his (Ahithophel) political maneuvering will backfire and his lack of loyalty to David will bring severe punishment. As a result, he travels home, puts his affairs in order, and ends his life.

Application
Most of us tend to think that we can offer good, sound advice and counsel. Whether someone even asks for our opinion, we are always glad to give it. It strokes our egos to be the "source of all wisdom and knowledge." But what happens when someone ignores our advice or rejects the counsel that we offer? How do we deal with such rejection? In the story of Absalom and Ahithophel, Ahithophel is devastated when Absalom ignores his advice. In fact, he is so defeated by the rejection, he takes his own life. Hopefully we would never resort to such action. Typically, when someone ignores our advice, we feel a little sting of rejection. We sulk. We display a little self-pity. And then we tend to hope that the person rejecting our advice will suffer as a result. "He/she will get what they deserve." It's as though we want fate to punish them for not listening to our "infallible" wisdom.

    Is there a better way to handle rejection? I think so. First, we need to remind ourselves that all we can do is offer our best thought. If someone chooses to head off in another direction, that's their choice. Second, we need to remember that a rejection of our counsel does not necessarily mean a rejection of who we are. Sometimes sane, rational people simply do not agree on how to solve an issue. Your counsel may enlighten and give perspective even if it is not the ultimate direction a person takes. Third, we need to recognize that no one, not even us, has all the answers. Hopefully we can learn together as we attempt to live wisely.

Prayer
Dear Father, teach us to learn positive lessons even amid rejection. Amen.

Day 285 — 2 Samuel 18: Dangerous Territory

> "The battle raged all across the countryside, and more men died because of the forest than were killed by the sword." 2 Samuel 18:8 (NLT)

Observation
This chapter tells the story of the battle in which David's son, Absalom, dies. As the scene opens, David places three men in charge of his soldiers. He is convinced not to lead in battle but to remain behind. David gives instructions, from fatherly sentiments, to "Deal gently with young Absalom." The forces of Israel and the forces of David battle in the thickly wooded and treacherous forest of Ephraim. At the end of the day, 20,000 men lose their lives. According to our focus verse, more died because of the dangerous terrain of the forest than by actual battle wounds. While riding his donkey, Absalom is caught by his hair in the thick branches of an oak tree. While suspended from the tree, Joab, one of David's generals, pierces his heart with three spears. Other soldiers finish the task of killing Absalom. His body is thrown into a deep pit and covered with stones. Two runners race back to David to share the news that his son has died. The chapter ends with David expressing deep sorrow and regret.

Application
As I write the words of this devotional thought, I tried to recall the most difficult terrain that I have ever encountered. I remember vividly a day when I, along with a group of several others, rode our way up a steep and rocky mountainside in the wilderness of Haiti. I also recall a time when I made my way through a dense thicket, a slippery creek, and a rocky hillside just to visit a prime fishing lake located on some rural land in central Kentucky. But even those experiences must pale in comparison to what the armies described in this Bible story had to encounter. Can you imagine a forest so dense and dangerous that it took the lives of thousands of men?

Let's take a moment to consider a different kind of dangerous territory—the lure of temptation. For the young man in Jesus' parable of the prodigal son, the dangerous territory was the "distant land" that promised a false freedom and a carefree life. It is my belief that the distant land doesn't really have to be that far away. It's the place we find ourselves anytime we are willing to step over the boundaries of godly conduct and decent thought. It's that dangerous territory where we no longer allow ourselves to hear God's Spirit directing our lives, choosing instead to listen to other voices or even to ourselves. The dangerous territory teaches us that ethics don't matter, that commitments can be broken, that peer pressure should rule the day. Whenever we allow ourselves to step into such a deep thicket of falsehood and deception, we expose ourselves to all kinds of dangers. Better mind your steps today. Make sure that you pay attention to where your journey leads.

Prayer
Dear Father, call us to righteous and distinct living that honors you. Amen.

Day 286 — 2 Samuel 19: A Swift Kick in the Pants

> "'Now go out there and congratulate your troops, for I swear by the Lord that if you don't go out, not a single one of them will remain here tonight. Then you will be worse off than ever before.'" 2 Samuel 19:7 (NLT)

Observation
As the scene opens in Chapter 19, David is grieving his son, Absalom. So deep is his grief that a sense of sorrow has spread all throughout the city. (The people sense the grief of their king, and they give him space to process that emotion.) There is a very negative side-effect. The soldiers who are returning from battle should have been celebrated for their great victory. There should have been parades and dancing and laughter. Instead, they enter the city without fanfare, as though they should have been ashamed by their actions. They feel as though their efforts have not been valued. It is Joab, commander of the army, who goes to David to encourage him to be more supportive of the troops. He actually commands him to go out and congratulate the men. David heeds the advice and in so doing, changes the spirit of the city. As the chapter continues, David is warmly welcomed back to Jerusalem with the full support of the tribes of Israel.

Application
Sometimes, we need a swift kick in the pants to get us to do the right thing. From time to time we need someone to speak truth into our lives so that we change our negative behavior into making better choices. For example, I just recently had a dental check-up and tooth cleaning. You know the routine… the dental hygienist pokes, picks, and flosses away all the built-up plaque. He or she gives your teeth a good cleaning, followed typically by a good scolding. "Have you been flossing each day? Have you been brushing regularly? Have you been eating too much candy?" It's a call to be more deliberate and careful in managing one's dental health.

Beyond the call to establish better habits that affect our physical selves, some of us may also need a little spiritual encouragement. It's easy to be lackadaisical when it comes to managing our spiritual disciplines. Let's be honest… it can be difficult to take the time to read, reflect, and pray every day. Interruptions to our schedules can occur at any moment and before we realize it, we have gone several days, or even a week, or maybe a month without tending to matters of faith. So, let me give you that swift kick in the pants today. You need to spend some time with the Word. You need to update your prayer list. You need to find a quiet moment to listen to what the Spirit of God is whispering. Growing in your faith will not happen by accident. It takes deliberate effort. Just in case you haven't been as faithful as you would like, don't beat yourself up this morning, but do make a fresh start. The effort will yield great results.

Prayer
Father God, may we have the discipline needed to grow in our faith this day. Amen.

Day 287   2 Samuel 20: The Power of Conversation

> "But a wise woman in the town called out to Joab, 'Listen to me, Joab. Come over here so I can talk to you.'" 2 Samuel 20:16 (NLT)

Observation
As the narrative begins in chapter 20, tribal feuding has increased between the 10 tribes in the north and Judah in the south. A man named Sheba, who is described as a "worthless fellow," leads a rebellion against the leadership of King David. He is eloquent and charismatic and soon many agree to support him. Abishai is sent by David to squash the rebellion. He will be joined in the effort by Joab. When David's forces catch up to Sheba, he is hiding in the city of Abel Beth-Maacah. A wise woman from that city engages Joab in a conversation. She is able to broker a deal. Instead of a complete destruction of the city, including the knocking down of the city wall, she agrees to rally the people within and have them kill Sheba. She will throw his severed head over the wall. Joab agrees to her plan and the deed is done. Sheba is slain and the city is saved. With the failed rebellion, David once again firmly establishes control of the kingdom.

Application
Never underestimate the power of a conversation. When people tend to talk directly to each other, disagreements often find resolution, tensions ease, perspective is gained, and problems get solved. Regrettably, most of us do more talking about people, typically behind their backs, than we do talking to those people. We need to remember that there is power in our conversations.

Years ago, while I served as pastor of the First Baptist Church of Gatlinburg, a restaurant owner wanted to develop a business on the property adjacent to the church. At the town council meeting, many people gathered to present their thoughts. There were lawyers and city planners, and a whole host of council members. Much had been assumed and many conversations had occurred behind the scenes. As the meeting went late and tensions grew, I simply asked the city manager if the council could recess for a moment and give me and the restaurant owner a few minutes to speak privately. Behind a closed door, I spoke to the owner about my concerns, and he expressed his solutions for those concerns. We agreed on a plan and quickly returned to the town council meeting for a quick resolution. What made the difference? The power of a conversation.

There are probably a few unresolved situations in your life this morning. Maybe there are some relationships that need a little work. Let me suggest a simple solution… just talk to each other. The direct and honest dialogue can solve a lot of problems.

Prayer
Heavenly Father, teach us the value of honest conversation. Amen.

Day 288 — 2 Samuel 21: Making Things Right

> "So let seven of Saul's sons be handed over to us, and we will execute them before the Lord at Gibeon, on the mountain of the Lord."
> 2 Samuel 21:6 (NLT)

Observation
This chapter reveals that a 3-year famine has occurred in Israel. David prays to God seeking a reason for it. The Lord reveals that the famine is the result of Saul's sin of murdering several Gibeonites. During the early days of the conquest, Joshua had made a covenant with the Gibeonites, promising to protect them (Joshua 9:3-27). David asked the Gibeonites what was needed to atone for the deaths of their kinsmen. They did not want financial reparations but asked that seven grandsons of Saul be executed to atone for the sins of Saul. Because Saul was already dead, he could not be executed for his crime. Seven grandsons are handed over and publicly executed by the Gibeonites. Their blood would pay the price for the sins of Saul. The demands of the law are fulfilled, atonement is made, and the famine ends. (The remainder of the chapter deals with David's defeat of four Philistine giants who had opposed Israel.)

Application
Obviously, this chapter deals with difficult issues. According to the narrative, the famine is a result of Saul's sin. By not keeping the covenant established by Joshua, his actions brought God's punishment in the form of a famine. We may be troubled by the notion that many had to suffer because of one man's sin. We can argue the unfairness of what occurred but certainly we cannot escape the vivid reminder of the rippling effects of our actions. We live in community with each other. When we choose to live well and honor God and others through our actions, the community thrives. When we choose disobedience and lawlessness, the community is lessened. In this case, Saul's sins resulted in a famine that caused many to suffer. In like fashion, our selfishly committed sins can cause many of those around us to suffer. The second difficult point is that of the execution of seven men to atone for the killing of the Gibeonites. One could read this passage and assume that God is somehow pleased by human sacrifice or execution because the famine ends when these men are slain. The takeaway, however, is not that God is a blood-thirsty tyrant, but that God cares about the way in which we keep our vows and the effort we must offer to make things right again with our neighbors against whom we have sinned. It is never easy to ask for grace amid mistakes. It is hard to confess when we have sinned. But beyond our confession must come the attempt to do whatever it takes to restore and heal the brokenness. I'm not suggesting the sacrifice of a family member, but I am suggesting that you take the effort to be reconciled to those who you have wronged through consistent and compassionate acts.

Prayer
Heavenly Father, help us to do the hard work of restoration. Amen.

Day 289 — 2 Samuel 22: The Power of Song

> "I called on the Lord, who is worthy of praise, and he saved me from my enemies." 2 Samuel 22:4 (NLT)

Observation

This entire chapter is a song of praise written by David on the day the Lord rescued him from all his enemies and from Saul. It is virtually identical to Psalm 18. The theme of the chapter reminds the reader of the sovereignty and deliverance of God. There are some commentators who suggest that the chapter may be out of order chronologically. The events described do seem to speak to an earlier period in David's reign when Saul was still alive and before David's transgression with Bathsheba. Throughout the chapter, David uses some very descriptive words for the power of God, describing him as rock, fortress, refuge, shield, horn, and stronghold. David reminds the reader that he has called on the Lord and has been saved from all his enemies.

Application

It is always interesting to me the power that a song can have. For example, ever hear a song first thing in the morning and it stays with you for the rest of the day? The notes and lyrics continue to echo through your mind all day long. You catch yourself humming the tune in your head and maybe when you are alone in the car, you even break out a few notes, believing that you're not such a bad singer after all. For some reason as I write this devotional thought, I have the melody of "Do You Hear the People Sing?" from Les Misérables, dancing around my head. (I like to think of myself as a true Renaissance man...) But songs can do that. They can have power over us. In fact, they can even speak power into our lives, or offer hope, or encouragement, or lift our spirits. They can inspire, teach, or offer comfort and grace.

I grew up in a traditional Baptist church where singing the great hymns of faith was a vital part of every worship experience. Unlike a lot of other churches, we even sang the third verse of every hymn! (You churchgoers in the crowd will understand that last sentence.) Singing was important. The hymns taught theology. If pressed on the matter, I can probably recite more hymn lyrics than I can quote Bible verses. That joining together of melody and lyric is a very powerful force. Let me invite you to do something a little different today... I want you to think about a hymn or a praise song that speaks to you in a special way. (Hopefully you have a favorite or two.) Take a moment to listen to the song. Pull it up on your phone or Google it on your computer. Let it just soak in for a moment so that it will float around in your head throughout the day. Let God speak to you through the power of a song. Pay attention to the words. Consider how the inspired lyrics offer you some insight into God's activity in your life.

Prayer

Father God, thank you for the gift of inspired music. Amen.

Day 290 — 2 Samuel 23: Giving Value to Sacrifice

> "David remarked longingly to his men, 'Oh, how I would love some of that good water from the well by the gate in Bethlehem.'"
> 2 Samuel 23:15 (NLT)

Observation

This chapter begins with the words, "These are the last words of David…" These are not the actual last words that he ever spoke, but the poetic lines which span the first seven verses are thought to be the last psalm written by David, composed shortly before his death. The psalm describes the way that the Lord had exalted David, taking him from shepherd boy to mighty king. He also describes God's everlasting covenant with the house of David. The second half of the chapter is devoted to a listing of David's mighty men. Thirty-seven different individuals are described in the chapter. David's three most valiant warriors are named along with some of their exploits. Their names are Jashobeam, Eleazar, and Shammah. In the listing of 30 other army "chiefs" an interesting story is embedded. At some point during David's reign, the Philistines, occupied the city of Bethlehem. David, who had found refuge in the cave of Adullam, longs to drink water from the well of Bethlehem. Three brave men risk their lives to break through the enemy lines to bring David the water he desires. When the water is presented, David refuses to drink it. He acknowledges that the water is too precious because it was obtained by three men who willingly risked their lives to bring it to the king. He pours it out as an offering before the Lord, giving great worth to the dedication of these men.

Application

Not that I'm still bitter about this, but I remember a story from the night of the annual high school Christmas dance. I bought my date a beautiful corsage to wear on her dress. Instead of pinning it to her dress, she pinned it to the winter coat that she decided to leave in the car. The flowers never made it to the dance and were in none of the pictures. I don't think she intentionally ignored the flowers, but she didn't value them or think of them as a gift. Again, I'm not bitter… not really.

Sometimes that happens. There are moments when someone does something special for us—they offer their time, their attention, their devotion—and we fail to see the worth and value of their gift. We treat their kind act as though it doesn't matter. What we are in effect saying at such a moment is that they don't matter. I like what David did when he received the gift of water. He held it in his hands like it was the most important gift he had ever received, too valuable to even drink. Imagine the worth and value his actions gave those men. Let me challenge you to be aware of even the seemingly small acts of kindness that people offer on your behalf. You will value them as you acknowledge the worth of their gift.

Prayer

God, may we be appreciative of the people around us and the gifts they bring. Amen.

Day 291 — 2 Samuel 24: Picking Out Your Switch

> "So Gad came to David and asked him, 'Will you choose three years of famine throughout your land, three months of fleeing from your enemies, or three days of severe plague throughout your land? Think this over and decide what answer I should give the Lord who sent me.'"
> 2 Samuel 24:13 (NLT)

Observation

This closing chapter of the book of 2 Samuel tells the story of a sin committed by David and the consequences it brought to Israel. The opening verse is a bit mysterious. It seems to indicate that God's anger is already burning against Israel, and David's action will bring about the punishment. In the narrative, David chooses to take a census of the men in Israel old enough to handle a sword. Though advised against taking the census, David pushes forward. It is apparently an act of pride on his part as he is tempted to think that his strength is found in the number of his soldiers. It takes 10 months to conduct the census. In all there are 1.3 million soldiers. As David begins to gain a sense of guilt and conviction about his actions, a prophet named Gad is sent to David to offer him three options to pay for his sins. He can choose between three years of famine, three months of fleeing from his enemies, or three days of pestilence throughout the land. He chooses the third option. An angel of wrath moves across the land and 70,000 people die. The destruction stops just short of Jerusalem. David builds an altar on the threshing floor of Araunah to offer atoning sacrifices for his sins.

Application

We've all heard a story about a misbehaving child being sent outside to pick out the switch with which they will be punished. These days the narrative is a bit different. Parents don't typically send their kids out to grab a branch off a tree so they can get a "whipping," but they do sometimes give their kids some options about punishment. For example, a teenager might get to choose their punishment: no cell phone for a week, no car keys for a while, or no activities outside of school for a week. Like this story of David, most would try to assess which punishment would be the least disruptive.

Think for a moment in terms of your own sins and acts of disobedience. Consider how God deals with your transgressions. God doesn't give us options for punishment. In fact, God gives us the option of not being punished. Through the atoning death of Christ, God offers us grace, mercy, and forgiveness. We don't have to pay the price of our sins because Christ has already provided the payment. The choice is whether to embrace him as Lord.

Prayer

Father God, thank you for providing a way of redemption from our sins. Amen.

Day 292 — 1 Kings 1: The King's Command

> "There Zadok the priest and Nathan the prophet are to anoint him king over Israel. Blow the ram's horn and shout, 'Long live King Solomon!' Then escort him back here, and he will sit on my throne. He will succeed me as king, for I have appointed him to be ruler over Israel and Judah."
>
> 1 Kings 1:34-35 (NLT)

Observation

This opening chapter to 1 Kings describes the transfer of the monarchy from King David to his son, Solomon. As the story begins, David is approaching the age of 70. His health and strength are in decline. In fact, he is unable to stay warm at night and a young woman is brought into the palace to hold him at night to keep him warm as he sleeps. As word begins to spread of his impending death, there is a scramble for leadership. Adonijah, David's second oldest son wants to take over the throne. He begins to build alliances with key leaders, including Joab, David's military commander. Three of David's most highly trusted leaders, including Nathan the prophet, go to David to tell him that Adonijah was trying to establish himself as king. David moves quickly to enact the oath he had made both to God and to Bathsheba, of anointing his son, Solomon, as king. The chapter ends with the new king firmly in place while Jerusalem erupts in celebration.

Application

When I was kid and questioning why I sometimes had to do the things I was told to do, my father would simply say, "Because I am your father and I said so." And that was it. The matter was settled. Why? Because he was the voice of authority. I had to do whatever he told me to do. As I grew older and had kids of my own, I heard those same words pour out of my mouth. There are those moments when parenting that you just have to pull out the "authority card." King David had vowed that his son Solomon would be the next king. When it came down to competing sons, each trying to enact their own will, he had to step in and declare Solomon's right to reign. David was the king and his commands had to be honored.

We often talk of the Kingdom of God. Jesus proclaimed it and the scriptures bear witness to it. The Kingdom is both reign and realm. It is the place in our heart and lives where Jesus reigns over us. It is also the physical place that will one day be established when he returns. But listen carefully… there can be no kingdom without a king, and there can be no king, unless there are servants committed whole-heartedly to obeying his commands. We have a King, and his name is Jesus. We are his servants. We live and act to fulfill his commands and to represent him well. We are not here on the planet to set our own agendas or to claim authority over our own lives. We are here to serve the King… this day, every day.

Prayer

Father, may we live out our spoken allegiance to the King this day. Amen.

Day 293 — 1 Kings 2: A Difficult Transition

> "Then David died and was buried with his ancestors in the City of David. David had reigned over Israel for forty years, seven of them in Hebron and thirty-three in Jerusalem. Solomon became king and sat on the throne of David his father, and his kingdom was firmly established."
> 1 Kings 2:10-11 (NLT)

Observation

If you just read the two verses printed above, you might believe that the transition of power from King David to King Solomon was smooth and relatively easy. That's not really the case. Although David clearly set forth his son Solomon as his successor, another son, Adonijah continued his attempt to seize the throne. The chapter opens with David giving counsel to Solomon, knowing that his days are drawing to a close. The rest of the chapter deals with several difficult situations and individuals that must be eliminated because of former deeds or current plots. Most prominent in the story is Adonijah's attempt to gain political advantage by asking for the hand of Abishag in marriage. Abishag was the virgin brought into David's chamber to sleep with him at night to keep him warm. By marrying his father's caregiver, Adonijah would strengthen his claim to the throne. He will be executed because of his political manipulations and the reign of Solomon will become firmly established.

Application

Transitions can be difficult. They are difficult because they represent change and all the upheaval, uncertainty, grief, and angst that change brings. Take for example the emotions that employees of a business go through when a new leader is named at the company. Questions swirl about leadership style and what changes will be made to the organization. Or think about the transitions within a family when teenagers grow into young adults and leave the nest to go to college or to begin a working career. Parents feel the pride of seeing their children succeed while also wrestling with the sense of sadness that life moves ahead so quickly. Also consider the transitions that come with old age. It is difficult to become more isolated, more infirmed, and less active. Transitions are a part of life. We move from one chapter to the next. The goal is to move with grace and ease, but seldom is the journey without a few bumps in the road. The greatest transition we are called to experience is the one that takes us from non-believer to Christ-follower. Paul says that such a transition will make us "new creations" (2 Corinthians 5:17). We walk from the darkness into his glorious light, yet not without difficulty. The transition requires that we surrender self and claim Jesus' authority. It requires a radical new way of living, thinking, and trusting that changes us into his likeness.

Prayer

Father help us to deal gracefully and meaningfully with the transitions of life. Amen.

Day 294 — 1 Kings 3: Be Careful What You Ask For

> "Give me an understanding heart so that I can govern your people well and know the difference between right and wrong. For who by himself is able to govern this great people of yours?" 1 Kings 3:9 (NLT)

Observation
This chapter reveals the beginning of one of the greatest monarchies of all time. As the story of Solomon's life is told, chapters 3 and 4 reveal his wise acts and 5 through 9 speak of his amazing building programs. Known world-wide for bringing Israel into world-class status, even the queen of Sheba will visit Solomon. In this chapter, Solomon has a personal encounter with God at Gibeon where he has gone to make sacrifices. When God promises to grant any request that Solomon makes, Solomon asks for wisdom to govern well. God is pleased by the response and promises Solomon not only wisdom, but also fame and riches. The first test of his wisdom appears very soon when two women come to Solomon, both claiming that the child they bring is theirs. Solomon skillfully reveals the identity of the true mother, and the child is given to her.

Application
"Be careful what you wish for… you just might get it." Typically, we view this statement in a negative light. The idea being that you might get exactly what you ask for only to discover that what you thought would be a blessing turns into a burden. It's an indictment on the foolish and selfish nature of many of our requests. Maybe we should take care to consider carefully what we really want to ask of God. Jesus once proclaimed, "If you abide in Me, and My words abide in you, ask whatever you wish, and it shall be done for you" (John 15:7 NASB). Knowing that God hears the prayers that we make, and knowing that God longs to provide, we should truly be careful when we petition God concerning our needs. If God met with you this morning in the private place of prayer and asked, "What shall I do for you?" how would you respond? Would you respond out of selfish motivation or foolish ambition? Would you respond in ways that reflected just "your" needs as opposed to some greater request? We should always treat our moments with God with great care and thoughtfulness. Rather than simply ask God to "bless" us or the people around us, maybe we should be specific. What do you really need from God this day? Do you need assurance? Courage? Wisdom about a big decision? Protection while on a trip? Healing in a broken relationship? Physical strength during a long day? A calm spirit to manage the chaos of the moment? Be careful what you ask for… you just might get it.

Prayer
Father, thank you for your willingness to give us what we need this day. Amen.

Day 295 — 1 Kings 4: Living in a Land of Plenty

> "The people of Judah and Israel were as numerous as the sand on the seashore. They were very contented, with plenty to eat and drink."
> 1 Kings 4:20 (NLT)

Observation

Chapter 4 speaks of the wise organizational structure that Solomon establishes to bring order and prosperity to his kingdom. He sets up a council of wise leaders that provides solid insight and counsel to the king. He also establishes 12 governors over the various demographic and agricultural regions of the kingdom to provide good administration that also included providing financial and agricultural support for the government and the needs of the palace. So grand was the extent of his kingdom, that the needs of the palace court alone required 300 bushels of flour, 600 bushels of meal, and hundreds of animals for meat each day! He also built up the military. He built huge stables to care for the 12,000 horses he owned. The closing verses describe Solomon's superior wisdom over many areas and his ability to write songs and proverbs.

Application

"They were very contented, with plenty to eat and drink." How blessed the people of Israel were during the reign of King Solomon. They truly lived in a land of plenty. Gone were the days of warfare, famine, and scarcity. Their needs were met, and they found contentment. I hope that they were grateful enough for the prosperity they enjoyed that they offered praises to God and learned to share out of their abundance.

I hope we are that grateful as well. In the midst of instability around the world, where many suffer from poverty, hunger, famine, and war, it is truly a privileged place to stand when we can say that we are contented, with plenty to eat and drink. Whenever we find ourselves in such a place, we really do need to thank God for the blessings we enjoy and then, we must learn to share out of our abundance. Any day that I am not hungry or cold or homeless or violated by injustice, I should remember those who are. With each lavish meal I eat, I should lavish a food pantry with donations. Whenever I unlock the door to my safe and warm house, I should volunteer to help build a house for someone who is struggling with safe and affordable housing. Whenever I reach in the closet for a warm jacket, I should consider the gift of a warm jacket to someone who shivers in the cold. You get the point. There is a burden that comes with blessing. It is the responsibility to share. It is the Gospel ethic that says I am to love my neighbor with the same passion with which I love myself. I have not been placed on the planet to merely enjoy my status… I am here to raise the status of others as well.

Prayer

Father, thank you for the ability I have to share with others in need. Amen.

Day 296 — 1 Kings 5: A Little Butter on the Biscuit

> "Therefore, please command that cedars from Lebanon be cut for me. Let my men work alongside yours, and I will pay your men whatever wages you ask. As you know, there is no one among us who can cut timber like you Sidonians!" 1 Kings 5:6 (NLT)

Observation
This chapter begins a long description of some of the major construction projects under the reign of King Solomon. Specifically, this chapter focuses on the initial preparations for the building of the Temple. King Hiram of Tyre was a friend of King David and even provided wood when David's palace was constructed. He is pleased that Solomon will rule in David's place and is anxious to establish a relationship. Solomon wanted the best wood for the Temple. He contacted King Hiram who was pleased to supply the timber. The logs were crafted into rafts and floated along the Mediterranean Coast to the south where they were disassembled and transported over land to Jerusalem. During the same time, stonecutters were employed to begin the excavation of stone for the Temple foundation. The project was massive. According to the chapter, 70,000 workers were used to transport the wood and stone, and 80,000 stone masons were also employed.

Application
Being the wisest of the wise, King Solomon knew how to carefully establish political alliances as well as how to arrange good business deals. Notice what he did in his conversations with King Hiram. He brags about the great work of the Sidonians. (A reference to the region over which King Hiram reigned.) "No one among us can cut timber like you Sidonians!" A little praise can go a long away. Surely the men in Hiram's work force took pride in King Solomon's mention of their good skills. Maybe his kind words even spurred them on to do really good work.

Everybody needs a little pat on the back occasionally. It costs nothing to affirm someone for the good and faithful work they are doing. A little praise can go a long way in helping someone feel valued and needed. You probably have a co-worker or two in your office setting that could benefit from a little ego boost today. Why not take a moment to praise them honestly for something that they continue to do well each day? It costs nothing to offer the compliment but could be just the kind word that person needs today. The same word of counsel applies to your spouse. Reminding your spouse that you are grateful for their constant contribution to your life could be very meaningful. Don't just brag about your husband or wife to others, say something positive to them. Let them know they are of great worth and that you appreciate the things they do each day to make life better.

Prayer
Father, teach us to be grateful and to express that gratitude often. Amen.

Day 297 — 1 Kings 6: Quietly Building

> "The stones used in the construction of the Temple were finished at the quarry, so there was no sound of hammer, ax, or any other iron tool at the building site." 1 Kings 6:7 (NLT)

Observation
Chapter 6 gives many details about the size, shape, and materials used to build the Temple. In the opening verse of the chapter there are several chronological markers to indicate when construction began. Most likely, construction started in 1447 B.C. It took 7½ years to complete the project. The Temple itself was a fairly small worship facility measuring 90 feet by 30 feet and standing 45 feet in height. The interior was completely lined with cedar and covered in gold. It was to be a place of reverence and functionality and was clearly a place of grandeur. Read the chapter carefully and you will notice that not only did God offer instruction about how Solomon was to build the temple, but also how Solomon was to build his heart. God commanded him to walk in the statutes and ordinances that had been established with his father David.

Application
As I read this chapter, I was struck by the seventh verse, which indicated that all the stone-cutting work was done off-site. The various stones were all cut and shaped to fit perfectly and then transported to the construction site where they were to be assembled quietly, with no sound of hammer, ax, or iron tool. It must have been quite an architectural marvel to carry out the construction this way. Here at Belmont University, over the past two decades, several amazing buildings have been constructed. To add needed parking space for campus, many of the newest buildings required deep holes in the ground to provide parking underneath. To build in such a way required a lot of blasting. The explosions were noisy, earth-shaking, and patience-testing for many of our neighbors. Unlike those early Temple builders, there was just no way to build our modern structures in silence.

As individuals longing to establish a firm foundation of faith on which to build our lives, we must pay attention to the construction techniques we employ. Building a strong faith does not happen quickly. It takes intentionality and careful discipline. We read the Word. We say our prayers. We listen for God's voice. We move at the Spirit's prompting. Interestingly, most of the construction happens in silence as we remove the distractions of life away from our hearts and minds so that we can discern the leadership of God. It is in those moments when we are still, contemplative, and thoughtful, that things come into focus. Be deliberate. Be still. Be pliable.

Prayer
Father, help us to grow strong lives of faith resting upon sure foundations. Amen.

Day 298 — 1 Kings 7: The Strong Foundations

> "From foundation to eaves, all these buildings were built from huge blocks of high-quality stone, cut with saws and trimmed to exact measure on all sides. Some of the huge foundation stones were 15 feet long, and some were 12 feet long." 1 Kings 7:9-10 (NLT)

Observation
This chapter describes the completion of the Temple along with the building of Solomon's palace. The palace would take 13 years to construct and was obviously an enormous undertaking. A portion of the palace was called the Palace of the Forest of Lebanon and it alone measured 150 feet by 75 feet and stood 45 feet tall. There was also a huge throne room called the Hall of Justice where Solomon settled legal matters. The focus verses describe the foundational stones placed underneath the palace. This chapter also tells the work of a man named Huram from Tyre who was gifted in casting objects from bronze. He made all the metal components of the Temple including the two massive pillars in the front of the Temple that were 27 feet tall and 18 feet in circumference. He also cast the "Great Sea," a huge water basin that could hold 11,000 gallons of water. This water was used in the sacrificial offerings. By the end of the chapter, the Temple was fully complete.

Application
If you know anything about architecture and building science, you know the importance of foundations. I recall the early stages of building our current home. The first phase of construction was not up, but down. A large backhoe was brought to the property to dig the footers. Once excavated, the footers were filled with concrete. It was upon that foundation that the house was constructed. We have lived in that home for the better part of 18 years now with no structural issues because of the attention paid to the foundation. Foundations are critical for a king's palace, for an office building, and for a residential home. But perhaps of even greater importance are the foundations we build for our lives. There are "foundational stones"—core values—that must continue to undergird our lives. These stones support our beliefs, define our ethics, form our values, and define our character. Foundational stones like honesty, integrity, and justice are the kinds of unwavering life positions that we must establish. In the face of ever-shifting cultural norms and political stances, it becomes vitally important for our witness to be consistent and our values to be rock-solid. I was recently speaking with a friend about the core values of her life. She mentioned that kindness was a defining virtue. Her desire to be kind in all relationships and transactions has become the governing principle for her life. Yours maybe be something entirely different. Without the strong foundations, your life will be unsteady and uncertain. Build carefully.

Prayer
Father, teach us the importance of the right "life foundations." Amen.

Day 299

1 Kings 8: The Mist of God

> "When the priests came out of the Holy Place, a thick cloud filled the Temple of the Lord. The priests could not continue their service because of the cloud, for the glorious presence of the Lord filled the Temple."
> 1 Kings 8:10-11 (NLT)

Observation

Chapter 8 tells of the moment when the Ark of the Covenant is brought to Jerusalem and placed in the Temple for the first time. The priests carried it on poles into the inner chamber of the Temple, referred to as "The Holy of Holies." According to this chapter, the Ark contained only the Ten Commandments. (At an earlier time, it also contained the Rod of Aaron and a jar of manna.) Once the Ark was set into place, the glorious presence of God filled the Temple in the form of a thick cloud. It was so thick that the priests had to suspend their normal duties. The presence of God could be seen and felt by those who experienced that moment. The final portions of the chapter record Solomon's prayer of dedication for the Temple and the actual dedication service. So grand was the week-long celebration that an almost countless number of animals were sacrificed as a peace offering before the Lord. The text mentions that 22,000 cattle and 120,000 lambs and goats were offered.

Application

When I was a kid, one of the ways our city officials kept the local mosquito population at bay was to spray billowing clouds of insecticide throughout neighborhoods. A truck would drive slowly down the street, spewing an enormous white cloud that blanketed everything for a few minutes. As kids, we would run out into the thick cloud and play in the opaque air. (I never claimed we were too bright as kids. And where were our parents while we ran around in an insecticide cloud? Once again, it was probably my brother who led the charge… but I digress.) Each time I read this story in scripture my mind brings up that image. What a moment to experience, when God's presence was that visible and powerful.

Think for a moment about a thick fog that surrounds you. You feel the moisture on your skin. You breathe the damp air into your lungs. It is in you and around you. It permeates everything. This reminds me of the presence of God. Though we cannot see God in visible form, surely we can feel God's presence. God lingers in the spaces we inhabit. He indwells our lives (1 Corinthians 3:16). He prods the heart to action and fills the mind with wisdom. We cannot escape God's presence, nor should we desire to do so. What comfort there is in knowing that God is indeed with us, around us, and in us. May you feel God's presence and guidance in your life this day.

Prayer

Father, thank you for the work of your Spirit in and around our lives. Amen.

Day 300 — 1 Kings 9: Hurting the Heart of God

> "I have heard your prayer and your petition. I have set this Temple apart to be holy—this place you have built where my name will be honored forever. I will always watch over it, for it is dear to my heart." 1 Kings 9:3 (NLT)

Observation
After Solomon completed the building of the Temple and his palace, the Lord appeared to him a second time. God was pleased with the Temple Solomon had built and said that it would be "dear to His heart." He also promised to establish a dynasty over Israel from the line of the king. Unless… There was warning in the words spoken by God. The blessings of future reign were contingent upon Solomon's obedience to the decrees and commandments of God. If Solomon or his sons failed to honor God or if they turned away to worship false gods, then Israel would be uprooted and the beautiful Temple itself would fall into ruin. The chapter then tells of the gift that Solomon made to King Hiram of Tyre for all the timber and gold he supplied during the construction process. Solomon gave him 20 cities in Galilee as a thank-you gift. The remainder of the chapter tells of various accomplishments, building projects, and the construction of a fleet of cargo ships.

Application
Notice again what God says about the Temple that Solomon had created. God said that it was set apart to be holy and that in that place, God's name would be honored forever. God also promised to always watch over it because it was dear to God's heart. Move the course of history along about 400 years and you will discover that this place of worship with all its splendor was destroyed in 587 B.C. when the Babylonians defeated the southern kingdom and destroyed Jerusalem. Today, not a single part of that original structure exists. It was destroyed and lost to the sands of time. How could something dear to the heart of God be destroyed? Simple. Because something even dearer to the heart of God was forsaken. There is nothing more important to God than creation. There is nothing more precious in God's sight than the heart of God's children. When God made the promise to watch over the Temple and to protect the reign of King Solomon, it was a covenant agreement. As long as Solomon obeyed God's commandments and decrees, and never bowed down to false gods, the covenant would be kept. As you know, Solomon slowly but steadily drifted away from his allegiance to God. The kingdom would fall, and the Temple was destroyed because of a lack of attention to the ways of God. So, what hurts the heart of God these days? The same thing… a lack of attention to the ways of God, from those of us who claim to be God's children. Surely when we forsake God's rule and reign in our lives, God's heart breaks.

Prayer
Father, forgive us when we fail to make godly obedience the priority of our lives. Amen.

Day 301 — 1 Kings 10: When Our Actions Honor God

> "Praise the Lord your God, who delights in you and has placed you on the throne of Israel. Because of the Lord's eternal love for Israel, he has made you king so you can rule with justice and righteousness."
> 1 Kings 10:9 (NLT)

Observation

Chapter 10 is an account of the splendor and majesty of King Solomon's reign. If you wanted a snapshot of when Solomon was at the top of his game, this would be the moment. His fame has spread to other nations. Kings and rulers longed to have an audience with him. This chapter tells of the moment when the queen of Sheba arrives to test his wisdom and to observe first-hand the splendor of his court. (Sheba is most likely in southwest Arabia near the modern-day country of Yemen. It is about 1,200 miles from Jerusalem.) The queen is overwhelmed by all that she observes. Never has she witnessed anything like the building projects and wisdom of Solomon. As she praises him, she also gives praises to the God responsible for his successes. She acknowledges that God has made Solomon great.

Application

There are moments as a father when the actions of my children bring me great joy and make my heart all but burst with pride. When I see the way my kids devote themselves to their spouses, their children, and to the Lord, I am so very grateful. When I see them act responsibly, and think critically, and serve joyfully, I am overwhelmed by the people they have become. Each time their actions are noble and their hearts are Christ-like it reflects well on my wife and me and the attempts we have made through the years to help them grow. And we are not alone in being proud parents. You have experienced the same emotions when your children act well. Their actions testify to who you are and the values you have instilled along the way.

Notice in our focus verse, that when Solomon was praised for his mighty deeds, God also received praise. The queen of Sheba was careful to acknowledge that all that was good in Solomon's life was the result of God's guidance and investment. I hope that the same will be said of us. I hope that when people see our lives, our attitudes, our passions, our convictions, that God will be praised. I hope that all of us live in ways that honor God. I hope that when people notice God's children, that the praise finds its way to the Father. This day, as you charge forth into the world to spend another day in pursuit of work, parenting, planning, etc., I hope that your goal will be that of bringing honor to God. I pray that God's Spirit would be so alive in you that your actions will reflect God's heart.

Prayer

Father, may the way in which we live this day, bring you both honor and joy. Amen.

Day 302   1 Kings 11: The Tipping Point

> "The Lord had clearly instructed the people of Israel, 'You must not marry them, because they will turn your hearts to their gods.' Yet Solomon insisted on loving them anyway." 1 Kings 11:2 (NLT)

Observation
Chapter 11 tells the story of the decline of Solomon's kingdom and legacy. The text records that Solomon loved many foreign women. In fact, he married women from Moab, Ammon, Edom, Sidon, and the Hittite region… 700 in all! God had counseled against doing so, indicating that they would turn the hearts of their husbands away from an exclusive worship of the Lord God. That's exactly what happened to Solomon. Soon, altars to several detestable gods were built across the land and sacrifices were offered. The Lord's anger was kindled against Solomon. God spoke to him and revealed that the kingdom would be torn away from him and his descendants. The remainder of the chapter begins to set the stage for the divided kingdom that will soon appear with Jeroboam leading a northern-tribe revolt.

Application
More than 30 years ago, I married my beautiful wife, Linda. She is an Auburn grad and I am a life-long Alabama fan. There were many who cautioned both of us against such a union. Would I be lured away from my devotion to the Crimson Tide? Would she be drawn away from her support of Auburn? I'm glad to report that it hasn't happened yet on either side. Hopefully, some things will never change! It's a silly illustration of the warnings once offered by God to Solomon. God knew that the foreign wives would steal the heart and the faithfulness of Solomon's fidelity away from the ways of God. It was this key distraction which caused him to lose sight of the obedience he was to have for the commandments of God.

    Regrettably, there is for most of us, a tipping point. There is something or someone that distracts our attention away from the boundaries and commandments of God. We never intend to step outside the lines. We don't enter a faith relationship with God ever meaning to betray it or to depart from it. But if we do not guard our hearts carefully, a destructive distraction will cause us to build our own pagan altars. The tipping point may arise in terms of scheduling. We let the busyness of our lives redefine our Sabbath agenda. Where we were once faithful in worship attendance each week, many of us have slipped into an "every-once-in-awhile" pattern. Or maybe the tipping point is determined by the time we spend surfing around the internet. We get into on-line social media arguments, or post words of hostility and anger. The tipping point could be anything that diverts our attention from God. God cares about our fidelity. Let's guard it carefully.

Prayer
Father, help us this day to see the destructive nature of our distractions. Amen.

Day 303　　　　　　　　　　1 Kings 12: Bad Advice

> "But Rehoboam rejected the advice of the older men and instead asked the opinion of the young men who had grown up with him and were now his advisers." 1 Kings 12:8 (NLT)

Observation

The chapter could be titled, "The Kingdom Divides," for it tells the story of the early stages of the divided kingdom. When the nation divides, the northern kingdom will be comprised of 10 tribes and will be called Israel. The southern kingdom will be comprised of just two tribes and will be known as Judah. Here's how it all began to unravel… Solomon's son, Rehoboam, is declared the new king. Jeroboam, who has led a rebellion against Solomon and fled to Egypt, hears the news of the coronation. He returns to Israel and appeals to King Rehoboam, asking him to lessen the difficult workload and expectations that King Solomon had imposed upon the people during the time of the huge building projects. Rehoboam seeks the advice of an older group of men who counsel him to ease the burdens and win over the nation. But he rejects the advice they offered and makes his appeal to a younger group who advise him to add even more to the oppressive workload. The people reject the idea and begin to place their loyalty behind Jeroboam. Soon, the northern 10 tribes will make Jeroboam their king. His reign will be short-lived due to the idol worship that he established throughout the land.

Application

Had King Rehoboam listened to the right group of advisors, he might have saved the kingdom from division. Sometimes when you ask for advice, you are not going to like what you hear. Such was the case of Rehoboam. Because he didn't like the counsel of the elders, he gathered a younger audience of men who would tell him what he wanted to hear. There are at least two important takeaways from this narrative. First, choose your advisors carefully. I find it interesting that those who attempted to offer the right advice, were a group of older men. These were men who had lived a lot of life and weathered a lot of experiences. Their perspective was important and their counsel was wise. This story says something to me about the value of a well-chosen mentor. All of us should seek the counsel of those who have lived long enough to learn from their life experiences. We would all do well to have a trusted confidant, older than ourselves, from whom we could draw insight and wisdom.

Second, if you are not going to listen to advice, then don't ask for it. Rehoboam didn't want advice, he simply wanted someone to validate his opinion. We sometimes do the same. There is always wisdom in listening to others. So, choose your advisors well and listen to them carefully. They could keep you from making huge mistakes.

Prayer

God, place insightful advisors in our lives and give us the wisdom to listen to them. Amen

Day 304 1 Kings 13: An Absent God?

> "The king cried out to the man of God, 'Please ask the Lord your God to restore my hand again!' So the man of God prayed to the Lord, and the king's hand was restored and he could move it again." 1 Kings 13:6 (NLT)

Observation
God had promised Jeroboam that obedience would bring an "enduring house" to his reign. But Jeroboam did not listen, and he suffered the consequences. A prophet of God is sent to Jeroboam to convict him of his disobedience. Two signs are used by the prophet to get the king's attention. First, the king's hand becomes paralyzed. (Our focus verse reveals Jeroboam's plea for it to be made whole again.) Second, the pagan altar on which the king is making a sacrifice is split apart and the ashes pour onto the ground. Though the moment was certainly traumatic for the king, the end of the chapter reveals that he refused to turn from his evil ways and as a result, his dynasty would be obliterated. This chapter also tells the story of the prophet's return to his home after confronting the king. He is deceived by another prophet who convinces him to defy God's command not to eat or drink in that place. Because of his disobedience, he is killed by a lion.

Application
Here's what caught my attention as I read this passage. Notice that when King Jeroboam cries out to the man of God, his plea is, "Please ask the Lord *your* God..." I find it interesting that here was a man who certainly knew God, in fact had dialogued with God (11:38), and yet he doesn't seem to know God any longer. So inadequate is his knowledge of God that he pleads with the prophet to ask *his* God to restore his hand. It is as though God is absent from his life. Ever feel that way? Ever think that you are far away and removed from the presence of God? Maybe you feel abandoned, cast aside, or even forgotten. There is nothing in scripture that hints that God will forsake you. In fact, it's just the opposite. The promises of God's continual and abiding presence are written about over and over again. Here's what happens… the only way God is distanced from our lives is when we choose to create that distance. It is not that God is ever absent from us, we choose to be absent from God. Go back to the story of the prodigal son in Luke 15. It is not the father who distances himself from the son. It is not the father who sends the boy away into the distant land. Not at all. It's the willful choice of the foolish young man to leave his father's presence. Read the story carefully and you will see the warm embrace that the "waiting father" longs to offer. So, if you think for a moment that God is no longer *your* God, think again. You are God's child, and you are not forgotten. Not even for a moment.

Prayer
God, thank you for your abiding presence in our lives. Amen.

Day 305 1 Kings 14: Trying to Manipulate God

> "Take him a gift of ten loaves of bread, some cakes, and a jar of honey, and ask him what will happen to the boy." 1 Kings 14:3 (NLT)

Observation

As this chapter unfolds, the consequences of Jeroboam's disobedience come to fruition. (Remember that Jeroboam is the first king of the northern kingdom. His actions of creating altars for idol worship were particularly egregious before God.) In this narrative, one of his sons is sick and he sends his wife to Shiloh to speak to the prophet Ahijah. He sends along gifts hoping to please the prophet and control or manipulate the prophetic message. The message is harsh from the prophet. Ahijah reveals that the Lord will end the reign of Jeroboam's family. The bodies of his offspring will be eaten by dogs in the street. The son about whom he is concerned will die as soon as his wife returns home. And further, the northern kingdom will quickly lose influence and will be overrun. The second half of the chapter tells the story of Rehoboam, who was ruling the southern kingdom of Judah. Under his rule, the Egyptian King Shishak, attacks Jerusalem and takes away all the treasures of the Temple and palace. Disobedience has led to destruction in both kingdoms.

Application

Read this story carefully and you will notice the way in which the king tries to "grease the skids" a little in the conversation with the prophet. No doubt he is fearful of the prophet's message. He knows that he has not obeyed the ways and commandments of the Lord. Hoping for a softer, more lenient message, he tells his wife to take along some provisions to give to the prophet. By doing so, he hopes to manipulate the message. What a foolish notion. It didn't work then, and it doesn't work now.

Here's the way it looks in our day. We try to manipulate God by attempting to strike a deal. We make foolish promises that we can never keep, hoping to buy God's favor. We say things like this, "I promise I will be in church every Sunday if you will just…" "I will give so faithfully if you can…" "If you will get me out of this jam this one time, I will do anything you ask." You've heard people make such promises. Maybe you have made a few of them yourself. What we so often forget is that we are already the objects of God's grace. God loves us. We are God's children. Rather than attempt to manipulate God's good favor, we would do well to simply ask for forgiveness when we have failed and pray for the courage to walk in God's ways. Sometimes we will indeed suffer the consequences of our sins. God allows that to happen, not because God enjoys punishing us, but because God knows that our actions at times need correction. So rather than trying to manipulate God, lean into the love God already has for you.

Prayer

God, help us to understand grace so that we stop making attempts at manipulation. Amen.

Day 306 — 1 Kings 15: The King's Feet

> "The rest of the events in Asa's reign—the extent of his power, everything he did, and the names of the cities he built—are recorded in The Book of the History of the Kings of Judah. In his old age his feet became diseased."
> 1 Kings 15:23 (NLT)

Observation
Beginning with this chapter, the remaining books of 1 and 2 Kings describe the quick succession of rulers both in the northern and southern kingdoms. Most are poor leaders, due primarily to spiritual compromise. There is also continued hostility and fighting between the North and the South. There are, however, a few good kings along the way. One is described in this chapter. He is Asa, king of the southern kingdom. Asa followed the reign of his wicked father Abijam. It is said of him that "he did what was right in the eyes of God." He was politically astute and attacked the idolatry in his land with great determination. He reigned for 41 years. Meanwhile, in the northern kingdom, Nadab and Baasha came to power, but the reign of each was short-lived due to continual spiritual corruption.

Application
I find it interesting that, as the story of Asa concludes, the last words spoken about him concerned his diseased feet. It's as though the writer is saying, "He did all of these good deeds and he was a good leader, and by the way, he had bad feet." Why the mention of the king's feet? According to 2 Chronicles 16:12-13, "In the thirty-ninth year of his reign, Asa developed a serious foot disease. Yet even with the severity of his disease, he did not seek the Lord's help but turned only to his physicians. So he died in the forty-first year of his reign" (NLT). Notice two things. First, it was this severe disease that apparently led to his death. Second, notice the problem with his approach to the illness. Rather than seek the Lord's healing and solution for his problem, he turned only to physicians for help. Although I am not making any judgment about the level of care these physicians could offer, I do think that it is interesting that a man seeking to lead the people of God would neglect to talk to God about his own needs. Was there a spiritual mindset that would have led the king to pray? Would God have intervened in a miraculous way? Who's to say?

Notice that it is his inattention to this one aspect of his life that eventually caused his death. The story reminds me that whenever we fail to give attention to even the small details of our lives, we can be wounded spiritually, crippled emotionally, and robbed of our joy. This lesson is not about foot care... it's about paying attention to our spiritual lives. We should never neglect our spiritual disciplines or act as though they don't matter. Whenever we fail to safeguard even the smallest aspect of our hearts and minds, we open the door to ruin.

Prayer
God, remind us that even the smallest details of our "faith walk" matter. Amen.

Day 307 — 1 Kings 16: Courage to Break the Cycle

> "But Ahab son of Omri did what was evil in the Lord's sight, even more than any of the kings before him." 1 Kings 16:30 (NLT)

Observation

Chapter 16 tells the story of continual spiritual decline within the northern kingdom of Israel and the quick succession of kings. The reader almost needs a diagram to keep up with the action. The narrative begins with a prophet giving a message to King Baasha reminding him that he has continued to commit the sins of Jeroboam, and as a result, his descendants will be destroyed. His son Elah becomes the next king, only to rule for two years before his assassination by Zimri. Zimri will rule for only seven days before committing suicide. Omri will become the next king and his 12-year-long rule will be one of increasing evil. His son Ahab will become the next king. Ahab marries Jezebel and will rule over Israel for 22 years. As the focus verse states, he too was an evil ruler… more so than any of the kings before him. And with the telling of his story, the prophet Elijah is about to emerge onto the scene.

Application

Patterns of behavior have a way of cycling through generations within a family. You may be a hunter who enjoys sitting in the woods in the fall hoping to kill your next meal. If you are a hunter, chances are that your father was a hunter and maybe his father before him. My family has a generational love for cars. My granddaddy loved to tinker with cars and so my dad learned to do the same. And then my brother and I followed in those footsteps. Our sons now share a passion for cars. Some patterns of behavior are not healthy. Let's say that your grandfather was a smoker. So, maybe your father smoked as well. And now maybe you smoke. The addiction has been passed along. Many of those who abuse alcohol grew up in a home where alcohol was abused. If you grew up in a broken home, there is a greater than 65% chance that you will one day walk away from your marriage. We get into those patterns of behavior for generations until someone has the courage to break the cycle. Look at the example of the kings of Israel. One after another, they sinned against God. Fathers did not provide an example for their sons. Disobedience in one generation led to disobedience in the next. Take a moment this morning to think about the negative baggage that you carry around, given to you by the generations before you. It might be an addiction. It might be an inappropriate emotional response to anger. It might be a disregard for the things of faith. Do you have the courage to break the cycle? Your children need your help. Be the leader you were meant to be.

Prayer

God, may we have the courage to end the unhealthy cycles in our families. Amen.

Day 308   1 Kings 17: What Happens in the Wilderness

> "Then the Lord said to Elijah, 'Go to the east and hide by Kerith Brook, near where it enters the Jordan River.'" 1 Kings 17:2-3 (NLT)

Observation

To fully understand the role of Elijah in this story, we need to remember that King Ahab and his wife, Jezebel, were firmly committed to the worship of Baal. They built pagan altars throughout the land and supported many priests. Baal was the god of the storm. Worshippers would pray to Baal to bring rain in times of drought or when seasonal crops needed watering. As this chapter opens, Elijah, prophet of the One True God—the God who alone has the power to direct the force of nature—goes to the king and declares that it will not rain again until Elijah gives the word for it to do so, according to the Lord's plan. In defiance of the king's god and in defiance of his leadership, Elijah makes his bold claim. As soon as that prophetic word is delivered, Elijah is told to "go and hide." God sends him out into the wilderness for both protection and for preparation.

Application

Let's talk about "the wilderness" for a few moments. For Elijah, it was a real wilderness. God sent him to a desolate and lonely place. God sent him there to prepare him for the great moment when he would take on the 450 prophets of Baal. For us the wilderness may not be a tangible location. It can be any place where we feel a little out of sync, a little broken, maybe a little despondent or forgotten. It's the distant land where we begin to think that God has cast us aside. It's interesting how we wind up in those places. Sometimes we push ourselves into the wilderness by our own poor choices. Our mistakes separate us from key relationships and normal living. Sometimes, we find ourselves in the wilderness by the actions of others. And sometimes, we find ourselves in the wilderness because God has directed us to that place—Moses in Midian, Jesus in the wilderness, Paul in Arabia after his conversion, Abraham in the land of Canaan. God sends us to the wilderness to prepare us for what is to come. Notice that every Bible character sent into the wilderness by God was being prepared for something great. Moses liberated his people. Jesus began his ministry. Paul became missionary to the world. Abraham started a nation. If you find yourself in the wilderness during this chapter of your life, remember two things. First, God will meet you there. God will heal, protect, and prepare you. God doesn't abandon you but eliminates the distractions to teach you. Second, God will send you from that place to do something great according to God's plan and purpose. So, if you are in the wilderness these days, rejoice. God is up to something big.

Prayer

God, help us to discover and embrace your plan in the wilderness. Amen.

Day 309   1 Kings 18: The Whisper of Hope

> "Then Elijah said to Ahab, 'Go get something to eat and drink, for I hear a mighty rainstorm coming!' So Ahab went to eat and drink. But Elijah climbed to the top of Mount Carmel and bowed low to the ground and prayed with his face between his knees." 1 Kings 18:41-42 (NLT)

Observation
Most of us have one or two truly defining moments in the course of our lives. For the prophet Elijah, this is his moment. As the chapter begins, God sends him to King Ahab to tell him that the drought is about to end. Through the mediator Obadiah, a meeting is set between Ahab and Elijah. Ahab calls Elijah, "the troubler of Israel." Elijah reminds Ahab that the trouble that Israel has experienced is not his fault, but rather the sins of the king. All the nation is assembled at Mt. Carmel. There are 450 prophets of Baal. Elijah is the lone prophet of God. Two altars are constructed and two bulls are sacrificed. The prophets of Baal spend the day attempting to call down fire from heaven. Despite their exhaustive efforts, there is no sound, no reply, no response, and no fire. Elijah then prepares his altar. As he prays, the fire of God falls from the sky and the people see proof of the power of the only true God. The prophets of Baal are slain. The story ends with the coming of the great rain.

Application
There is a typical pattern that announces the coming of a summer storm. First the wind begins to pick-up. Then the scent of rain begins to fill the atmosphere. In the distance, streaks of rainfall can be seen falling from the sky. And finally, the stillness of the moment is interrupted by the pity-pat sound of drops striking the ground. Within seconds, the falling rain produces a mighty roar. I love this moment when Elijah tells the king, "You need to get ready; a huge storm is coming. I can hear it." To be honest, I doubt that Elijah actually heard the rain. In fact, the small cloud had yet to appear on the horizon. What Elijah heard was the whisper of hope. His belief in God's presence and the fulfillment of God's promises was so strong that he could hear beyond the audible. In the depths of his mind and heart, he heard the rain declaring the victory of God. As people of faith we are sometimes called to hear those things that are not yet audible, see things that are not yet visible, imagine things that are not yet possible, and hope for things not even plausible. We walk by faith and not by sight. It is our hope that sustains us through difficult moments, challenging times, and the darkness of uncertainty. We hear, we see, and we imagine because our faith is fixed on the God who will bring all things to pass. Take a moment to listen in the distance today. You just may hear God marching your way.

Prayer
God, thank you for the power of faith that helps us to see beyond human understanding. Amen.

Day 310 — 1 Kings 19: The Unexpected Voice

> "And after the earthquake there was a fire, but the Lord was not in the fire. And after the fire there was the sound of a gentle whisper. When Elijah heard it, he wrapped his face in his cloak and went out and stood at the entrance of the cave." 1 Kings 19:12-13 (NLT)

Observation
To say that Elijah had stirred up a hornet's nest is putting it mildly. Ahab returns to his palace to tell Jezebel all that Elijah has done and how he killed all the prophets of Baal. She is enraged and swears vengeance, promising to kill Elijah. Out of fear, Elijah runs for his life. He races out into the wilderness of Beersheba and beyond. An angel sustains him along the journey. He travels 40 days and nights and finally arrives at Mount Sinai where he hides in a cave. The Lord speaks to him and says, "Elijah, why are you here?" God must wonder why he cowers in fear just days after God's display of power and strength. God brings a strong wind, an earthquake, and then a fire to get his attention. He then speaks to Elijah in a gentle whisper. Elijah is told to go back... there are things to do, places to go, and kings to anoint. The chapter ends with Elijah visiting Elisha, upon whom he will place his mantle.

Application
Our family pet, Zaccheus, is a small, white, Maltese dog. He's been in the family for 15 years. For the most part, he gets along well to be so old, but we have noticed that he doesn't hear as well as he once did. When I come home in the afternoons, I can unlock the door, put down my stuff, and walk all the way through the house before he realizes that I am there. In early days, he would hear my car pull up outside and race to meet me at the door. When we need to get his attention these days, we have to shout "Zac!" pretty loudly to get his attention.

Sometimes, we all can be a little hard of hearing in terms of our spiritual lives. I often tell people that the reason we don't always hear from God is *not* because God isn't speaking, it's because we aren't listening. At least, not very well. How does God speak to us? A lot of ways... a preacher's message, a passage of scripture, the words of a friend, an inspired book. And yes, sometimes using a gentle whisper. I've been a believer for more than half a century and never once have I heard an audible voice booming from the heavens, but I have heard from God many times. It's the quiet voice of the heart. It's the whisper of the Spirit that offers insight and direction. It's that still small voice that prompts me to go speak to a friend, or to pray for a need, or volunteer to help with a ministry initiative. I have felt that gentle whisper many times and each time that I respond, God uses me in some way that I didn't expect. It can be your story as well. Listen closely today, you just may hear it.

Prayer
God, speak to each of us today through both the great and small voice of your Spirit.

Day 311　　　　　1 Kings 20: The Dangers of Trash Talking

> "The king of Israel sent back this answer: 'A warrior putting on his sword for battle should not boast like a warrior who has already won.'"
> 1 Kings 20:11 (NLT)

Observation
As this chapter opens, the story of King Ben-hadad of Aram comes to the forefront. He has set up an alliance of 32 kings and vows to attack Samaria, the capital of Israel. Ahab, the king of Israel, attempts a peace agreement by submitting to his demands. Not satisfied, Ben-hadad makes a second set of demands. Acting on the advice of his elder advisors, Ahab stands up the king and an attack becomes eminent. A prophet is sent to Ahab telling him that God will deliver the Israelites. After two separate attacks, the armies of the Arameans are defeated. More than 100,000 soldiers are killed. Ahab is able to capture Ben-hadad but later chooses to release him after Ben-hadad makes a number of concessions. Another prophet is sent to Ahab to deliver a message of God's judgment because of Ahab's failure to destroy Ben-hadad as he had been told.

Application
Early in the narrative, Ahab stands up to Ben-hadad with the words of our focus verse. Ben-hadad has sworn to reduce the city of Samaria to dust. It is Ahab who responds with a little advice… "don't boast like you have already won."

Let's be honest, most of us who are a little competitive, like to offer a little "trash talk" from time to time. We like to boast about how we will win, or in how our team will surely claim victory. We boast and brag as though our arrogance will ensure a victory. The problem with trash talking is that sometimes things don't turn out like we had planned and suddenly we are left trying to offer weak excuses for our defeats.

I am afraid that there are those occasional moments when we fail to realize the strength of our spiritual opponents. We forget the power of temptation… its cunning, continual, and relentless assault in our lives. We think we can control its power. We believe that it won't get to us, trap us, or destroy us. We claim all kinds of Bible verses that remind us of the superior power of the Spirit within us. "Greater is He who is in you than he who is in the world" (1 John 4:4b NASB). "No temptation has overtaken you except what is common to mankind. And God is faithful; he will not let you be tempted beyond what you can bear. But when you are tempted, he will also provide a way out so that you can endure it" (1 Corinthians 10:13 NIV). There is nothing wrong with those verses. They promise great strength to defeat our opponent. However, it is one thing to recite those verses… it is another to allow the Spirit of God to claim authority over your life to give you the ability to win. Be strong. Be bold. Lean on God's power, not your own.

Prayer
God, may we understand the power of temptation and look to you daily for help. Amen.

Day 312 — 1 Kings 21: Clinging to God's Gifts

> "But Naboth replied, 'The Lord forbid that I should give you the inheritance that was passed down by my ancestors.'" 1 Kings 21:3 (NLT)

Observation
A man named Naboth owned a vineyard on a plot of land that adjoined King Ahab's property. Ahab wanted the land to grow vegetables. He approached Naboth and offered to purchase the land at a good price. Naboth refused to sell the land because it had been in his family for generations. In fact, it had been promised to his ancestors when God entrusted the land to God's people (Leviticus 25:23). The king returns to his palace, depressed and saddened that he cannot own the land. When Jezebel realizes the reasons for his sadness, she takes matters into her own hands. She sends fake letters to the elders of the community telling them to accuse Naboth of wrongdoing. She signed them with the king's autograph. The plan works. Naboth is accused and stoned to death. Jezebel then tells the king that he can have the land because Naboth is dead. About that time, Elijah shows up to confront Ahab about the evil he has done. God pronounces judgment on Ahab and all his descendants.

Application
Naboth was tenacious. Here was a man who owns a piece of land, passed down to him through generations. Even though the king offers him a fair price, he refuses to sell. He stubbornly clings to that which God had provided.

Most of us have a few items in our possessions with which we will forever refuse to part. They are family heirlooms. They have great sentimental value. They are important to our lives and so we protect them carefully. Maybe you have some old photographs you cherish. Maybe a piece of furniture, or an old clock are among the "passed-down" items that you love and will keep forever. Now turn this conversation in the direction of faith. Consider for a moment some of the gifts that God has promised. He promises to fill us with love, joy, peace, patience, kindness, goodness, gentleness, faithfulness, and self-control. That's part of our Spiritual inheritance. Those qualities have been embedded into our lives for safe keeping. Why would we let anything take those gifts from us? But we do. When we allow selfishness, anger, or hatred to establish a foothold in our hearts, we lessen our grip on these treasures. When we fail to forgive, or when we refuse to share our blessings, do we not begin the process of giving away God's good gifts? Your life has been filled to overflowing with the blessings of God. Defend them. Protect them. Refuse to surrender them. Ask for the heart of Christ to motivate your actions and the wisdom of the Spirit to determine your thoughts.

Prayer
God, may we stubbornly cling to the treasures of faith entrusted to us. Amen.

Day 313 — 1 Kings 22: The Painful Truth

> "But Micaiah replied, 'As surely as the Lord lives, I will say only what the Lord tells me to say.'" 1 Kings 22:14 (NLT)

Observation
This final chapter of the book of 1 Kings, tells the story of King Ahab's death. For three years, there had been no war between the nations of Israel and Aram. When King Jehoshaphat of Judah goes to visit King Ahab of Israel, Ahab asks Jehoshaphat to join him in attacking Aram, insisting that they needed to retake the city of Ramoth-gilead. Jehoshaphat insists that they should seek counsel from the Lord before undertaking an attack. Ahab gathers 400 prophets who insist that the time is right for battle. Jehoshaphat is apparently able to see through the guise of these false prophets and insists that Micaiah, a prophet of God, be consulted. Micaiah predicts destruction and the death of Ahab. The words do not sit well with Ahab. He goes to battle in spite of the warnings and is mortally wounded by an arrow. When the bloody chariot is washed, the dogs come and lick up the blood as promised by an earlier word of the Lord (21:19).

Application
Maybe the line from the movie *A Few Good Men* should have been shouted at King Ahab… "You can't handle the truth!" When Ahab didn't like the words of the prophet, he chose to listen to the voice in his own head, which ultimately led to his death. Sometimes the problem is not in "hearing the truth," but is in the failure to "accept the truth." We are guilty of doing the same thing. We make up our minds and we plan our lives, according to our own wisdom. We do what we think is right. We really don't want anything to complicate our plans… not even a word from the Lord.

So, take a moment to consider the boldness of this prophet named Micaiah. He refuses the temptation to tell the king what the king wants to hear. He declares that he will only say what the Lord tells him to say, regardless of whether it is the politically expedient thing to say. Oh, how we need such people in our lives. We need people to speak honesty and truth to us, even if the truth is a difficult word to hear. We need people who love us enough to tell us the truth consistently, and hopefully, in a compassionate way. And yes, we need to become those people in the lives of our friends, co-workers, and families. We must be willing to share with people what the Lord would have us say, rather than what we think they might want to hear. Such a challenge dictates that we are well-invested in our faith… that we have spent time with God, that we have searched God's word, and that we have prayed for God's wisdom. There may be someone in your circle of influence today that needs a word from God. Be that person.

Prayer
Father God, give us wisdom and courage to be your representative today. Amen.

Day 314 — 2 Kings 1: The Anger of God

> "But the angel of the Lord told Elijah, who was from Tishbe, 'Go and confront the messengers of the king of Samaria and ask them, 'Is there no God in Israel? Why are you going to Baal-zebub, the god of Ekron, to ask whether the king will recover?'" 2 Kings 1:3 (NLT)

Observation
As 2 Kings opens, Ahaziah rises to power as the new king of Israel. For some unexplained reason, he falls through the latticework of an upper room in his palace and is seriously injured. He sends messengers to the Temple of Baal-zebub of Ekron (Philistine city) to inquire about his recovery. An angel of the Lord tells Elijah to confront these messengers about the sinfulness of their journey. He confronts them and sends word to the king that he will not recover. He will die in his bed. When the king hears this word, he sends 50 soldiers to arrest Elijah. When they arrive at the spot, Elijah calls down fire from heaven and all 50 are consumed. A second group of 50 are then sent to make the arrest, and again, the same scenario plays out. A third and final group of men are sent to arrest Elijah. The captain of the guard falls on his face before Elijah and pleads for the lives of his men. Elijah agrees to go with them and delivers the same message of judgment to the king that he had earlier given to the messengers sent to Ekron.

Application
Want to make God angry? Just deny who God is and put someone else in God's place in your life. Ahaziah was foolish to think that the prophets of Baal-zebub could do anything about his injury. He was foolish to seek their advice and counsel over and against the wisdom and power of God. The king's idolatry would bring God's punishment. After hearing about the experiences of all the foolish kings that are mentioned in the book of 1 Kings, you would think that someone would finally wise-up and say "no" to the influence of pagan deities. But the pattern continued.

It happens in our lives as well. We are quick to abandon our trust in, and our allegiance to, Almighty God that we will seek counsel and favor in any number of places. We listen to the voice of popular culture. We gauge the winds of human intellect that swirl about us that attempt to redirect our morality and ethics. We knock on wood as a preventative from some evil, as though the wood has the power to save. We flip a coin as though there is wisdom in the random spinning of minted metal. We consult an attorney, a life coach, or a financial planner to guide us in the best course of our decision making. We continue to place our trust in things and not in the power and presence of the Living God. When will we ever learn? We sometimes act as though there is no God in Israel. Don't be so stupid. Be faithful instead.

Prayer
Father God, forgive us when we place our trust in anything but you. Amen.

Day 315

2 Kings 2: And the Beat Goes On

> "When the group of prophets from Jericho saw from a distance what happened, they exclaimed, 'Elijah's spirit rests upon Elisha!' And they went to meet him and bowed to the ground before him." 2 Kings 2:15 (NLT)

Observation

There are several very dramatic events that take place in this narrative. The overall focus of the story is the transition of the prophetic ministry of Elijah to Elisha. The two men travel together throughout the day. They go first to Bethel, then to Jericho, and finally to the Jordan River. Elisha is under no illusions. He knows that this is the appointed day when God will remove Elijah from the earth. With 50 fellow prophets watching, the two men cross the Jordan River in dramatic fashion. Elijah touches the water with his cloak and the river ceases to flow. Once on the other side, Elisha asks for a double portion of Elijah's spirit to rest on him. Elijah indicates that he will know if God answers that request if Elisha is able to see Elijah depart into the heavens. Suddenly a chariot of fire appears, and Elijah is taken away into the heavens. Elisha takes up Elijah's cloak and parts the waters of the Jordan. It is evident that he now possesses the prophetic power of God. Before the chapter ends there are two miracles performed by his hand... one is the purification of a river and the other is the bizarre story of bears coming out of the woods to maul a group of boys who have mocked the prophet.

Application

God always has a plan of succession. God always works from one generation to the next, conveying God's will, speaking God's message, redeeming God's people. Just as Elisha took up the prophetic ministry of Elijah and carried it forward, God will continue to raise up men and women to continue God's redemptive work through all generations. Just as all of us are the recipients of those faithful believers who have come before us, the next generation will benefit from the faith-legacy that we extend to them. The question is never one of God's willingness to continue to work with creation. The question is whether we will choose to join God in that work. What an amazing privilege and responsibility we have of being invited into God's plan. God longs to use our lives to reach the next generation. How willing are you to hear God's call and take up the mantle of responsibility that is placed upon your shoulders? To leave a legacy of faith, you and I have to "live" a legacy of faith. Faith will not be important to our children if it is not first important to us. So, if you care about the next generation... live intentionally, practice your faith diligently, love extravagantly, forgive abundantly, follow Christ devotedly.

Prayer

Father God, give us a contagious passion for following you. Amen.

Day 316 — 2 Kings 3: The Lord Speaks Through Him

> "Jehoshaphat said, 'Yes, the Lord speaks through him.' So the kings of Israel, Judah, and Edom went to consult with Elisha." 2 Kings 3:12 (NLT)

Observation
As this chapter opens, Jehoram begins his reign as the king of Israel. He soon faces his first test of power when Mesha, the king of Moab, refuses to pay the annual tribute that was required of Mesha as a vassal. Jehoram decides to go to battle against Moab and as he does, he asks Jehoshaphat, king of Judah, to join him. It is a logical request since Jehoshaphat's son had married Jehoram's sister. The combined armies travel through the wilderness of Edom on their way to fight the Moabites. But after seven days without water, the kings become desperate. They consult Elisha to seek a prophetic word from the Lord. Elisha promises that water will flow into the land of Moab and the troops, horses, and cattle will have plenty. The miracle unfolds and water is provided. The kings then fight against Mesha and his army. The Israelites score a resounding defeat of their enemy.

Application
Most of us have a favorite preacher we like to hear or favorite Christian author we like to read because we have a sense that God speaks through that person. There is something so consistent about their words and insight, that we conclude that God uses them in an effective way. In the story of ancient Israel, when the kings needed a word from God, they consulted Elisha. They knew that he was a "man of God," and that God would speak through him.

How does a person earn the reputation of being a "person of faith?" How does a person become the "mouthpiece" of God? First, the person must be led by the Holy Spirit. As believers in Christ, we are promised the indwelling of the Spirit at the moment we profess faith in Jesus. However, it is one thing to be Spirit-filled and quite another to be Spirit-led. Those who allow God to speak through them have long abandoned self-reliance and personal opinion in order to proclaim the truth provided by the authoritative Spirit in their lives. Second, to become a trusted mouthpiece of God, a person must live a life of consistency. Faith cannot be worn like a winter coat at some moments and then discarded at others. Faith requires allegiance, consistency, and obedience over the long haul. We prove ourselves in both the great and small aspects of our lives. Third, we become the voice of God when we are willing to surrender to that responsibility. A whole lot of prophets got stoned to death for speaking the truth of God. There is no guarantee that your words will be welcomed by the world to whom you preach. But the calling is not optional. It is who you are once you surrender to that responsibility. Accept the challenge. Let God speak through you.

Prayer
Father God, give us both consistency and courage that we might represent you well.

Day 317   2 Kings 4: The Miracle of Multiplication

> "'What?' his servant exclaimed. 'Feed a hundred people with only this?' But Elisha repeated, 'Give it to the people so they can eat, for this is what the Lord says: Everyone will eat, and there will even be some left over!'"
> 2 Kings 4:43 (NLT)

Observation

This chapter tells of four miracle events that unfold at the hand of Elisha. The Lord's Spirit abides in him as he is able to do extraordinary things. The first miracle involves a poor widow with a great amount of indebtedness. Her two sons are about to be sold into slavery to pay off the creditor. Elisha instructs her to keep filling pots and jars with the oil from her flask that seemingly becomes inexhaustible. She is able to sell enough to pay the debts and have money to live on. The second miracle involves a woman from Shunem who had provided the prophet with a place to lodge. Her son dies and Elisha brings him to life again. The third miracle involves a pot of stew. A group of prophets were eating stew during a famine only to discover that some of the plants in the stew were poisonous. Elisha throws flour in the stew to purify it. The fourth miracle is the feeding of 100 people with just a small amount of food. Clearly, God is at work in the life of the prophet.

Application

Read the focus verse again. Of what does it remind you? I immediately think of the great miracle of Jesus recorded in all four Gospels… the feeding of the 5000. You remember how God took the small offering of two fish and five loaves from a young boy and with it, fed the multitude. In this story, Elisha takes a very meager gift of grain and bread from a local man and is able to feed a large crowd. In both this experience and in the story from the Gospels, two lessons come to the forefront. #1—There is a miracle of multiplication when we offer God even meager amounts of resources. God has a way of taking our willingness, our obedience, and our offerings, and using them to bring hope and to meet the needs present in the lives of others. Though God certainly does not need our small gifts to make the miracle unfold, by accepting and using our gifts, God allows us to participate in miraculous events. Do not ever discount even the small offerings you make. #2—The Spirit of God transforms lives and situations. Elisha did powerful things because the Spirit rested on him. Elisha wasn't anything great. The Spirit of God made him great. That same Spirit abides in us. If we will lean into the prompting of the Spirit and rely upon God's authority and guidance, great things can happen through our efforts. So, gather up your best gifts and talents today and head out at the bidding of the Spirit. You just never know what miracles are waiting to be claimed.

Prayer

Dear God, may we become Spirit-reliant and miracle-expectant. Amen.

Day 318 — 2 Kings 5: Sacred Soil

> "Then Naaman said, 'All right, but please allow me to load two of my mules with earth from this place, and I will take it back home with me. From now on I will never again offer burnt offerings or sacrifices to any other god except the Lord.'" 2 Kings 5:17 (NLT)

Observation
Naaman was the commander of the army for the king of Aram. He was a mighty warrior, but he suffered from leprosy. An Israelite slave girl told Naaman's wife that he should go and visit the prophet of Elisha. Naaman goes to find Elisha, taking with him a number of valuable gifts to present to the king. The king realizes that he has no power to offer in response to Naaman's disease but sends him on to Elisha. Elisha tells Naaman to wash in the Jordan River seven times. At first, he is reluctant. It seems like too simple of a thing to do. But he obeys and is cured of his leprosy. Elisha refuses to accept any gifts from Naaman. But Gehazi, Elisha's servant, overhears the conversation and tries to trick Naaman into giving him some of the gifts that he has brought. When Elisha discovers his deed, Gehazi is struck with leprosy.

Application
The first and only trip my Grandfather Roebuck ever made by plane was a trip to visit the Holy Land when he was in his early eighties. He took with him on the trip several small glass bottles with a screw-on lid. He wanted to collect samples of water from the various holy sites. He collected water from the Jordan, the Sea of Galilee, the Dead Sea, along with other places including Jacob's Well. He wanted to bring back a little piece of the Holy Land… small samples of water that Jesus had visited. (My father baptized him in the Jordan.) My grandfather felt it was important to bring back home a little of the sacred spirit of the Holy Land. Notice what Naaman does in our focus verse. He loads up two donkeys with soil from Israel to take back to Aram. It was a common idea in the ancient world that a deity could be worshiped only on its own home soil; so Naaman wanted to bring home with him the soil of Israel. His motives may have been good, but his understanding of God was perhaps a bit immature. I do like the thought, however, that he connected the sacred soil with the presence of the Living Lord. He wanted a tangible reminder of the place where God once healed his life. Maybe you have a sacred place in your heart and mind that connects you to something that God has done in your life. I have a few keepsakes and souvenirs from a number of mission trips that I have taken through the years. One is a small stone on which these words are written, "I am not forgotten." It's from an orphanage in Haiti where students had spelled out that same message in stones embedded in the cement of their playground. It was a word of hope to them and remains so to me. I hope you too have something sacred to hold and cherish.

Prayer
God, thank you for tangible reminders of those places where you have acted. Amen.

Day 319

2 Kings 6: More of Us

> "'Don't be afraid!' Elisha told him. 'For there are more on our side than on theirs!'" 2 Kings 6:16 (NLT)

Observation

This chapter opens with another miracle of Elisha. In this case, while felling trees along the banks of the Jordan River, an iron axe head flies off the handle of one of the workers who happens to be a member of a local prophet group. He is distraught. The axe was borrowed and was certainly a valuable tool. Elisha throws a stick in the water and commands that the axe head float to the surface, where it will be retrieved. The second half of the chapter deals with Elisha's efforts at frustrating the army of the Arameans. The king of Aram had planned several attacks on Israel. Elisha perceives his plans and warns the king of Israel. After this scenario plays out several times, the king of Aram sends an army to capture Elisha. The city of Dothan is surrounded, and it seems that the prophet is in peril. Elisha's servant is fearful until Elisha prays for his servant's eyes to be opened. He sees chariots of fire all around on the surrounding hillside. The army of the Arameans is struck blind by God and Elisha leads them to Samaria. When their eyes are opened, they realize their efforts have been wasted and they return home.

Application

When faced with a huge opposing army, Elisha tells his servant, who is shaking with fear, "Don't be afraid!" Notice what he says next: "For there are more on our side than on theirs!" The armies of God far surpass the meager number of the enemy's forces. That's an important word for us to hear. Sometimes we get a little overwhelmed by the threat of evil in our world. We worry about terrorism and those who plan heinous attacks. We worry about the rise of militant groups and the radicalization of many even within our own land. We stress over foreign nations who are led by vicious madmen who seem to act unilaterally. It's easy to see the evil that surrounds us. What we fail to remember at times is this simple truth, "There are more on our side than on theirs!" I'm not talking about American soldiers, police officers, or NATO peacekeeping forces. I'm talking about the armies of God that are spread all around the globe in every nation, every city, and in every town. This army is not armed with missiles, guns, and chemical weapons. They are armed with a greater power... the power of Christ's love. Deeply embedded into every believing heart is the capacity to forgive, heal, redeem, and love. The darkness of warfare will never win out against the forces of such light. There are more of us than there are of them. The darkness does not win. Evil can only triumph when we allow the light in us to fail. Live the Gospel and win the battle. The light has come.

Prayer

God, grant us the courage of the light to defeat the darkness of our age. Amen.

Day 320 — 2 Kings 7: The Sin of Silence

> "Finally, they said to each other, 'This is not right. This is a day of good news, and we aren't sharing it with anyone! If we wait until morning, some calamity will certainly fall upon us. Come on, let's go back and tell the people at the palace.'" 2 Kings 7:9 (NLT)

Observation

The long narrative of this chapter actually begins to unfold at the end of chapter 6. King Ben-hadad of Aram musters his entire army and besieges the city of Samaria. The siege lasts so long that life is difficult and dangerous within the city. Essential goods are scarce. Exorbitant prices are demanded. People turn to desperate measures. One woman had agreed with another woman to both slay their children and eat them. Once the first child was sacrificed, the other mother refused to honor their agreement. The king senses the desperate situation within his city. He blames God for his plight and longs to kill Elisha as God's representative. But Elisha prophesies to the messenger of the king that every dire situation will be solved by the following day. Then the story switches to four lepers who decide to sneak away from the city and surrender to the Arameans, believing that their lives could not be worse. They discover that the Aramean army has fled their encampment, leaving everything behind... food, vegetables, livestock. They return to Samaria to inform the others within the city. The crowds rush out and find provisions and the prophecy of Elisha is fulfilled.

Application

Notice the actions of these four leprous men who discover the empty Aramean camp. As soon as they realize there are plenty of provisions to share that will certainly save the lives of their fellow citizens, they rush back to share the news. They felt that some calamity would surely befall them if they failed to share their message.

Let's draw a Gospel parallel to this story. All of us who claim the Christian faith have found great provision for our lives in the world's scarcity. In Christ, we discover an abundance of love, joy, peace, and security. Everything the world craves, we have in abundance through our relationship with Jesus Christ. How sinful is it for us to have made such a discovery and then fail to share this good news with others? Is it not the heart of God's saving strategy to use those of us who have found real, meaningful, and abundant life to share the story with others? How dare we become silent! People all around us live desperate lives. We have a story to tell, a hope to offer, a grace to extend. We have answers. God intends for each of us to tell His story. Jesus, himself, made Gospel proclamation the number one commandment of his kingdom. The world cannot wait on our silence. Proclamation is not an option.

Prayer

God, give us the boldness needed to share the story of Christ consistently. Amen.

Day 321 — 2 Kings 8: Killing the King

> "But the next day Hazael took a blanket, soaked it in water, and held it over the king's face until he died. Then Hazael became the next king of Aram."
> 2 Kings 8:15 (NLT)

Observation

Chapter 8 opens with the story of the woman from Shunem whose son Elisha had raised to life. Elisha had warned her of the upcoming famine in the land of Israel and so she had fled to the land of the Philistines where she lived for seven years. When she returned, she appealed to the king about reclaiming her property. The king, impressed with her story as it intertwined with the story of Elisha, restored all her possessions and even compensated her for the value of any harvested crops while she was away. The remainder of the chapter continues the sad narrative of the succession of kings in the north and south as they continue to do evil in the eyes of the Lord. The main story of the chapter centers on the assassination of King Ben-hadad of Aram who is killed by Hazael. Elisha had predicted that the king would recover from an illness only to die in another way. Our focus verse reveals the fulfillment of Elisha's prophecy.

Application

As I read this chapter, the one verse that seemed to leap off the page was our focus verse, in which Hazael smothers the king. It's hard to avoid it, right? And it gives rise to other questions. Did anyone see him do it, and if so, why didn't they stop it? How did Hazael have such access to the king with no servants close by? And what about the details? Someone had to witness the event to tell the story in such detail. So maybe there's more than meets the eye. Perhaps there was a conspiracy to kill the king, and many were involved.

Most of us would never desire to be a part of a conspiracy, especially one that involves the killing of a king. But maybe we are not as guiltless as we would like to be. If I were to ask, "Who's to blame for Jesus' death?" Perhaps we'd answer, "It's the fault of the Romans. They are the ones who nailed his body to a cross." Or "Blame the Jews. They're the ones who incited the riots and made all those false accusations." But aren't we surely part of the problem? Was it not our sins that drove his sacrifice? Was it not because of our disobedience that "God made Christ, who never sinned, to be the offering for our sin, so that we could be made right with God through Christ" (2 Corinthians 5:21 NLT)? How do we continue to smother the king? Whenever we fail to forgive, extend grace, or care for the needy, are we not smothering his Gospel and tamping down his message? Let's stop killing the king. Let's proclaim him instead.

Prayer

God, forgive us when our actions betray the faith we claim to celebrate. Amen.

Day 322 — 2 Kings 9: A Hornet's Nest

> "Find Jehu son of Jehoshaphat, son of Nimshi. Call him into a private room away from his friends, and pour the oil over his head. Say to him, 'This is what the Lord says: I anoint you to be the king over Israel.' Then open the door and run for your life!" 2 Kings 9:2-3 (NLT)

Observation
This chapter marks the beginning of a new era in the history of the kings, sometimes referred to as the fourth dynasty. This chapter tells of Jehu's rise to power. Elisha summons a member of the group of prophets and sends him to Ramoth-gilead. He is told to take a flask of oil and anoint Jehu as the new king of Israel. He instructs the young prophet to anoint Jehu in private and as soon as he does so, he is to run for his life! The young prophet does as he had been told. Jehu is anointed and instructed to purge the evil from Israel by destroying the entire household of Ahab. Very quickly, support begins to build around Jehu's leadership. He kills Ahab in battle and has his men kill Ahaziah, king of Judah during the same military campaign. When he arrives at the king's palace, he convinces former servants of Queen Jezebel to throw her out of a window. She falls to her death. Very quickly, through his servant Jehu, God begins the process of purging the land from those who continue to worship false gods.

Application
We've all done it as kids. Someone discovered a hornet's nest clinging to the eave of a house and dared you to throw a rock or a dirt clod at it. You mustered up the courage, picked out a sizable stone, and you threw it at the nest, knocking it from its position. As soon as you did, the nest exploded with angry hornets. Then you and your friends ran in all directions hoping not to be stung. Why did we do such things? Was it the thrill or was it because someone "double-dog dared" us? Maybe this is why Elisha told the young prophet to deliver his message and then run for his life. He knew that the action of anointing the new king was like stirring up a hornet's nest. The young prophet was setting into a motion, a series of events that would shake up all of Israel.

I sometimes wonder if, in our stoic and well-rehearsed practice of Christian baptism, we have lessened the impact of what we are asking of a candidate. Normally, at least in Baptist tradition, we ask the person standing in the water to confess faith, and then we lower them into and raise them from the water, and everyone says, "Amen." But there really should be more to it than that. We are asking that person to not only profess faith in Christ, but to pledge to live in obedience and loyalty to him. It is no small step. It is the kind of decision from which there is no turning back. And yes, it also represents the engagement of battle. We take on the armor of Christ knowing that in terms of satan's design for humanity, we have stirred up a hornet's nest.

Prayer
God, give us a bold and enduring faith that strengthens us for life. Amen.

Day 323 — 2 Kings 10: Close, but No Cigar

> "But Jehu did not obey the Law of the Lord, the God of Israel, with all his heart. He refused to turn from the sins that Jeroboam had led Israel to commit." 2 Kings 10:31 (NLT)

Observation

If you are the least bit squeamish, you may not want to read this entire chapter. It continues the story of Jehu's purging of the family of Ahab and the destruction of the practice of Baal worship in Israel. Former King Ahab had 70 sons living in the city of Samaria. God told Elisha that all of them needed to be eliminated. The guardians over these 70 sons were ordered to behead them. Their heads were brought to the town of Jezreel and piled at the city gate to signal a change in terms of leadership and pagan worship practices. Later in the chapter, all the prophets of Baal are tricked into gathering in a pagan temple, believing that Jehu is going to lead them in worship. Instead, Jehu orders the prophets of Baal be slain and the instruments of Baal worship destroyed. Jehu brought serious reform to the nation, but "he refused to turn from the sins that Jeroboam had led Israel to commit." He brought upheaval and change but failed to live in full obedience before God.

Application

You may be familiar with the expression, "Close, but no cigar." It dates back to the mid 20th century here in America when cigars were given out as prizes at county fairs and carnivals. If someone won a game at a booth or stall, they were awarded a cigar. But there was no prize for second place.

Jehu came close to being the king that God needed on the throne. In fact, according to verse 30, he was so successful that God promised his sons would sit on the throne for four generations. But he fell short of being all that God demanded. He was almost faithful, almost obedient, almost a great king. He came close, but no cigar.

I wonder if the same will be said of us in terms of our faith commitments. Most of us get it "right" most of the time. We are fairly consistent in our practice of faith. Most of our thoughts are pure. Most of our motivations honor God. Most days we live consistently. But there are times when we miss the mark. There are moments when our faith convictions seem non-existent and our moral compass spins like a top. It's proof of our humanity, whether we want to admit it or not. We are not flawless. We are far from perfect. But we are claimed by Christ and that's a game changer. We are embraced by a Savior Who loves us in spite of our flaws and weaknesses. And even when we don't always get it right, we are always loved.

Prayer

God, thank you for the grace of Jesus who makes the unworthy, acceptable. Amen.

Day 324   2 Kings 11: Protecting the King

> "Form a bodyguard around the king and keep your weapons in hand. Kill anyone who tries to break through. Stay with the king wherever he goes."
> 2 Kings 11:8 (NLT)

Observation
As soon as word about the death of King Ahaziah begins to spread, a scramble for power and control begins to break out across the land. Athaliah, the mother of Ahaziah, seizes control and proclaims herself queen. She then begins a systematic process of killing off any remaining potential heirs to the throne. Ahaziah had an infant son named Joash. When Joash's nurse hears of the queen's killing spree, she hides Joash in the Temple where he will remain in seclusion until he is six years old. Jehoiada, who is serving as the high priest, rallies military commanders, mercenaries, and palace guards to show their support for Joash as future king. They protect him and crown him king. He is ushered to the royal palace and Queen Athaliah is executed. Joash is seven years old when he begins to reign. Meanwhile, Jehoiada leads the people to destroy the Temple of Baal and tear down all the altars and idols of Baal.

Application
Notice how the military commanders surrounded the Temple and later surrounded the new boy king as they took him to the royal palace. They had sworn out an absolute oath to protect him and guard him with their lives. It's the kind of scene that you would expect of a team of secret service agents who are assigned to protect the president. You've seen the way such a team surrounds the president, not only guarding him with the latest technology and weaponry, but even acting as human shields at times, ensuring that the president is closely guarded.

    Let's talk for a moment about protecting our king, whose name is Jesus. How do we ensure, in our culture and context, that his commandments are carried forth, that his love is spread, and that his grace is offered to those who have lost their way? How do we protect the king? First, we protect him with every authentic proclamation of the Gospel that we make. Every time we tell his story and teach his message, we protect all that he came to share. Second, we protect him by making disciples. Whenever we lead others to accept him in faith, we safeguard the Christian story and preserve it for future generations. Third, we protect the king each time that we act in his name. When we serve the needs of others, forgive those who have wronged us, and share abundantly with those in need, we honor the king. Like those early soldiers who protected young Joash, we must give the oath that faith demands, that we will surround, defend, and protect the one we call king. Let's be authentic about our practice of faith even this day. Let's honor Christ as Lord.

Prayer
Father, may we be found faithful as defenders of the faith. Amen.

Day 325

2 Kings 12: Who's on Your Team?

> "All his life Joash did what was pleasing in the Lord's sight because Jehoiada the priest instructed him." 2 Kings 12:2 (NLT)

Observation

This chapter provides some detail concerning the reign of Joash, king of Judah, who first came to the throne at the age of seven. He reigned a total of 40 years and did what was pleasing in the sight of the Lord. His success was due, in large measure, to Jehoiada the priest, who obviously gave him much wise and godly counsel through the years. Of note, Joash endeavored to repair the Temple. According to the text, he diverted a lot of money to the project and made sure that good, honest workers were employed and well paid. During his reign, a very serious political threat arose from King Hazael of Aram who had vowed to attack Jerusalem. Joash was able to avert the crisis by paying the king a large sum of money. Joash's reign ended on a sad note. He was assassinated by Jozacar and Jehozabad, who were both described as being trusted advisors to the king.

Application

You know how poems and song lyrics have a way of hanging around in your memory… Here's one that I have had stored away in the back of my mind for a long time. I think my dad used to quote it in a sermon and maybe that is how I first encountered it. It's called "The Pig Got Up and Slowly Walked Away," written by Benjamin Hapgood Burt in 1933: "One evening last October, when I was far from sober, And dragging home a load with manly pride, my feet began to stutter and I fell down in the gutter, and a pig came up and lay right by my side. Then I mumbled, 'It's fair weather when good fellows get together.' Till a lady passing by was heard to say, 'You can tell a man that boozes by the company he chooses,' Then the pig got up and slowly walked away." It's not some great Shakespearean sonnet, but the message is well-conveyed. Those with whom we cast our lot, will make or break both reputation and success.

Young Joash had success because Jehoiada was a wise and supportive friend. Jehoiada was able to speak truth and wisdom into the life of the king. It begs the question, "Who has your attention? Who are those persons in your life that speak truth into your heart?" It is vital for all of us to develop relationships that encourage us, feed us, and nurture us. It is important that those relationships are ones of honesty through which we can see ourselves and understand our actions more clearly. We may not always enjoy the critical voice or the word of correction that a good friend can offer, but how we much we need it! I pray that you will know the counsel of wise people in your life and that you will be that same voice for others.

Prayer

Father, surround us with friends who will speak the truth as they point to you. Amen.

Day 326   2 Kings 13: When God's Spirit Rests in Your Life...

> "Once when some Israelites were burying a man, they spied a band of these raiders. So they hastily threw the corpse into the tomb of Elisha and fled. But as soon as the body touched Elisha's bones, the dead man revived and jumped to his feet!" 2 Kings 13:21 (NLT)

Observation
This chapter outlines the stories of several bad kings who came to power during the final days of Elisha's life. In describing the reign of King Jehoahaz, the text mentions a "deliverer" who continued to give aid to Israel and offer moments of peace amid political upheaval. Most Bible scholars believe this is a reference to Elisha and his continual prophetic ministry to the nation. It is believed that his prophetic ministry lasted for 56 years. It was apparent that God's Spirit rested on his ministry, both in life and in death. One of the most bizarre stories about Elisha unfolds at the end of this chapter. Elisha dies and is buried. And as our focus verse states, when a group of mourners, trying to escape from some Moabite bandits, throw a dead body into the tomb of Elsha, the dead man comes to life! It is symbolic of the role of Elisha who attempted for decades to call the Israelites back to life from the spiritual decay caused by their disobedience.

Application
Let's talk Holy Spirit for a moment. There is an important difference in the role the Spirit displayed in the Old and New Testaments. The Spirit has been eternally present as a part of the Trinity. Genesis 1 speaks of the Spirit of God moving across the waters during creation. In the Old Testament, the Spirit was placed in the lives of specific individuals at specific moments to do specific things. The Spirit rested on the judges of Israel as they sought deliverance of Israel from those nations that oppressed them. In the time of the great prophets like Elijah and Elisha, the Spirit gave ordinary men the ability to perform extraordinary miracles as they attempted to bring the nation into godly compliance. In the New Testament, the Spirit was suddenly given to all Christians at the moment of conversion. Manifested on the Day of Pentecost as tongues of fire, the Spirit became and remains an indwelling presence of God in the life of every believer. As promised by Christ, the Spirit abides with us, teaching us, correcting us, empowering us, and ministering through us. It is vital that we understand that God's eternal Spirit, along with his power, now rests in our lives. And when the Spirit rests in each of us, we can do extraordinary Kingdom acts. We produce Kingdom fruit. We challenge the stronghold of evil. We bring the presence of Christ to the world. We are mighty in His name. You are stronger than you think.

Prayer
Father, thank you for the gift of the indwelling Spirit. Amen.

Day 327 — 2 Kings 14: Pride Goeth Before a Fall

> "You have indeed defeated Edom, and you are very proud of it. But be content with your victory and stay at home! Why stir up trouble that will only bring disaster on you and the people of Judah?" 2 Kings 14:10 (NLT)

Observation

By this point in the narrative, the names and deeds of all the kings tend to get a little confusing. In this chapter Amaziah, king of Judah, is described as a good king, mostly obedient to the Lord. Jehoash, king of Israel, is described as a bad king. Though they share the same heritage, land, and language, these two kings continue a civil war. Amaziah, after winning a decisive battle against Edom, decides to challenge Jehoash and demands they meet in battle. Jehoash responds with a parable in which a mighty cedar tree is challenged by a thistle bush. He warns Amaziah not to attack him. Amaziah is too prideful and will not back down. He attacks Jehoash and is badly defeated. (The remainder of the chapter briefly describes some of the final remaining kings who will come to power prior to the Assyrian conquest.)

Application

Pride… a little of it builds your self-worth and confidence. Too much of it destroys your life. Because he had been victorious over the Moabites, Amaziah foolishly thought that he was ready to take on the world. His foolish pride forced him into making a bad decision, one that cost a lot of lives. It's the same for us. Though we will probably not challenge the king of Israel to a battle anytime soon, we will have those moments when too much pride will force us into making some bad decisions. We get a little cocky at times. We get a little "too big for our britches."

Here's where the sin of pride gains the strongest foothold in our lives. We grow up and begin to settle into a mentality that proclaims that we have made it on our own. We've pulled ourselves up by the bootstraps. We've worked hard, earned an education, and by our own savvy, we have had success. Somewhere along the line we move away from God-dependency and slip into a self-sufficiency. We forget that "every good and perfect gift is from above" (James 1:17 NIV). We trick ourselves into thinking that we are who we are and have obtained what we own, because of our abilities. What foolish and sinful pride. We are totally dependent upon God. All that we have is a result of God's blessings in our lives. The ability to learn, to work, to survive, are all gifts of grace. If we do not take a moment each day to acknowledge God's sovereignty and offer our gratitude, then maybe we have gotten a little too big for those pants.

Prayer

Father, keep us humble in the midst of your blessings in our lives. Amen.

Day 328 — 2 Kings 15: The Loneliness of Leadership

> "The Lord struck the king with leprosy, which lasted until the day he died. He lived in isolation in a separate house. The king's son Jotham was put in charge of the royal palace, and he governed the people of the land."
> 2 Kings 15:5 (NLT)

Observation
Much of this chapter is devoted to the stories of four kings who reigned in Israel (northern kingdom) as the rise of the Assyrian empire continues and begins to influence the political climate in Israel. All four of these kings were very ineffective as leaders, one of them reigning only for a month. None of them honored the Lord by their actions. In contrast to what was going on in the north, the southern kingdom was led by King Uzziah. Uzziah was 16 when he came to power and would rule for the next 52 years. He brought stability by doing "what was right in the sight of the Lord." (His son, Jotham, would succeed him on the throne and would rule for 16 years.) One interesting backstory of Uzziah's reign is this mention of his leprosy. According to 2 Chronicles 26:16-21, the reason for God's punishment involved Uzziah having once arrogantly entered the Temple to burn incense, usurping the role of a priest. From the text, the reader can assume that much of his leadership was carried out in isolation.

Application
William Shakespeare wrote, "Uneasy lies the head that wears the crown" (King Henry IV, Part II, Act III, Scene 1). He's right. There is both an uneasiness and loneliness to those who lead others. Whether it's a CEO of a Fortune 500 company, the president of a nation, the manager of a retail chain, or even the pastor of a local church, there are some downsides to being in charge. Authority is always questioned. Decisions are always second-guessed. Responsibilities continue to grow with each year of leadership. Expectations increase to super-human levels. And… there are always those who want to unseat the leader in the hope of taking his/her place. So… it is indeed a little lonely at the top.

In the story of King Uzziah, one must add the burden of disease to his résumé. Though he served for more than half a century, surely many of his days were spent in isolation, depression, and silent suffering. It was not easy being the king. It's interesting how many of us view those in authority over us. We envy the big salary and spacious office. We covet the luxurious vacations and the ego-boost that power provides. It seems like a great life that anyone would want to live. But there are always criticisms, pressures to perform, and expectations. Here is my challenge for you today. Pray specifically for your boss, whomever he or she might be. Pray for their health and well-being. Pray that they would have wisdom. Pray for the safety and health of their family. Your encouragement can mean a great deal. Trust me on that.

Prayer
Father, thank you for those who have been called to lead. Grant them grace. Amen.

Day 329

2 Kings 16: Back to the Future

> "Instead, he followed the example of the kings of Israel, even sacrificing his own son in the fire. In this way, he followed the detestable practices of the pagan nations the Lord had driven from the land ahead of the Israelites."
> 2 Kings 16:3 (NLT)

Observation

Just when it seemed there was some hope emerging in the southern kingdom of Judah because several kings had been more faithful in pointing the nation towards God, along comes Ahaz who does just the opposite. He acted more like the wicked kings of the northern kingdom who practiced idolatry and pagan worship rites. Ahaz even went so far as to offer his son as a burnt sacrifice to a pagan deity. When attacked by Israel and Aram, Ahaz formed an alliance with Tiglath-pilser, king of Assyria to help in the battle. Though successful in turning away the threat, 120,000 soldiers of Judah were killed in a single day. Ahaz agreed to allow Judah to become a vassal state under Assyrian rule. When visiting the king of Assyria, Ahaz took note of a special altar for worship and had a duplicate built to replace the main altar at the Temple. In addition, he made other modifications at the Temple including the removal of the Great Bronze Sea from the shoulders of the bronze oxen that supported it. All these actions indicated a very strong drift away from God.

Application

As many of you know, I had double-knee replacement surgery in late December of 2015. Things continue to progress well with each passing month. Range of motion is good and normal activities get easier all the time. One thing that I can no longer do is get on my knees. The design of the joints is such that doing so is painful. But every once in a while, I forget. Without thinking, I will bend down to work on something and forget that I can't put the weight on my new joints. The pain reminds me very quickly to alter my behavior. But I will probably do it again, and again. Sometimes it's just hard to "unlearn" a behavior that you have done for years.

From a spiritual standpoint, we have been called to newness. There should be a clear "before and after" picture of our behavior because of our walk with Christ. We are called to transformation. And yet, from time to time, the old life beckons us back. We slip-up. We make a poor choice. We let the lure of temptation draw us in. There are days when we seem to live as though we have never met Christ, nor pledged fidelity to him. It's the old "one step forward and two steps backward" mentality. The truth is that we are but human and we will make our mistakes. The key is not being dominated by those poor choices. Promise this day, that you will live with greater resolve and more fidelity to your faith.

Prayer

Father, give us wisdom that will keep us from making the same old mistakes. Amen.

Day 330 — 2 Kings 17: Cause and Effect

> "Finally, in the ninth year of King Hoshea's reign, Samaria fell, and the people of Israel were exiled to Assyria. They were settled in colonies in Halah, along the banks of the Habor River in Gozan, and in the cities of the Medes." 2 Kings 17:6 (NLT)

Observation
This chapter describes a pivotal moment in the history of the northern kingdom of Israel. Hoshea will be captured after a nine-year reign and will have the distinction of being the last king of the northern kingdom. Hoshea had continued the pattern of the kings before him in doing evil in the eyes of the Lord. Because Israel had become a vassal state of Assyria, Hoshea attempted to form an alliance with the king of Egypt against Assyria. King Shalmaneser of Assyria heard about the plot and arrested Hoshea and placed him in prison. In 722 B.C., the Assyrians invaded the northern kingdom and besieged the capital of Samaria for three years. The people were captured and taken away into exile. Verses 7 through 17 speak of the primary reasons why God allowed the exile to occur. Verse 7 states, "This disaster came upon the people of Israel because they worshiped other gods. They sinned against the Lord their God, who had brought them safely out of Egypt and had rescued them from the power of Pharaoh, the king of Egypt" (NLT).

Application
I watched a horrific video on YouTube that contained footage of a thrill-seeker in China who had gained a huge, world-wide following by climbing to the top of very tall structures and dangling hundreds of feet in the air. This stunt called for him to hang over the edge of a tall building by just his fingertips. After doing a few pull-ups, his grip weakened, and he fell to his death. It was a tragic and senseless loss of life. It was also predictable. There was a cause and effect.

The ancient Israelites had been warned again and again to forsake the pagan gods and heinous worship practices of the people who had once inhabited the land of Israel. But a failure to rid the land completely of all pagan influences forced a compromise of belief and a lack of fidelity to the Lord. Though God continued to send prophets to warn the people, their admonitions fell on deaf ears and defeat was the result. The tragedy is that it did not have to happen. Changes could have been made and hearts could have remained loyal. It's easy to blame the ancients with their moral failures and lack of fidelity, but lest we be too quick to judge, let's consider our own patterns of faith engagement. Do we give daily attention to our faith pursuits? Do we pledge anew our fidelity to our Sovereign God? Are we careful to rid our lives of false gods and attention-demanding idols? It takes intentionality. It takes discipline.

Prayer
Father, may we remain faithful and obedient, this day and every day. Amen.

Day 331 — 2 Kings 18: What Are You Trusting?

> "Then the Assyrian king's chief of staff told them to give this message to Hezekiah: 'This is what the great king of Assyria says: What are you trusting in that makes you so confident? Do you think that mere words can substitute for military skill and strength? Who are you counting on, that you have rebelled against me?'" 2 Kings 18:19-20 (NLT)

Observation

Chapters 18 through 20 describe the last era of the southern kingdom (Judah). The chapter opens on a very hopeful note as Hezekiah comes to power. He will reign for 29 years, most of which occurs during the dominance of Assyria on the world scene. He did what was right in the sight of God and found favor with God for having done so. He is favorably compared to King David. He removed the pagan altars from the land and tore down the Asherah poles. He even destroyed the bronze snake Moses had once used in the wilderness because the people had turned it into an idol. He prospered as a king. He defeated the Philistines and strongly opposed Assyria. When King Sennacherib of Assyria came to power, suddenly Assyria began to turn the heat up on Judah. He demanded an oppressive assessment not to invade Jerusalem. This chapter ends with a representative of Sennacherib threatening the people of Judah.

Application

"Who are you counting on?" That was the rhetorical question that the Assyrian chief of staff posed to Hezekiah. Maybe that's a question that we should ask ourselves. Where do we put our trust? Who are we counting on to bring us hope, prosperity, and safety? I have a good doctor who manages my care. Whenever I go to him with a medical concern, I always feel better after he has made his diagnosis and offered a remedy. But is he the one who can really control my well-being? I have a good insurance man from whom I have bought many policies. I have life insurance, homeowner's insurance, and car insurance. I sleep a little better at night knowing that my assets are protected, but can State Farm really give me a better quality of life? I have a good banker who helps to watch over my financial world. He offers advice that directs the funds into which I place my retirement money. But can he really predict the future? I am tempted to place my trust in a lot of people, businesses, and financial institutions. What a foolish notion. "What are we trusting in that makes us so confident?"

Doesn't it make so much more sense to place our trust, hope, and allegiance in a God who loves us like a father, who controls the destinies of all men, who has unlimited resources, and who has the time to listen to our every concern, fear, and need? How foolish it is to give the total care of our lives to temporal things and flawed human beings, when the eternal God offers us real life, sustaining hope, and boundless resources.

Prayer

Father, teach us to place our trust and reliance solely in you. Amen.

| Day 332 | **2 Kings 19: Laying Down One's Burdens** |

> "After Hezekiah received the letter from the messengers and read it, he went up to the Lord's Temple and spread it out before the Lord."
> 2 Kings 19:14 (NLT)

Observation
As this chapter opens, King Hezekiah understands the severity of the threats that King Sennacherib of Assyria has made, and he turns to the Lord for help. He does two things. First, he seeks the counsel of Isaiah, the prophet of God who was ministering to Judah at this time. (Isaiah has been on the scene since the death of Uzziah although this is the first mention of him in 2 Kings.) Second, Hezekiah takes the threats of the Assyrian king, which had been delivered in the form of a letter, and spreads them out in the Temple before the presence of the Lord. Meanwhile, King Sennacherib continued to taunt Judah, suggesting that the God of Israel would be powerless to defeat Assyria. Isaiah prophesies about the defeat and death of Sennacherib. An angel of the Lord struck and killed 185,000 soldiers in the middle of a single night. The king is forced to flee back to Assyria where he is killed by his own sons.

Application
Ever get into one of those situations when you don't know what to do, how to pray, or where to turn? King Hezekiah was in one of those situations. But notice what he does. He takes the written threats of the enemy and he lays them in front of the altar of God knowing that he (Hezekiah) is powerless to "fix" his problem. He acknowledges his dependency upon God and leaves his petition before the altar.

I am reminded of a story I once heard of a young girl who had been sent off to bed by her mother, instructed to remember to say her prayers. As the mother walked past her daughter's room, she heard her daughter saying the letters of the alphabet and nothing more. So, she stopped and asked her daughter what she was doing. The sweet, young girl responded, "I didn't know what to say to God tonight and so I was just giving God the letters, knowing that God could put the words together." Sometimes, that's all we can do. We find ourselves falling on the altar of God saying, "I can't fix this... I can't carry this burden any longer... I don't even know what to pray." And maybe it is in those moments when we offer ourselves completely to God in total humility and dependency that we voice our best prayers. Sometimes we just need to lay out our burdens and seek God's help. Romans 8:26 reminds us that in those moments of anguish, we have a helper... "In the same way the Spirit also helps our weakness; for we do not know how to pray as we should, but the Spirit Himself intercedes for us with groanings too deep for words" (NASB). I don't know what enemies threaten you today, but I do know you alone are powerless to defeat them. Isn't it time to lay them before the altar of God and let God work?

Prayer
Father God, hear our humble prayers and grant us courage for this day. Amen.

Day 333 — 2 Kings 20: A Speedy Response

> But before Isaiah had left the middle courtyard, this message came to him from the Lord: "Go back to Hezekiah, the leader of my people. Tell him, 'This is what the Lord, the God of your ancestor David, says: I have heard your prayer and seen your tears. I will heal you, and three days from now you will get out of bed and go to the Temple of the Lord.'"
>
> 2 Kings 20:4-5 (NLT)

Observation

This chapter tells of the final days of King Hezekiah. The king becomes deathly ill. Isaiah shows up and tells the king that he is going to die, that he will not recover from his illness. Hezekiah weeps bitterly, perhaps reflecting on the error of his ways. He pours out his heart to God in prayer. And the prayer is heard and answered… immediately. Before Isaiah can even leave the palace, he hears from the Lord, directing him to return to the king and announce that he will become well again and will live for an additional 15 years. As proof of God's deliverance, the shadow on the king's sundial moved backwards that day. The chapter closes with the details of an envoy from Babylon who visit the king to wish him well in his recovery from his illness. Hezekiah shows them the extent of his riches and wealth. Obviously, this visit foreshadows the continuing rise of the Babylonian empire.

Application

Talk about an immediate answer to prayer… this has got to set some kind of record, right? Hezekiah is lying on his death bed. He pleads for God's intervention. And as soon as the words get out of his mouth, Isaiah is told to return to the king and pronounce his recovery. Don't you wish all your prayers were answered that quickly? Most of us can proclaim with absolute certainty, an answer to some prayer that we have made. In God's response to our prayers we are reminded that God always listens and responds in ways that are best for us. And yes, sometimes those prayers get answered very quickly. But sometimes, slowly. I have some prayers that I have prayed on behalf of others that took years to receive an answer. I have other prayers that I make with regularity that have yet to be answered at all.

I wonder sometimes about the timing of God's answers. I wonder about the reasons for the delay, or about the ways in which some prayers are not answered in the ways I thought they should have been. I have to remind myself that God's ways are not always my ways and that God's timing is not always dependent upon my schedule. I simply have to trust that God knows what is best in every situation, and that God has heard my petition and understands my needs. I can't tell you when your prayers will be answered; I can tell you that God has heard.

Prayer

Father God, thank you for hearing and responding to our prayers. Amen.

Day 334 — 2 Kings 21: Like Father, Like Son

> "He did what was evil in the Lord's sight, just as his father, Manasseh, had done. He followed the example of his father, worshiping the same idols his father had worshiped." 2 Kings 21:20-21 (NLT)

Observation
When King Hezekiah died, his son Manasseh became king. He was only 12 years old at the time. He would rule for the next 25 years. He was the polar opposite of his father. He had little-to-no-regard for the things of God. He rebuilt pagan shrines and constructed altars to Baal. He bowed down before all the gods of the earth and even sacrificed his own son. He even placed pagan objects of worship in the Temple itself! He also murdered a number of individuals. When he died, his son Amon, took the throne at the age of 32 but only reigned for two years. He behaved just like his father by doing extraordinary evil in the eyes of the Lord. His own officials conspired against him and killed him.

Application
King Amon worshipped the same idols that his father had worshiped. Why would he not? It was the way he had been raised. It was the example that had been set. It was how his father modeled how to do life. It was a cycle of disobedient behavior that quickly ended his reign on the throne. In a perfect world, sons learn a lot of good and noble things from their fathers. In that same perfect world, fathers are kind, honest, patient, courageous, and faithful. I know a few men who have been privileged to live that kind of life, and because of the godly influence and righteousness of their fathers, they grew up to become good and decent men. But I have also seen men who have not turned out well as adults, because their fathers modeled terrible behavior. I know of a young man in his early twenties who has abused both alcohol and women because he saw his father do both of those things as he was growing up. Sure, we are responsible for our own actions. But unfortunately, we are, in many ways, the product of our environment. I sometimes describe this process of growing up like wearing a tool belt. In a perfect world, a child grows up with all the essential tools needed to become a well-balanced, responsible adult. But in many cases, some of the tools are missing. I know a lot of men and women who spend decades as adults, trying to add tools to their belts that they were never given. No one taught ethical behavior. No one modeled a healthy marriage or good parenting techniques. No one explained how to be considerate of others. Maybe you need to break a destructive cycle in the history of your family. Your children are watching. Be responsible.

Prayer
Father God, help us to become the role-models that our children need. Amen.

Day 335 — 2 Kings 22: Going by the Book

> "'Go to the Temple and speak to the Lord for me and for the people and for all Judah. Inquire about the words written in this scroll that has been found. For the Lord's great anger is burning against us because our ancestors have not obeyed the words in this scroll. We have not been doing everything it says we must do.'" 2 Kings 22:13 (NLT)

Observation

After the death of wicked King Amon, his son Josiah rose to power. He was eight years old when he took the throne and he reigned for 31 years. Unlike his father and grandfather, Josiah did what was pleasing in the eyes of the Lord. He never turned away from following God. A definitive event occurred when he ordered the restoration and repair of the Temple. Hilkiah, the high priest, discovered the Torah scroll that had apparently been hidden or cast aside during some of the previous moments when pagan gods were worshiped in the Temple. He took it to the king and read it to him. The king realized how badly the nation had perverted the ways of God. Then Hilkiah consulted the prophet Huldah. She predicted the utter destruction of Jerusalem but told the king that God would spare him from witnessing the event. She prophesied that he would be buried in peace before that moment came.

Application

Reach in the glove compartment of your car and take out the owner's manual. Flip to the back and you will see a recommended maintenance schedule. It will advise you on how often to change the oil, rotate the tires, replace filters, drive belts, etc. To be honest, most of us never even glance at those instructions. We just get the oil changed whenever it feels like it's about time, and we take care of the other items when and if there is a problem. I would imagine that if we really did "follow the rules," that most of our cars would give us much better service over a much longer period

The people of Judah discovered that they had been living for a long time without consulting the Scroll of God on which God's instructions were written. Because they seldom read the words, their behaviors quickly lost focus and destruction was the result. The same mistakes get repeated by our generation. Whenever we neglect the reading, studying, and meditating of God's Word, we will quickly veer away from the paths that God has outlined for our lives. Bible study is not a casual activity. It cannot be a "hit or miss" kind of thing. It has to take priority so that our lives stay grounded and our actions remain pleasing in the eyes of God. As grateful as I am for your willingness to read this book, I really hope that it is only a supplement for your own time spent in the Word. If you have to make a choice, put down this book and read your Bible.

Prayer

God, give us a passion for your Word that motivates us to read it consistently. Amen.

Day 336   2 Kings 23: Personal Responsibility

> "Then the king summoned all the elders of Judah and Jerusalem. And the king went up to the Temple of the Lord with all the people of Judah and Jerusalem, along with the priests and the prophets—all the people from the least to the greatest. There the king read to them the entire Book of the Covenant that had been found in the Lord's Temple."
>
> 2 Kings 23:1-2 (NLT)

Observation

As the story of the southern kingdom of Judah begins to wind down, one of its greatest kings come to power. His name was Josiah and he carried out extensive religious reforms that changed the culture of the nation. Notice the focus verse... He personally summoned all the religious leaders to the Temple along with all the people of the land. There, he himself, read the entire Law of Moses to the nation. He renewed the covenant of the Lord. He pledged to obey the word of the Lord with all his heart and soul. This chapter gives a lengthy description of all the actions he took to purge the land of pagan deities and their influence. He tore down pagan altars, smashed the shrines that housed idols, and destroyed every Asherah pole. He reinstituted the celebration of Passover, which had been neglected for generations. He got rid of mediums and psychics. True to his pledge, he kept the law of Moses. Unfortunately, when he died, his sons turned back to the earlier evils which had plagued the nation.

Application

Sometimes, as a leader, you just have to take charge. Josiah didn't try to delegate responsibility. He refused to play the blame game. He avoided the temptation to sit back and hope that time would heal all wounds. He gathered the people and he read the Law and then he set into motion all that would be required to live according to it. I am intrigued by the image of the king himself, reading every bit of the Law to his constituents. It is always a powerful moment, when the person given the authority to lead, actually takes the initiative to do so.

Everyone reading this devotional thought is a leader in some context or another. You may lead a business, a professional office, a school, a company, or an organization. You may lead a family, a group of co-workers, children, or neighbors. Please don't protest and suggest that you have no influence or responsibility over others, because we all do. We influence the lives of those around us either by a stated job description, or by circumstance. So, the question becomes one of how well you are taking on that responsibility? Do you take initiative and seize opportunities, or do you sit back and wait for someone else to carry the load that you have been tasked to carry? It's time take personal responsibility and lead others to take faith steps.

Prayer

God, may we become the leaders we were meant to be. Amen.

Day 337 — 2 Kings 24: Creating Distance

> "These things happened because of the Lord's anger against the people of Jerusalem and Judah, until he finally banished them from his presence and sent them into exile." 2 Kings 24:20 (NLT)

Observation

As this chapter unfolds, the demise of the southern kingdom of Judah is imminent as King Nebuchadnezzar of Babylon comes to power. The Babylonian king invades the land. The current king of Judah, Jehoiachin, is captured and exiled. Nebuchadnezzar strips the royal palace and the Temple of all the treasures that remained from the days of King Solomon. He also takes with him 10,000 soldiers, craftsmen, and artisans to Babylon. Only the poorest of the poor are left behind. (Those left behind at the Exile will become known as the Samaritans and will be despised by the exiled Jewish population.) Nebuchadnezzar installs Zedekiah as the last king of Judah. It is important to note that all these things occurred because of the wrath of God. It was God's choice to send the people into exile because of their sinfulness.

Application

The Exile lasted about 50 years. Many positive things happened during this dark time. Faithful Jews began to reclaim important worship practices. Bloodlines were purified. Places of assembly were created called "synagogues" so that the reading of the Torah and the practice of meaningful community could continue. The time away from the promised land and the Temple gave the people new perspective and insight into their own lives and into their need to reestablish their relationships with God.

Sometimes distance can be a good thing. Human relationships can be difficult at times. Even with those that we love, sometimes there can be a strain, a brokenness, or an anger. And sometimes in such moments, a little "cooling off" period can help. At times, the space created by time and distance allows for our anger to subside, our tensions to ease, and our thoughts to become clear again. The distance can give us a little perspective, a little patience, and a little longing to be reconciled again. Please don't misunderstand me... I am not suggesting that the best way to solve all quarrels, anger, disagreements, and misunderstandings is to run from the problem. I am merely suggesting that sometimes we need a little space so that we can think clearly and react redemptively. God is never pleased by brokenness in our lives and longs for us to "set things right again." Sometimes the path to reconciliation has to take a few days to allow tensions and anger to cease. So, don't be afraid of creating a little distance when needed. Just don't be content to stay there for very long.

Prayer

God, may we be reconciled to each other through the work of grace. Amen.

Day 338 — 2 Kings 25: The Edge of Hope

> "On August 14 of that year, which was the nineteenth year of King Nebuchadnezzar's reign, Nebuzaradan, the captain of the guard and an official of the Babylonian king, arrived in Jerusalem. He burned down the Temple of the Lord, the royal palace, and all the houses of Jerusalem. He destroyed all the important buildings in the city." 2 Kings 25:8-9 (NLT)

Observation

This final chapter of 2 Kings has to be among the most difficult chapters to read from the perspective of the Jewish faithful. It describes the final siege of Jerusalem, which includes the destruction of the Temple, the royal palace, and all the homes. King Nebuchadnezzar ordered the captain of his army to go into the city and complete the task of burning it all to the ground. As a part of his assault on the Temple, he even took the bronze elements used for worship and broke them apart and sent them back to Babylon. The king of Judah had to watch as his sons were killed and then the Babylonians gouged out his eyes. The land was decimated. The Temple was destroyed. It seemed that the very presence of God was gone. The people were led to Babylon with only the smallest glimmer of hope remaining.

Application

One of the most difficult places to stand is on the edge of hope. Maybe you have stood there. The edge of hope is that place where all the strongholds of your life have been stripped away and there is all but nothing left to keep you going. Maybe a chronic illness has invaded your life. You have tried every treatment, taken every pill, and prayed every prayer and still no relief. You just don't know how to carry on for one more day. Or perhaps grief has taken you to the edge. Some catastrophic loss in your life crushes your spirit to the point that you don't know how you will ever move forward. The pain is too real, the loss is too great, the sorrow is too profound. Maybe a broken relationship has taken you to your wit's end. Maybe the pain of addiction has pushed you farther than you could have ever imagined. Maybe an unfulfilled dream, a lost vision, or promise broken has you standing on the edge, asking questions about life, purpose, worth, and even the existence of God.

You're not the first to stand on the edge where hope is all but diminished. Christ felt it at Gethsemane and then on the cross. "My God, My God, why have You forsaken ME" (Matthew 27:46 NASB)? But remember the rest of the story. God had not forgotten him, nor has God forgotten us. Through our periods of exile, abandonment, and despair, the Great Shepherd is still watching over the sheep. We will see in a mirror dimly for a while, but our story is not done. Take courage. God is sovereign and you are not forgotten. Not for a moment.

Prayer

God, even during our darkest days, may we see the glimmer of your presence. Amen.

Day 339   1 Chronicles 1: The Cliff Notes

> "Eber had two sons. The first was named Peleg (which means "division"), for during his lifetime the people of the world were divided into different language groups. His brother's name was Joktan." 1 Chronicles 1:19 (NLT)

Observation
I like to think of the books of 1 and 2 Chronicles as sort of a "CliffsNote" version of the history of Israel: short and concise. Probably written by Ezra (circa 400 B.C.), these books contain somewhat of a revisionist history of the nation up until the time of the exile. The first nine chapters deal with genealogies and the rest of the chapters describe the Deuteronomic history of the nation. The chronicler wants to paint a portrait that all nations are linked as a part of God's creation. He also wants to carefully trace the line of David, connecting his story to the coming Messianic age. Our focus verse briefly describes the events that occurred during the life of a man named Peleg. It was during his lifetime that the Tower of Babel event occurred (Genesis 11), which led to the creation of various languages and the dispersion of people to the various ends of the earth.

Application
Just in case you are not familiar with "CliffsNotes," let me offer a brief word of explanation. The Cliff Note company, which has been around for a long time, offers condensed versions of hundreds of works of literature, including study guides and background information. Although they are intended as a supplement to someone's study of a book, the lazy student will sometimes read the Cliff Notes to get the gist of a book rather than reading the full version. (Yes, I will have to admit that in high school I dodged a few summer reading assignments by just reading these notes. Graduated with high honors… thank you very much.) It is important to note that the writer of 1 and 2 Chronicles assumes that the reader has a thorough knowledge of the history of Israel. His brief account of all that has occurred up to this point in the history of the nation is not intended to be a substitute history but rather a supplement. He wants to remind the reader of the important moments so that the reader can more clearly trace the redemptive work of God through the context of the narrative. My fear is that many of us want to "Cliff Note" our way through the Bible. We want to know the highlights and few of the great stories in the hope that this limited knowledge will get us by. The problem is that when we "shortcut" our knowledge of God's redemptive narrative, we "shortcut" our knowledge of God. I challenge you to invest heavily into God's Word so that you might discover the God whom it describes. Read all of it. Read it carefully. Let it change your life.

Prayer
Father God, give us a passion for your Word so that we might know you. Amen.

Day 340 — 1 Chronicles 2: Bad Boys, Bad Boys

> "Judah had three sons from Bathshua, a Canaanite woman. Their names were Er, Onan, and Shelah. But the Lord saw that the oldest son, Er, was a wicked man, so he killed him." 1 Chronicles 2:3 (NLT)

Observation
The chronicler begins the chapter with a list of the 12 sons of Jacob (Israel). Though listed in birth order in verse 1, the chronicler begins tracing descendants with the sons of Judah, who was certainly not the firstborn. But again, the focus is on Judah because all the kings of Israel came from this line of descendants. Most notably, it is the ancestral line from which King David descended. The three sons of Judah are named, Er, Onan, and Shelah. Some detail to this story is told in Genesis 38. What is unclear, however, is what Er did that brought the wrath of God. All that is known of his story is that he was once married to Tamar. Because he was slain by God, the law of levirate marriage required that his brother Onan marry Tamar and provide offspring to further his brother's line of descendants. Because of his disobedience, Onan would also be slain by God.

Application
As they say in the deep south, sometimes you can "outgrow your raising," meaning that even those individuals with a bad upbringing can grow up to become something great. We've all known stories of people who grew up in horrible conditions only to become a great politician, or lawyer, or doctor. Certainly, Judah's line didn't start out all that well with two of his sons being killed by God because of their wickedness. But further along in the story the great king of Israel, King David, was a product of this family. This story says to me that though our early experiences can certainly shape our psyche and distort our values, there does come a day when we become responsible as adults for the decisions we make and the values we hold dear.

I am certainly blessed to have been raised by wonderful, godly, loving parents. They modeled so many important lessons and provided me with the essential life-tools that have helped me as an adult. Unfortunately, not everyone has such an experience. There are many who grow up in broken homes. Some are raised in abusive situations. Some are raised in families where addictive behavior is chronic and passed along to each new generation. But the scriptures promise that in Christ, you are a new creation (2 Corinthians 5:17). Because of the saving, redemptive, life-changing love of Jesus, you don't have to be defined by how you were raised or what life skills you weren't provided. Christ has come to make all things new… including you. May God bless the new life you have in Christ.

Prayer
Father God, thank you for the new life we have in Christ. Amen.

Day 341 — 1 Chronicles 3: Who Knew?

> "These six sons were born to David in Hebron, where he reigned seven and a half years. Then David reigned another thirty-three years in Jerusalem. The sons born to David in Jerusalem included Shammua, Shobab, Nathan, and Solomon. Their mother was Bathsheba, the daughter of Ammiel. David also had nine other sons: Ibhar, Elishua, Elpelet, Nogah, Nepheg, Japhia, Elishama, Eliada, and Eliphelet. These were the sons of David, not including his sons born to his concubines. Their sister was named Tamar."
>
> 1 Chronicles 3:4-9 (NLT)

Observation

This chapter outlines the sons of King David. (Remember that one of the priorities of the chronicler was tracing the Davidic line because of the promises made to David in terms of land, kingdom, and presence.) Though all the sons born to his various wives are named, the primary focus is on the lineage as it extends through Solomon and then on to Zerubbabel. The line of descendants is traced all the way to the time in which the chronicler wrote this account... approximately 400 B.C. If you add up the all the names you will discover that David had a total of 19 sons and at least one named daughter, Tamar. There were, apparently, other sons and daughters born to concubines that are unnamed and unnumbered in this account.

Application

Want to win a Bible trivia contest? This might be a great fact to remember. How many sons did King David have? Answer: 19. (At least that he could talk about... there were a few others born to women who were not his wives.)

If you trace my family heritage back a couple of generations, it gets a little crazy. On my paternal grandmother's side of the family, there were 13 brothers and sisters. One of the last times that we gathered for a family reunion, hundreds of descendants gathered at Beulah Baptist Church in Snoddy, Alabama. The members of my father's generation were called the "numbered cousins." Whenever a child was born into the extended family, they were given a number according to the birth order of that generation. My dad is number nine and my uncle is number 18. (I think there were 43 in all!) I've often wondered if my great grandparents could remember all those names. And what of the generations of King David? How many total descendants would there have been and who could even remember all their names? I can give you that answer as well... God. God knows our stories and remembers our names. Why? Because we are important. Every one of us. So, if you ever feel a little insignificant and wonder if anyone even knows who you are, be comforted by the fact that the one who matters most knows you better than you even know yourself.

Prayer

Father God, how thankful we are that each of us is vitally important to you. Amen.

Day 342   1 Chronicles 4: A Little Abuse Goes a Long Way

> "There was a man named Jabez who was more honorable than any of his brothers. His mother named him Jabez because his birth had been so painful. He was the one who prayed to the God of Israel, 'Oh, that you would bless me and expand my territory! Please be with me in all that I do, and keep me from all trouble and pain!' And God granted him his request."
>
> 1 Chronicles 4:9-10 (NLT)

Observation

This chapter lists the descendants of two of the tribes of Israel. The first half of the chapter lists all the descendants from the tribe of Judah. The second half of the chapter is devoted to the tribe of Simeon. According to the ancestral land grants, these two tribes lived closely to each other and may explain why the chronicler chose to list one right after the other. Embedded within the list of names is this short narrative about a man named Jabez that is our focus passage. A lot has been made of his prayer. It was a simple request and promise of reliance upon God. God heard Jabez and responded favorably, according to the text. I am also intrigued by this man's name, Jabez. It literally means, "pain," and was given to him by his mother because of the pain she experienced in childbirth. Although I can certainly understand the reasons for the name, I wonder, if later in life, when he turned from being a pain to becoming a blessing, if his mother ever regretted the name she had given him.

Application

Sometimes we imprint characteristics and qualities into the psyche of our children at a very young age. A little positive feedback and nurturing can go a long way. Unfortunately, a little abuse and negativity can also stay with a child for a very long time. Years ago, in a church I pastored in central Kentucky, I met a woman who told me some of the hurtful things that had happened to her as a child. She grew up in a very poor region in Appalachia. Her parents sold her to another family where she was treated very much like a slave. She was not allowed to attend school. Her role was to clean the house, do the cooking, and wash the clothes. Whenever her "owners" were displeased, they would say, "You're not worth the money we paid to get you!" You can imagine the pain and abuse that she suffered. She was well into her seventies when she told me her story. By the grace of God and the love of Christ, her life had improved. She had met a wonderful man who removed her from that situation. She raised a family of her own and was a sweet and kind person. She was a faithful member of the church, but even all those years later, when she talked about her childhood, her voice would crack and the tears would flood her eyes. She continued to carry the abuse of her past. So be careful what you say to your children. Affirm them. Love them.

Prayer

Dear Father, may we live a legacy of affirmation and encouragement. Amen.

Day 343 — 1 Chronicles 5: That Which Is Within Us

> "The oldest son of Israel was Reuben. But since he dishonored his father by sleeping with one of his father's concubines, his birthright was given to the sons of his brother Joseph. For this reason, Reuben is not listed in the genealogical records as the firstborn son." 1 Chronicles 5:1 (NLT)

Observation

Continuing his listing of the various generations of the 12 tribes of Israel, the chronicler traces the lineage of the three tribes of Reuben, Gad, and the half tribe of Manasseh. Remember that these three tribes were those granted land east of the Jordan even before the conquest of Canaan began. They received the land agreeing to fight with their fellow Israelites throughout the conquest. This chapter names many descendants, along with some of the battles fought and victories won by this group of tribes. According to the record, there were 44,760 warriors within this group, all well-trained and well-equipped for battle. Focus is placed on Reuben. Although he was the first-born of Jacob, he is not given the prominence typically afforded the first-born son. The birthright was stripped from him because of a sin described in Genesis 35:22 where he had relations with one of his father's concubines.

Application

Let's take a moment to remember a little about Reuben. As stated in our focus verse, he committed a grievous sin by sleeping with Bilhah, one of his father's concubines. This very dark blot on his life record certainly cost him both prominence and the blessings of his birthright. But let's also remember that it was Reuben who argued for the life of his brother Joseph when the other brothers longed to execute him. It was his suggestion to throw him into an empty cistern rather than take his life. He had secretly planned to rescue him and return him to his father (Genesis 37:21-22). So, you find within the heart and mind of Reuben the ability to do both evil and good. He had the capacity to act poorly and to act nobly. Such a dichotomy is deeply embedded into us as well.

We all have our good days and our bad days. There are days when we are led by the Spirit, when our actions are pleasing in the eyes of God and beneficial to everyone within our sphere of influence. But then there are those days in which we act poorly. We are driven and prodded along by the darker prompting of our psyche. Our actions result in the betrayal of our best intentions and noble character. Most of us hope to be remembered at our best moments and not by our worst decisions. So maybe we need to show a little grace to those around us who struggle with living in the tension of good and bad behavior. Let's celebrate and rejoice when the good wins out, and lovingly admonish and encourage when it doesn't.

Prayer

Heavenly Father, may our lives be governed by a golden rule ethic. Amen.

Day 344 — 1 Chronicles 6: The Task Before Us

> "Only Aaron and his descendants served as priests. They presented the offerings on the altar of burnt offering and the altar of incense, and they performed all the other duties related to the Most Holy Place. They made atonement for Israel by doing everything that Moses, the servant of God, had commanded them." 1 Chronicles 6:49 (NLT)

Observation

There are 81 verses in chapter 6 that describe both the descendants of Levi and the allotment of land given to this tribe. Remember that the tribe of Levi was the priestly tribe. The chronicler traces the lineage from Levi, to Aaron, to Jehozadak who was the high priest at the time of the exile. It is important to the chronicler to show the continuity of qualified priests serving in leadership roles in the tabernacle. One interesting character in the listing is Zadok. Mentioned in the narrative of 2 Samuel, Zadok was a key figure in David's administration who supported David during Absalom's rebellion. This chapter also gives a nod to the Temple musicians who were assigned by David to "minister with music" at the tabernacle. Our focus verse is a reminder that only the direct descendants of Aaron served as priests. There was a very important distinction between the Levites and the priests. All priests were Levites, but not all Levites were priests. The priests alone (direct descendants of Aaron), were responsible for the actual duties of making offerings and sacrifices. The Levites supported them in their work. For example, the Levites would have prepared animals for sacrifice, maintained the tabernacle structure, and performed any number of menial tasks.

Application

It is important to note that the descendants of Aaron had a very specific, important, and vital role to play. That was their task and calling. God had clearly set them apart for this work. So, let me ask a rather existential question. "Why are you here? Why has God placed you on the planet?" I would suggest that God's purpose for your life is just as clearly defined as that of the ancient Levites. You are here to glorify God and to do the special work that God has designed you to accomplish. No, you probably have not been called to offer burnt offerings at the Temple, but you have been called to influence lives and heal the brokenness of humanity. Sometimes we fret and wonder at God's specific plan for our lives. We may or may not discover it. There are times when God places us at just the right place, at just the right moment, at just the right time to make a huge difference in someone's life. Whether you ever become aware of that moment is not essential. What is vital is to know is that God is using your life. You are making a difference in God's Kingdom. Be grateful for the role you play whether you are conscious of it or not.

Prayer

Father God, thank you for your calling in our lives. May we be found faithful. Amen.

Day 345   1 Chronicles 7: Black Sheep of the Family

> "The descendants of Ephraim were Shuthelah, Bered, Tahath, Eleadah, Tahath, Zabad, Shuthelah, Ezer, and Elead. These two were killed trying to steal livestock from the local farmers near Gath."
> 1 Chronicles 7:20-21 (NLT)

Observation
Chapter 7 gives a very quick look at the remainder of the tribes that have not been listed in the early chapters. The descendants of six tribes are listed: Issachar, Benjamin, Naphtali, Manasseh, Ephraim, and Asher. It is interesting to point out that only a single verse is devoted to the descendants of Naphtali (first generation only) and there is no mention of the descendants from the tribes of Zebulun and Dan. It is theorized that perhaps some of the scrolls were damaged at the point at which they were being copied, or that they were lost or destroyed when Tiglath-Pilesar attacked and exiled these tribes.

Application
Our focus passage deals with a short narrative concerning two of the descendants from the tribe of Ephraim. One has to assume that the two men described in verse 21 are the last two listed in verse 20. Apparently Ezer and Elead were horse thieves or cattle rustlers. We can only fill in the blanks with our imaginations, but obviously, some type of skirmish occurred with local farmers as they attempted to steal some livestock. Ezer and Elead were killed in the process and their names have forever been recorded as being disreputable men. They became the black sheep of their family and were probably remembered at family reunions with more than a little disdain.

Well, we've all got family. There are colorful and sordid stories that swirl around every family on the planet. We've all got a crazy uncle or a sister who's nuts. One of the legendary stories in my family is the tale of my great uncle Renny who once put his wife on a bus to head to Birmingham for surgery. He was too cheap to pay for the gas and the hotel expense that he would have incurred if he had taken her himself. To make matters worse, he bought her a one-way ticket in case she didn't make it! True story. My people...

Ever wonder if you are the "black sheep" of your family? Are you the one who has sullied the name or ruined the reputation? Don't think in terms of your physical family, but your spiritual one. How well have you carried the name of Christ in your words and actions? How much honor have you brought to the Kingdom? Let's admit that all of us are far from perfect. We've all "stolen a little livestock." But let's stop looking at the past and look ahead to the new reputation we can forge. Let's strive for honor, for character, for civility, and for grace.

Prayer
Father God, help us to lean into a bright future, not mired by the sins of the past. Amen.

Day 346 — 1 Chronicles 8: Teaching Your Children

> "Ulam's sons were all mighty warriors and expert archers. They had many sons and grandsons—150 in all. All these were descendants of Benjamin."
> 1 Chronicles 8:40 (NLT)

Observation
In this chapter the chronicler expands his genealogy of the Tribe of Benjamin that he had first introduced in Chapter 7. This tribe is possibly singled out because the Tribe of Benjamin is the tribe from which King Saul will originate. He is mentioned briefly in the narrative of this chapter. The lineage is further traced through his oldest son, Jonathon. The narrative also adds that all these descendants lived in and around Jerusalem. It is important to note that only a small portion of land was given to the descendants of Benjamin, but from a strategic location point-of-view, this portion was vital. The city of Jerusalem was in this territory. (The Tribe of Judah was given land just to the south and contained the city of Bethlehem.) Our focus verse is the last verse in the chapter. It gives a brief word about the sons and grandsons of Ulam. Ulam is the son of Eshek and is distantly related to King Saul. The reader is told a couple of key facts: these men were mighty warriors and they were many in number.

Application
When I was young, a lot of days were spent running around the neighborhood playing cowboys and Indians. Half of us carried six-shooters and half of us carried bows and arrows. The six-shooters, of course, never fired anything and the arrows had rubber tips. Mostly we just ran around and acted like kids used to do before the days of Xboxes and Phone apps. At lunch time, the cowboys and Indians would declare a peace treaty and dive into a good peanut-butter and jelly sandwich.

I would think that Ulam must have taken great pride in the skillset that his sons and grandsons had developed. It was no small thing to say of them that they were, "expert archers." They developed a skill that brought pride to their family and safety to their nation. It is obvious that the fathers taught the sons the skills they had developed. It begs the question, "What skills are you teaching your kids?" Some parents teach their children how to cook or grill. Some teach how to quilt and sew. Some teach how to play sports or work on a car. Nothing wrong with any of that. But are such skills enough? What about the skills of patience, civility, and common courtesy? What about the skills of marriage, parenting, or faith-development? What about the skills of loving a neighbor and giving aid to those in need? Such important life-skills are best taught from parent to child. If they don't get them from you, from where will such instruction come? Invest in the life of your children. Teach the essential skills.

Prayer
Father God, give us the strength and wisdom to teach our children well. Amen.

Day 347　　　　　　　　　　　　　　1 Chronicles 9: Gatekeepers

> "The four chief gatekeepers, all Levites, were trusted officials, for they were responsible for the rooms and treasuries at the house of God. They would spend the night around the house of God, since it was their duty to guard it and to open the gates every morning." 1 Chronicles 9:26-27 (NLT)

Observation
Chapter 9 begins with a summary statement by the chronicler, indicating that all pre-exilic Israel was listed in the genealogical records. He further states the reason for the exilic period. "The people of Judah were exiled to Babylon because they were unfaithful to the Lord" (vs. 1 NLT). Following that statement, he begins to list all the families who returned to Israel following the exile. They "repopulated" the land with God's people. This list includes commoners (vs. 3-9), priests (vs. 10-13), Levites (vs. 14-16), and gatekeepers (vs. 17-27). The chronicler wants to send a very clear message that Israel had survived the exile. All the people needed to govern, lead worship, and do the work of restoration had been brought back to the land. He mentions that 212 gatekeepers were in the returning group. Our focus verse indicates that there were four chief gatekeepers whose job it was to guard the rooms and especially, the treasuries of the house of God.

Application
Gatekeeping is an important responsibility. Those who "keep the gate" are the first line of defense against any outside threats to an organization, home, or family. For example, one of the fast-growing businesses these days is cyber security. Concerned about the threat of identity theft and all that goes along with that, millions of people pay millions of dollars to safeguard their on-line presence and personal information. Many insist on "gatekeeping" at their homes. I have a neighbor who not only has an alarm system on her doors and windows, but an elaborate network of cameras mounted all around her house so that she can monitor what's going on even from a remote location. Airports, courthouses, schools, and emergency rooms use metal detectors. We understand the importance of gatekeeping… or do we? I wonder how well we are guarding our hearts and minds? How well do we monitor the intake? We are often lulled into a false sense of security thinking that the "world" won't really get to us. We think we can handle the violence we watch, the angry politicians we monitor, and the onslaught of racy images that splash across our screens. We foolishly think that we can keep the dangers at arms-length. We need to provide better security for our lives. We do that by establishing a daily reliance upon the Spirit to give us wisdom and discernment throughout each day. There are constant threats, and we need to stay vigilant.

Prayer
Father God, help us to guard carefully the gates to our hearts and minds. Amen.

Day 348 — 1 Chronicles 10: Lessons Learned

> "So Saul died because he was unfaithful to the Lord. He failed to obey the Lord's command, and he even consulted a medium instead of asking the Lord for guidance. So the Lord killed him and turned the kingdom over to David son of Jesse." 1 Chronicles 10:13-14 (NLT)

Observation

In just a very few verses, the chronicler quickly rushes through a history of the reign of King Saul. There is an assumption that the reader has a knowledge of the story. Because the chronicler wants to move quickly into the story of King David, he only speaks of what he sees as being the only significant part of Saul's reign... the ending. He lists a few scant details of Saul's last battle with the Philistines. He speaks of the providential moment, when Saul is mortally wounded by an archer's arrow, which will usher in the reign of King David. At the end of the chapter, he sums up the reasons why the "Lord killed him." He was unfaithful to God. He did not obey God's word. And he did not seek the Lord in his decision making.

Application

I often counsel with people and remind them that the tragedy is not necessarily in making mistakes, but in not learning from them. Oh, to be sure, none of us would ever want to make a mistake. We would love to have enough vision, wisdom, and insight to never make a bad decision or lean into a poor choice. But the truth of the matter is that we are human, and we will make a few mistakes along the way. We need to own up to our humanity enough to realize that truth. The key is to learn from our mistakes and correct our behavior. The real tragedy is making the same mistakes over and over again. Take another look at the life of King Saul. In his telling of the story, the chronicler listed at least three reasons, or mistakes, which brought the end of Saul's life. Had he learned from any of his errors, perhaps he could have corrected his behavior and mentality, and have brought greater success to his reign.

I know a lot of people who spend years in regret and shame over some past mistake. They can't seem to forgive themselves and let go of the guilt. That's not what God intends. In fact, God sent Christ to forgive us of our sins and cleanse us from all unrighteousness (1 John 1:9). Paul goes so far as to write in Romans 8:1, "Therefore there is now no condemnation for those in Christ Jesus" (NASB). There is a freedom offered... a wiping clean of the slate. Sometimes however, we abuse such grace by repeating the same mistakes over and over again. How many times do we have to feel the pain of regret and sorrow over repetitive action until we start changing our behavior? Let me challenge you this morning to learn from your mistakes. Rather than beating yourself up because of a mistake, take a moment to unpack the reasons behind it, and then chart a course for a better life. Learn and grow.

Prayer

Father God, help us to learn and change in ways that honor you. Amen.

Day 349   1 Chronicles 11: The King's Wish, Our Command

> "David remarked longingly to his men, 'Oh, how I would love some of that good water from the well by the gate in Bethlehem.'"
> 1 Chronicles 11:17 (NLT)

Observation

As the chronicler opens chapter 11, he chooses not to rehash the negative aspects of Israel's history during the time of the transition between King Saul and King David, but instead chooses to accentuate the unifying spirit that swept the land during David's reign. In verse 1 of this chapter, he goes so far as to say that "all" of Israel gathered before David as a show of unity and support. The theme of national unity would be especially important to the context in which the chronicler wrote this narrative. Remember that he writes during the time the Israelites were returning from the exilic period. National unity would become a very important theme. This chapter also includes a listing of David's mighty warriors. Our focus verse is drawn from a brief story told in this chapter that involved David's three elite commanders.

Application

David and his men were battling the Philistines. The Philistines occupied the city of Bethlehem, the place of David's birth. David looks across the valley filled with Philistine soldiers and into the village of Bethlehem. He longingly looks towards the well in Bethlehem, whose water he surely had tasted numerous times over the course of his life. His wish is for a taste of the cool, clean water. His three elite commanders hear his desire. They strap on their armor and break through the enemy lines and are able to draw water from the well and bring it to the king. Knowing that these men have risked their very lives to obtain the water, David refuses to drink it, but instead pours it out on the ground as an offering before the Lord. The water had become too precious to drink, but instead had become fit to use in worship before the Lord.

Here's the takeaway… what the king longed to have, his servants risked their lives to obtain. His wish really did become their command. What does our king long to see happen in our world? What does he wish to see accomplished in our generation? Surely Jesus wishes for reconciliation among men, forgiveness of injury, healing in the midst of brokenness, love in the midst of divisive hatred. He wishes for everyone to hear the Gospel story. He longs for all men to live in a right relationship with God. He wants all to come to salvation. So his wishes must become our marching orders. We have to proclaim his story of grace, salvation, and love with both our words and our actions. If we are truly his servants, then nothing else matters. Our focus, our priority, and our thoughts each day must be that of Kingdom proclamation. How can I represent him today? How can I bear his image before the nations and before my sphere of influence? How can I fulfill his wishes this day?

Prayer

Heavenly Father, teach us how to make Jesus' wishes our priorities for this day. Amen.

Day 350   1 Chronicles 12: Understanding the Times

> "From the tribe of Issachar, there were 200 leaders of the tribe with their relatives. All these men understood the signs of the times and knew the best course for Israel to take." 1 Chronicles 12:32 (NLT)

Observation
As he had done in Chapter 11, the chronicler is once again emphasizing Israel's unity behind the leadership of David. In this chapter, he flashes back before David was king. He describes the periods of time when David was encamped first at Ziglag and then at Hebron. Verse 22 indicates that "day by day" more and more men rallied behind David as their leader. This chapter give specifics in terms of the number of men from each tribe that joined forces with David. It is very much a growing momentum. Three times in the chapter, the tribe of Benjamin was mentioned. This is significant because King Saul was a member of this tribe. The chronicler was pointing to the fact that everyone, including those who should have sided with King Saul were giving their allegiances to David.

Application
The chronicler mentions that there were men among the tribe of Issachar who "understood the signs of the times and knew the best course for Israel to take." They understood that God's hand of providence was evident in David's life and so they encouraged others in Israel to join with them in rallying behind his leadership. In today's language, we might suggest that these men possessed a wisdom to both perceive what God was doing and to follow His leadership. Let's admit that all of us have struggled to "understand the times." We wonder about this chapter in the life of our nation and culture. We wonder where issues of ethics, morality, and civility are headed. We fret. We fear. We question. We attempt to tighten the moorings of our core values and wonder if the knot will hold. The problem is that we "see in a glass dimly." We tend to see only through human perspective and wisdom and not through the lens of faith. If we read the Biblical record closely, we will discover that God has never abandoned His people. We are still the objects of His good grace, and He wills that which is best for us. So maybe we should look at the times and see the opportunities for Kingdom advancement where some only see moral depravity and a hopeless abandonment of all things sacred. I believe that God is continually in the process of arranging people, place, and moments for God's purposes. In other words, God's always at work, pushing us ever forward into God's plan of redemption. So, let us understand these times, not as moments for despair, but as moments into which God is going to do great things. May we have the wisdom to see God at work and give our allegiance to God each day.

Prayer
Heavenly Father, may we see a glimpse of your work, even this day. Amen.

Day 351   1 Chronicles 13: Details Matter

> "They placed the Ark of God on a new cart and brought it from Abinadab's house. Uzzah and Ahio were guiding the cart." 1 Chronicles 13:7 (NLT)

Observation
King David attempted to promote unity within the nation of Israel by giving attention to the Ark of the Covenant and to worship celebrations. Knowing that the Ark represented the very presence of God among the people, David took care to consult all the leaders of Israel before transporting the Ark to Jerusalem. For many years, the Ark had remained at a place called Kiriath-Jearim, a city about 20 miles west of Jerusalem. The reader may recall that the Ark had been left in this city after the horrible incident when it had been captured by the Philistines and taken to some of their cities. David's desire was to house it in Jerusalem. He prepared the people for a huge celebration as the Ark was moved. But notice the detail in our focus verse… "they placed the Ark of God on a new cart…" This was the exact same way the Philistines had returned it to Israel. Unwittingly, David violated the exacting commandments for moving the Ark. God had proclaimed that it was to be carried on poles, placed on the shoulders of the Levites. As the journey progressed, the oxen stumbled, and the Ark shifted on the cart. A man named Uzzah reached to steady it. The Lord struck him dead the moment he touched the Ark. His action, though noble, was a violation of God's law.

Application
Details matter. Sometimes we discover such things the hard way. Several years ago I owned a BMW 320i automobile. It was a great car that reflected the best of German engineering. In those days, I always performed oil changes myself. I had read that BMW recommended a Bosch oil filter that was quite expensive. I substituted a Fram filter at a fraction of the cost. On a cold, windy Louisville morning, while driving to work across the bridge that connects Kentucky to Indiana, my wife heard an awful noise and watched as a massive amount of smoke billowed behind the car. The pressure caused by the cold temperatures had blown the oil filter off the car. I discovered that the Bosch filters had a release valve to eliminate such a problem. Lesson learned. Details matter.

According to our focus passage, details especially matter in terms of worship. Our worship of God is not a casual affair. It requires that we bring our best selves to the moment. It makes a difference how well we prepare for the service. Those who preach must offer the gift of their best labors. Those who lead in worship must be prepared and rehearsed, ensuring that God receives our best attempt at excellence. Those who participate as congregants, should be alert, non-distracted, and ready to encounter God. Details matter. Worship matters.

Prayer
Heavenly Father, may we always remember the importance of worship. Amen.

Day 352 — 1 Chronicles 14: Abandoning Your Gods

> "The Philistines had abandoned their gods there, so David gave orders to burn them." 1 Chronicles 14:12 (NLT)

Observation

This chapter lists three examples of God's blessings, poured out in the life of David. These blessings helped to confirm to David that God had established him as king. The first blessing mentioned involves the actions of King Hiram of Tyre. He sent lumber, stonemasons, and carpenters to build a palace for David. The second blessing involves the number of sons born to David while in Jerusalem. Married to multiple women, David had 13 sons born during this point in his life. Fertility was a sign of blessing. The third blessing involves David's decisive victories over the Philistines. He did what King Saul had failed to do and part of the reason why, was connected to the fact that David inquired of the Lord for wisdom each time that he faced a threat.

Application

In his decisive battle over the Philistines that is recorded in this chapter, the chronicler mentions that the Philistines, who had apparently brought into battle with them their pagan idols, abandoned these idols on the battlefield where David's men would later burn them. This action was an act of obedience to what God had declared in Deuteronomy 7:5, "This is what you must do. You must break down their pagan altars and shatter their sacred pillars. Cut down their Asherah poles and burn their idols" (NLT). It is interesting to me that as soon as the Philistines discovered their gods had no power nor influence over the battle, they abandoned them, leaving them strewn across the battlefield.

Think with me for a moment about the gods we carry with us as we take on the battles we face each day. We put a lot of hope and trust in idols that we mistakenly think will give us strength and victory. We trust in our wealth. We trust in our education. We trust in our intuition. We trust in our connections. We trust in our luck. Being rather arrogant, we think that in our own strength, we can take on the enemies that seek to disrupt our lives. We are strong enough, wise enough, rich enough... or so we think. And not long into the battle, we discover that we are without help and without hope. We discover our self-crafted idols are of little support. Maybe it's time for us to abandon a few gods of our own. The trappings of self-sufficiency lull us into a false security. Our true strength, wisdom, and provision comes from God alone. Remember the musings of the psalmist... "I will lift up my eyes to the mountains; From where shall my help come? My help comes from the LORD, Who made heaven and earth." (Psalm 121:1 NASB). Abandon your idols and embrace your God.

Prayer

Dear God, may we look to you alone to provide the help we need. Amen.

Day 353   1 Chronicles 15: Learning to Celebrate

> "David also ordered the Levite leaders to appoint a choir of Levites who were singers and musicians to sing joyful songs to the accompaniment of harps, lyres, and cymbals." 1 Chronicles 15:16 (NLT)

Observation
This chapter could be titled, "Moving the Ark: The Second Attempt." You may recall that a couple of chapters ago, David attempted to move the Ark of the Covenant to Jerusalem but with terrible results. He had not adhered to the very specific instructions given to Moses as to how the Ark was to be moved. This time, the instructions were carried out with exacting details. The Levites were singled out as the only ones who could carry the Ark. They carried it on their shoulders using long poles, just as Moses had once outlined. With shouts of joy and wonderful songs, the Ark made its way into the city. David himself, led the procession, skipping along and laughing with joy. His wife Michal, the daughter of Saul, look upon him with contempt. She had no appreciation for his enthusiasm because she had little understanding of the value and meaning of the Ark of the Covenant.

Application
Our focus verse indicates that David appointed a choir, along with musicians, to sing joyful songs while the Ark was carried into the city. He appreciated the value of celebration in the context of what God was doing in their midst. Perhaps one of the great shortcomings of the modern church is the failure to celebrate the work of God in the life of each congregation. To be sure, most of us know how to celebrate the important moments in our lives. We plan special meals, wear special clothes, and cook special food for celebrations like weddings, birthdays, and anniversaries. I have a friend who threw a party for his family and friends when he paid off his mortgage! Many families will gather in joyful celebration of a graduation from high school or college. Yet in terms of the local church, how well do we celebrate the work of God in our midst? I must confess that often in my pastoral ministry, I was so focused on the next event, the next mission trip, or the next financial goal that I often failed to lead the people in an appropriate moment of celebration. Oh, we would stop in a service to clap for a goal achieved, or to give a plaque to someone for a job well done, but did we really celebrate with joy all that God was doing? Things like baptisms and child dedications and calls to special ministry are a big deal. They are the evidence of God moving among God's people. When steps of faith are taken, it is a reminder of God's continual work. So, let me challenge you as an individual and as a part of a body of Christ, to take the time and energy to truly celebrate the big moments. You honor God whenever you do.

Prayer
Dear God, teach us to celebrate your work in our lives. Amen.

Day 354 — 1 Chronicles 16: Party Favors

> "Then he gave to every man and woman in all Israel a loaf of bread, a cake of dates, and a cake of raisins." 1 Chronicles 16:3 (NLT)

Observation
This chapter describes the scene as the Ark of the Covenant is brought to Jerusalem and placed in a special tent that David had prepared for it. In a spirit of both celebration and worship, the people offer sacrifices and peace offerings. David blesses the people and gives gifts to all the men and women who gathered for the celebration. The musicians play and David offers a song of praise. In his song, David offers several imperatives that the people of God should undertake in their worship of God. He uses words like, "give thanks, make known, sing, speak, seek, and remember." In his song, David also recalls the Abrahamic covenant and speaks of God's continual blessing on the nation. The chapter also describes the great care given to ensure proper attention and detail are provided for the care and security of the Ark. David also provides a second place of worship at the city of Gibeon, about five miles from Jerusalem.

Application
When I was a kid, going to birthday parties for friends was always fun. There was cake and ice cream along with games to play. There were bowling parties, skating parties, and even pool parties. And... at the end of each well-hosted party the guests were always given a party favor... some small gift offered to each participant. Turn again to our focus verse. Those who attended the celebration when the Ark was brought to Jerusalem were given party favors. Every man and woman received a loaf of bread, a cake of dates, and a cake of raisins. And notice who gave out the gifts... King David himself. The king rewarded those who participated in the celebration with extravagant gifts. Can you imagine as the people returned to their homes and villages and reported that the king had placed these gifts in their hands?

Our King does the same. Because each of us has accepted the gracious invitation to come to the banquet prepared as a part of Christ's Kingdom, we receive amazing gifts. Because we place our trust in Christ and because we have been welcomed into his presence, God gives us eternal life. God gives us grace. God gives us peace and assurance. God gives us the gift of the indwelling Spirit. The gracious host longs for you to celebrate the life offered to you and to all those who have joined their hearts to Christ. From time to time I hear theologians speculate about the riches of heaven. Are some rewarded more than others? Do some get better party favors? Doesn't matter. The joy is being included in the party.

Prayer
Dear God, thank you for inviting us to your eternal celebration. Amen.

Day 355 — 1 Chronicles 17: Taking God on the Journey

> "I have never lived in a house, from the day I brought the Israelites out of Egypt until this very day. My home has always been a tent, moving from one place to another in a Tabernacle." 1 Chronicles 17:5 (NLT)

Observation

Chapter 17 opens with David settling into his beautiful palace. He is concerned that he lives in such splendor, while the Ark of the Covenant, which represents the presence of God, is housed in a canvas tent. He speaks to Nathan the prophet and tells Nathan of his desire to build a house for God. That same night, Nathan hears from the Lord who instructs Nathan to tell David not to build a house for the Ark. That responsibility will fall to his son. However, God will build David a dynasty of kings. David receives this word from the Lord with gladness and offers a song of praise.

Application

Portability is a huge consideration in the electronics industry. As consumers, we want to be able to take along our work, our files, and our data. In fact, we get a little miffed when the WIFI connection is weak or we find ourselves out of cell phone range. I can still remember the first laptop computer that I ever saw. A friend, doing PhD research at UAB, had been given one to use by the school. It used those 3.5-inch diskettes and it was a game changer. Suddenly everyone wanted the ability to take along their "portable office." Laptops morphed into iPads which then morphed into smartphones. Everywhere we go these days, we have access to the web, to our work, to our email, to our pics, and to our contacts. We would become bewildered without the ease of portability.

In God's design for the Ark of the Covenant, God commanded the construction of a portable tent to house the Ark. As you may recall, it was always set-up in the center of the Israelite encampment. Portability was intentional. God wanted the people to have the ability to take it along on every step of the journey. They, in a very real sense, carried God with them to every place they went. They never had to leave God's permanent dwelling place behind as they packed up and journeyed onward. Because of God's desire to be omnipresent in our lives, God has taken portability to the next level by placing the Holy Spirit deeply within each of us. We are never separated, not even for a moment, from the presence, protection, and providence of God, who walks the journey with us. Wherever you go, God goes. In every storm you encounter, God protects you. In every decision, God counsels you. In every dream, God inspires you. In every fear, God comforts you. From every enemy, God shields you. Remember the name Immanuel. God with us.

Prayer

Dear God, thank you for always being present with us. Amen.

Day 356 — 1 Chronicles 18: Home Depot

> "King David dedicated all these gifts to the Lord, along with the silver and gold he had taken from the other nations—from Edom, Moab, Ammon, Philistia, and Amalek." 1 Chronicles 18:11 (NLT)

Observation
Chapter 18 offers an accounting of the various military battles that David fought to expand his kingdom. According to verse 6, all of David's victories came about because, "the Lord helped David wherever he went." He defeated the Philistines, the Moabites, and the Edomites. As he claimed territory, lands, and armies, he collected spoils along the way. He gained chariots, horses, soldiers, golden shields, as well as large amounts of bronze and silver. Remember that David had been told by the prophet Nathan that he would not be chosen to build the Temple that would house the Ark of the Covenant. That responsibility would fall to his son, Solomon. But David was to raise capital and material for the future construction project. Read this chapter carefully and you will discover that the chronicler specifically mentions the ways in which some of the materials taken in battle will be later used by Solomon to build the Temple.

Application
I live conveniently close to a Home Depot store... maybe too close. I find myself in the store a lot... dreaming of the next home improvement project that I want to undertake. I'm a "Do-It-Yourself" kind of guy and places like Home Depot are a favorite hangout. A few Christmases ago, my daughter gave me a Home Depot gift card. I walked the aisles for hours trying to figure out the best way to spend the card! I make a lot of quick trips to the store to get that special bolt or screw or part that I need to fix something at the house. Because the store is well-stocked, I always find what I need.

Consider the life of King Solomon for a moment. His father David made his life so much easier by "stocking" much of the materials needed to build the Temple. Timber, stones, and precious metals were all there when Solomon needed them. His father had made careful provision. Our Heavenly Father has done the same for us. Because God knows us intimately—knows every need that we will encounter, every problem that we will face—God's storehouse is well-stocked. The shelves are bowed with an abundance of grace, compassion, forgiveness, peace of mind, love, and joy. All that we need to survive, to build the Kingdom, to raise our families, and to change the world, is freely and abundantly waiting for our use. God is waiting to meet your needs. Take a moment this morning to consider the biggest problems you will face today. Ask for God's help and then be grateful for God's answer.

Prayer
Dear God, thank you for supplying every need that we will face this day. Amen.

Day 357   1 Chronicles 19: No Good Deed Goes Unpunished

> "Some time after this, King Nahash of the Ammonites died, and his son Hanun became king. David said, 'I am going to show loyalty to Hanun because his father, Nahash, was always loyal to me.'"
> 1 Chronicles 19:1-2 (NLT)

Observation
King David not only proved to be a fierce and successful military leader, but he also had powerful diplomatic skills and was cordial to friends and allies. At the death of Nahash of Ammon, David sends a delegation of consolation to convey the king's sadness at the death of Nahash and to express his desire for continued good relations. The Ammonites had been an enemy of King Saul. This once "icy" relationship had begun to thaw under David's leadership. Hanun's advisors misinterpreted David's intent. The Ammonites sent the delegation home in humiliation after shaving their beards and cutting their clothing in an immodest way. This action resulted in an escalation of conflict. The Ammonites prepared to go to battle against Israel and enlisted the help of the Arameans to fight with them. The Arameans soon experienced the might of the Israeli army as 40,000 foot-soldiers were killed in a single battle. Because of this huge loss, the Arameans withdrew their support of the Ammonites.

Application
Sometimes, when you try to do something nice for someone, it backfires. In this Biblical text, King David was simply trying to offer condolences to the son of a foreign leader. His act of kindness was misinterpreted and soon conflict resulted. Going to war with the Ammonites was certainly not King David's intention. Ever have a similar experience? You try to do something nice for someone, maybe offer a gift or a compliment and the next thing you know, instead of making things better, you have created a bigger divide. Such moments point to the problems of communication and the lack of understanding that sometimes disrupt human relationships. What we might offer as a "kind and generous act" can be perceived as being something quite different. It's not a perfect world and sometimes our good deeds get punished. It happens even in those moments we extend grace to others. Sometimes our offer to forgive and move forward is not well received. That leaves us with a choice. On the one hand, we can become bitter and decide that we will not extend further forgiveness or make any attempt at healing brokenness. The other choice is to doggedly pursue peace in our relationships and continue to offer kindness even when it is rejected or misinterpreted. Which is the better choice? Which is more Christ-like? Whenever we choose to base our actions on resentment, revenge, or rejection, we lessen ourselves. The Christ ethic demands that we love our neighbor and pray for our enemies, even when our actions are misinterpreted.

Prayer
Dear Father, help us to do the right thing at the right time, every time. Amen.

Day 358   1 Chronicles 20: Be Careful of the Crown

> "When David arrived at Rabbah, he removed the crown from the king's head, and it was placed on his own head. The crown was made of gold and set with gems, and he found that it weighed seventy-five pounds. David took a vast amount of plunder from the city." 1 Chronicles 20:2 (NLT)

Observation
Chapter 20 is a concluding record of David's victories. Two nations—Ammon and Philistia—are mentioned in the account. David's general, Joab, had led the initial battle against the Ammonites. (David had stayed behind in Jerusalem; 2 Samuel: 11 tells the story of his affair with Bathsheba.) Once David arrives on the scene, he takes the crown from the head of the Ammonite king and places it on his own head. Notice the description… "he found that it weighed seventy-five pounds." He also took a vast amount of plunder from the city and enslaved all the Ammonites. The later part of the chapter deals with the Philistines. Though they are many and possess superior weaponry, by the power of God at work, David and his men defeat them.

Application
I've never worn a crown on my head, and doubt that I ever will. The heaviest item I have placed on my head for any period of time had to be a football helmet that I wore in high school. It carried both physical and psychological weight. The average helmet with a face mask weighs about 4.5 pounds. That was not too heavy to carry physically, but the weight of what it meant to wear it was important. To strap on the helmet meant preparation for battle. It meant giving your all for the team. It meant playing the game as a competitor. I imagine that David got quite a shock when he placed the Ammonite helmet on his head. It weighed 75 pounds! But more than just the sheer weight of the gold was the weight of responsibility that it brought. He would take over the leadership of the nation. He was responsible for the lives of his captives. He was accepting the role of leadership. It was a "weighty" task. The apostle Paul tells us to "Put on salvation as your helmet…" (Ephesians 6:17 NLT). We typically talk of that passage in terms of the helmet being a protective piece of equipment… we protect our minds from evil forces by covering our heads with the protection of salvation through Christ. But what if putting on the helmet also meant accepting the weight of responsibility that it brings? What if it meant accepting the fact that challenges are going to come? What if it meant preparing for battle? What if it meant we were accepting responsibility for leading the nation God has placed around us? It is no small thing to put on the helmet of salvation. It's a call to duty, leadership, and responsibility. Be careful of the crown.

Prayer
Dear Father, teach us to accept the roles of leadership you bring to our lives. Amen.

Day 359   1 Chronicles 21: The Problem of Pride

> "So David said to Joab and the commanders of the army, 'Take a census of all the people of Israel—from Beersheba in the south to Dan in the north—and bring me a report so I may know how many there are.'"
> 1 Chronicles 21:2 (NLT)

Observation

As this chapter opens, David orders a comprehensive census be taken of all the tribally occupied land in his kingdom. Our focus verse gives a hint at the problem of ordering this action. Notice the phrase, "so I may know how many there are." Perhaps this is a subtle clue to his motives. Maybe he wants to congratulate himself on the expansion of the kingdom or perhaps he wants to pat himself on the back for his military achievements. His actions suggest that the people were his to claim and not God's. Joab recognized that his actions would be seen as sinful in the eyes of God and tried to stop the process. But the king insisted, and the census revealed that more than 1.5 million warriors were living in the land. God spoke to David through his seer, Gad. God gives David the choice of three punishments: 1) Three years of famine; 2) Three months of destruction by Israel's enemies; 3) Three days of a severe plague. David chooses the third option and 70,000 die as a result. David repents and the Lord relents. David builds an altar that will become the location of the future Temple.

Application

Move the story of David's life forward a few years. His son, Solomon, will become the next king and will build the great Temple. Known for his wisdom, Solomon will also write many wise sayings that are recorded in the Book of Proverbs, including this verse, "Pride goeth before destruction, and a haughty spirit before a fall" (Proverbs 16:18 KJV). In our modern usage, we have shortened the verse to read, "Pride goes before a fall." Is it possible that Solomon wrote these words with the story of his father's foolish actions rolling around in his mind? David's pride certainly cost the nation dearly. Pride remains a destructive force in our lives. It makes us think too highly of ourselves. It makes us commit foolish actions. It makes us over-extend, over-inflate, and over-react. It also forces us to push the wisdom and counsel of God to the sidelines so that our own thoughts and plans take prominence. And as in the story of King David, our pride always demands a cost. Hopefully, your pride won't cost the lives of 70,000 fellow citizens this morning. But it might lead to broken relationships, a lack of trust, or the loss of a job or some other important title. The Bible counsels that our boasting should be in the Lord and not in ourselves. I invite you to look at your life this morning and ask, "Is my pride becoming a destructive force?" Name it and tame it before it is too late.

Prayer

Dear Father, may we see the destructive nature of our pride. Amen.

Day 360 — 1 Chronicles 22: Preparing the Next Generation

> "David said, 'My son Solomon is still young and inexperienced. And since the Temple to be built for the Lord must be a magnificent structure, famous and glorious throughout the world, I will begin making preparations for it now.' So David collected vast amounts of building materials before his death." 1 Chronicles 22:5 (NLT)

Observation

The remainder 1 Chronicles and the beginning of 2 Chronicles shifts the focus of the narrative to the Temple and its construction. The chronicler will first describe David's preparation followed by Solomon's actual construction project. The materials for the Temple have to be gathered and the Levites and priests have to be organized. There is a zeal and excitement about the impending work that the chronicler hopes to capture. Remember that he is writing years later as the Israelites return from exile. He hopes that by telling the story of the construction of the first Temple, that people will be motivated to rebuild the Temple and kick-start formal worship observances. In his preparation, David collects iron, bronze, and cedar logs. Solomon, who most likely is in his early twenties, is inexperienced. He has never run a government, nor taken on such a daunting project. Therefore, part of David's preparation for building the Temple includes preparing his son for all that he will face.

Application

Ever notice that the things toward which we devote our attention become part of the legacy that we pass along to the next generation? I have friends whose fathers were sharp in business and so they developed a business acumen of their own. Others I know followed their parents' modeling in various careers like nursing, law, or medicine. What parents are passionate about often become the passions of their children. Even our pastimes and hobbies get retained by the next generation. My son certainly shares my love for college football. My dad's love for cars found its way into the DNA of my brother and me. But there are some things that can't be assumed or left for chance. There are some qualities and lessons that must be shared with intentionality.

King David realized that his son needed to expand his view of God and understand how essential obedience to the Lord would be to the success of Solomon's future reign. And so, he "prepared" his son. He taught him. He spoke to him. He modeled behavior. How well are you preparing your children for the life of faith that they need to embrace? Do you talk of spiritual things? Do you model the disciplines of faith? Do you emphasize the importance of worship? Do you demonstrate what servanthood on behalf of others resembles? You need to prepare your children. Be intentional and faithful.

Prayer

Dear Father, as parents, may we carefully prepare the next generation. Amen.

Day 361   1 Chronicles 23: The Pros and Cons of Growing Older

> "These were the descendants of Levi by clans, the leaders of their family groups, registered carefully by name. Each had to be twenty years old or older to qualify for service in the house of the Lord."
> 1 Chronicles 23:24 (NLT)

Observation

Chapters 23 through 27 highlight David's administrative abilities. Widely known as a great military leader and songwriter/musician, David also displayed tremendous skills in organizing and leading the nation. The basic organizational structures that he established served his successors for centuries. Of note is David's structuring of the Temple leadership. He was convinced that those who served God in leadership capacities were as important as the architectural splendor of the buildings in which they served. Therefore, he gave forethought and attention to both. (Most scholars believe that these organizational structures were put into place during David's last year of life, probably 970 B.C.) Our focus verse describes an age requirement for the Levites who served in the Temple. They had to be at least 20 years of age.

Application

There are pros and cons of growing older. When we are young, we await the progression of age with anxious impatience. At 16 we are allowed to drive. At 18, we leave high school and explore new freedoms and rights, like the right to vote and let our voices be heard. Somewhere along the way we become old enough to marry, to have kids, or to own a house. But did you notice along the way, that with each freedom came great responsibility? Having a license meant you were responsible for driving safely and protecting those in the car with you. At 18, you may have registered for the draft and to vote. At 21, you were considered as an adult in every context, no longer able to blame the immaturity of youth for your poor choices. Getting older also meant bearing responsibilities that previously rested on the shoulders of your parents. You had taxes to pay, a mortgage to manage, a job to keep, and kids to raise. With each coming year, freedoms and responsibilities magnified.

I imagine that as a young Jewish boy growing up in the tribe of Levi, the age of 20 was one of those defining moments. You were handed the keys to the kingdom, or at least, the keys of serving in the Temple. What joy. What excitement. What responsibility. Surely it marked the beginning of a life of maturity and requirement. It was the moment when many "came of age." No matter your age as you read this devotional thought, there are responsibilities on your shoulders. My hope for you is that you will take each one seriously and provide the kind of leadership that is expected of you. Pray for wisdom as you need it. Heed the call when you hear it. Revel in the joy as you experience it.

Prayer

Father God, call us to faithfulness in all our responsibilities. Amen.

Day 362   1 Chronicles 24: Avoiding Favoritism or Embracing It?

> "All tasks were assigned to the various groups by means of sacred lots so that no preference would be shown, for there were many qualified officials serving God in the sanctuary from among the descendants of both Eleazar and Ithamar." 1 Chronicles 24:5 (NLT)

Observation
This chapter is devoted to the duties of the priests who serve in the various capacities of Temple worship and practice. Remember that the priests, who alone attended to the altar and performed service "inside the veil" (Numbers 18:1-17), were all direct descendants of Aaron. The various tasks to be performed were assigned to various divisions of Aaron's descendants. In order that no favoritism be shown among these 24 divisions, lots were cast in the presence of David, the officials, Zadok the priest, Ahimelech son of Abiathar, and the family leaders of the priests and Levites. The casting of lots determined the assigned duties.

Application
Let's admit that it's hard to make a completely impartial choice without showing a little bias. There is nothing wrong with considering all factors when making a wise choice, but to choose without prejudice or influence is difficult. The court of David used a system of casting lots to determine randomness. In our day, we might simply put all the names in a hat and do a blind draw, or simply flip a coin. I've noticed that one of the local television stations here in Nashville broadcasts the selection of the lottery numbers for each day. The short commercial shows the numbers tumbling around and falling into place to assure that there is no bias in the process. But sometimes… it's a wonderful thing to know that certain decisions, choices, and selections are more than just a random rolling of the dice.

A pastor friend was once preaching a revival in a small community in Kentucky. To build interest and excitement among the youth of the community to attend the meetings, a local car dealer donated a used car to the church to be given away on the last night of the revival. Names of eligible students were to be drawn from a large fishbowl. Each night that a student attended, his or her name would be added and so the more a student attended, the greater the chances of winning the car. One family in the community had experienced job loss, illness, and many other difficulties. The high school son in that family needed a car but had no hope of owning one. On the night of the big draw, he won! My friend made this comment about the event, "Was it more exciting to see him win, or more exciting to know a bunch of kids all put his name on their slips of paper to make sure that he would win?"

Prayer
Father God, we are grateful that in Christ, we have been chosen as your children. Amen.

Day 363 — 1 Chronicles 25: The Praise You Offer

> "David and the army commanders then appointed men from the families of Asaph, Heman, and Jeduthun to proclaim God's messages to the accompaniment of lyres, harps, and cymbals." 1 Chronicles 25:1 (NLT)

Observation

Music was obviously close to David's heart. He was a musician of renown with the ability to play instruments, write lyrics, and perhaps even lead in worship experiences. This chapter tells of the duties entrusted to certain men to "proclaim God's message" with music. David knew, as we too have experienced, that music can elevate devotion, soothe a troubled mind, inspire a brave heart, and motivate the masses. Music was and is a powerful tool to remind us of the workings of God in our lives. And so David appointed key leaders to proclaim God's message with lyres, harps, and cymbals. David required a sense of excellence from these leaders. These were to be "skilled" musicians who could lead well. Worship was too important not to offer God the best of their talents and abilities. The same should hold true today in any context of worship, whether formal, traditional, or contemporary. What we do with our music should honor the Lord and inspire people. There is never an excuse for mediocrity. All those who proclaim God's message, either with spoken word, expressed prayer, or musical notes, should offer their best.

Application

Notice the interesting wording of our focus verse. These appointed leaders were to "proclaim God's message." Some translations use the word, "prophesy." To "prophesy" meant more than the foretelling of future events. It also meant to "forth tell" the truth about God. David was demanding that these leaders boldly and carefully proclaim the news of God through the instruments in their hands. Interesting concept, right? They were to take whatever talent and instrument they possessed and play it in a way that God would be honored and glorified.

Let's just tell it like it is… not everyone is a musician. Not everyone can play an instrument. Not everyone can match pitch or carry a tune. That's not my point. The point is to consider carefully what gift, talent, or ability that God has placed in your life and use that gift it in a way that glorifies God. If it is a musical talent, then offer a performance worthy of the king who sits in your audience. If it is the power to speak, then preach with the conviction that what you say and how you say it might save a person's life. If it is the ability to build with your hands, demand excellence in all that you do. If it is a talent to teach, do it as unto the Lord. If it is the ability to manage a company, run a business, or heal a wound, then "proclaim God's message" in all that you do. There is no time for mediocrity. God is worthy of our best praise.

Prayer

Dear God, may we take whatever ability we have and praise you with it. Amen.

Day 364   1 Chronicles 26: Guarding the Strategic Places

> "These divisions of the gatekeepers were named for their family leaders, and like the other Levites, they served at the house of the Lord. They were assigned by families for guard duty at the various gates, without regard to age or training, for it was all decided by means of sacred lots."
> 1 Chronicles 26:12-13 (NLT)

Observation
Chapter 26 is devoted to the various "gatekeepers" assigned by the king to safeguard the city, the Temple, and the Temple treasures. These men are described as being "mighty" and "valiant." They were essentially the security detail for the king and the city. They were assigned to strategic spots. Some were stationed at the actual gates of the city. Others protected the Temple itself, while still others guarded all the treasures in the Temple, including both offerings and the spoils of war... "anything that had been dedicated to the Lord."

Application
Several years ago, I had the honor of leading a mission team to a remote spot in the Dominican Republic. We worked with local missionaries who had established a Christian school for the children of the area. On the day that our team flew home, one of the young, local teenagers, who had been raised and educated by the missionaries, was joining us on our flight back to the U.S. She was heading off to college. Having never traveled to the U.S., she was anxious, excited, and a little intimidated. I was standing with the missionary mother as she spoke her final words of farewell to this young woman whom she had helped to raise. She hugged her tightly and said, "Don't give away your heart to anyone." Those words have stuck with me since that tender parting at the airport. Don't give your heart away. I think the missionary's advice was that of protecting her heart and mind from all the influences and even people she would encounter who might draw her focus away from the Lord and from her priorities as a student.

I am reminded that it is important to guard the strategic places in our lives. There are always those influences that attempt to divert our attention and rearrange our priorities. Those influences distract us, confuse us, and change us. And so, it is vital to do the difficult work of safeguarding. We need to make sure that we have made a strong defense around our hearts, our minds, our eyes, and our attitudes. We have to make sure that we have considered carefully what we read, what we watch, and even what we explore on the internet. Are the influences that we allow in our lives positive or negative? Do they make us better? Do they honor the Lord? Do they build character? Have we safeguarded our hearts or are we giving them away too quickly? Post the gatekeepers strategically in your life.

Prayer
Dear God, knowing that we represent you, keep us distinct and holy. Amen.

Day 365   1 Chronicles 27: Who's Teaching Your Sons?

> "Jonathan, David's uncle, was a wise counselor to the king, a man of great insight, and a scribe. Jehiel the Hacmonite was responsible for teaching the king's sons." 1 Chronicles 27:32 (NLT)

Observation

This chapter provides a list of military and civil authorities along with the tasks to which they were called. There are four groups listed in the text. The first are the commanders of the army. There are 12 divisions, each with 24,000 soldiers. Each division was to serve for a month at a time. Next, the chief officer of each tribe is listed. Then, the text lists those in charge of the king's property. There is a specific listing of the men in charge of everything from donkeys to camels. Finally, there is a list of David's cabinet advisors and closest associates. This organizational structure, implemented by King David, helped to bring unity to the nation as well as providing a shared vision for the construction of the Temple.

Application

In selecting the right people for just the right tasks, King David chose a man named Jehiel as a tutor for his sons. Although little is known about this person, perhaps there is a clue as to why he was chosen contained in his name. The name Jehiel means, "God's Living One." If I can read between the lines a little… perhaps this man was chosen because the Spirit of God rested within him, and he represented the characteristics, heart, and passion of God to those around him. Who better for David to choose in the raising of his sons than someone whose life reflected such an allegiance before God? I would hope that most of us believers understand the important role we have as parents in the raising of our children. We should understand that we have been commissioned by God to raise them in the "nurture and admonition of the Lord." It is our sacred obligation to lead them in matters of faith. We are to teach God's Word, live out our Christian values, and ensure that they hear about the love of Christ, early and often. Most of us get it. We understand the role of Christian parenting. But here's my question this morning… "Who are you choosing to include in your circle of teaching associates?" There are many outside influences that will affect the shaping of your child's morality, ethics, and character. Who will you include in that loop? It is important to establish the kinds of relationships with others that are a positive influence for your children. Though you cannot control every voice they hear, you can choose the relationships that you hold close… those that will influence the lives of your children as they influence your heart and mind. In other words, *your* friends will make a difference in the lives of your children. Choose them carefully for their sake.

Prayer

Father God, may we surround our children with those whose lives are dedicated to you. Amen.

Day 366 — 1 Chronicles 28: An Intimate Knowledge of God

> "And Solomon, my son, learn to know the God of your ancestors intimately. Worship and serve him with your whole heart and a willing mind. For the Lord sees every heart and knows every plan and thought. If you seek him, you will find him. But if you forsake him, he will reject you forever." 1 Chronicles 28:9 (NLT)

Observation

In these last two chapters of 1 Chronicles, King David offers a final address to the nation. Most of his conversations and instructions up to this point had dealt with the physical and material preparations for the kingdom and the Temple. He now turns to the spiritual preparations needed for the nation to succeed. He longs to steer the hearts and minds of the people in a godly direction. He calls for strict obedience and loyalty before God. He reminds the people that his son will build the Temple because he is a "man of rest," whereas David had been a "man of war." In this address to the nation, David gives several specific charges to his son, Solomon. In our focus verse, David challenges Solomon to know the God of his ancestors intimately.

Application

How can you have an intimate knowledge of a God you can't see, or hear, or touch? All my spiritual life, I have heard pastors and teachers talk of an intimacy with God. My mind often drifts into thoughts of having some mystical, contemplative, meditative relationship with God in which I am drawn into some spiritual trance or other-worldly experience. Surely you have wondered about what it means to "get close to God." So, how do we get to know God intimately? What does that even mean? There are certain things about which I have an intimate knowledge. I drive a Mini Cooper automobile. I have examined every inch of that car, read every page of the owner's manual, checked under the hood dozens of times, and meticulously washed it till you think the paint would rub off. I know that car inside and out. I have an intimate knowledge of my yard. I have been cutting that lawn, trimming those hedges, and watering those plants for 18 years. There is not a single square inch that I haven't addressed over these many years. So how do we gain an intimate knowledge of an invisible God? We touch the invisible as we touch that which is visible, tangible, and representative of God. To have an intimate knowledge of God means we must have an intimate knowledge of scripture. It means we must have lifelong relationships with godly people. It means we must welcome the Holy Spirit through worship. It means we must stand in God's presence with daily, dedicated prayers. I can experience God as I touch, hold, and read those items through which God is revealed. It must become an intentional passion for us all.

Prayer

Father God, may each of us have an intimate relationship with you. Amen.

Day 367 — 1 Chronicles 29: You Can't Take It with You

> "And now, because of my devotion to the Temple of my God, I am giving all of my own private treasures of gold and silver to help in the construction. This is in addition to the building materials I have already collected for his holy Temple. I am donating more than 112 tons of gold from Ophir" 1 Chronicles 29:3-4a (NLT)

Observation

This final chapter of 1 Chronicles represents the ending narrative of David's life and reign and will end with a very brief account of David's death. In the earlier portion of the chapter, David writes about the provision he has made and will make to the construction of the Temple. As our focus verse indicates, he not only gives a huge sum of gold to the effort, but he challenges the leaders of Israel to give sacrificially to the effort, which they are glad to do. They will give "freely and whole-heartedly." The middle portion of the chapter is devoted to a prayer that David offers that both praises God for abundant grace and offers petitions for Solomon, that he will dedicate himself to the building of the Temple. The chapter then closes with a summary of David's reign.

Application

King David's passion for the building of the Temple was so strong that he gave all his private treasure to the effort. The narrative lists not only this huge sum of gold, but silver and various precious stones as well. In great leadership style, David challenges the people to do as he has done. He chose to lead by example and the people were inspired by his generous giving.

The mantle of leadership is both a blessing and responsibility. It is certainly fulfilling to have the ability to lead others in the critical directions and decisions of their lives. But true leadership never says, "Go and do this…" but instead, says, "Follow me." Consider for a moment the areas of leadership that fall on your shoulders as a parent, a spouse, a friend, or neighbor. To be exceptional in your leadership requires a willingness to invest self, time, energy, and even resources to inspire others. I recently read a good definition of leadership… "To know if you are a leader… look around and see if anyone is following you!" Leaders always have followers. And I believe the best form of leadership always involves personal input and action. For example, if you want your children to be strong in their faith commitments, *you* have to be strong in your faith commitments. If you want your spouse to be loving and gentle, then *you* must be loving and gentle. If you want to be respected by your co-workers, *you* must respect *them*. You get the point, and you see the pattern. To be an effective leader, you must lead by example. It is the pattern you set that will lead others to follow.

Prayer

God, thank you for giving each of us places of leadership. May we be faithful. Amen.

Day 368   **2 Chronicles 1: A Temporary Tent?**

> "Then he led the entire assembly to the place of worship in Gibeon, for God's Tabernacle was located there. (This was the Tabernacle that Moses, the Lord's servant, had made in the wilderness.)" 2 Chronicles 1:3 (NLT)

Observation
The Book of 2 Chronicles opens with the beginning of King Solomon's reign. The first verse of chapter 1 reveals the reasons for Solomon's present and future success. God "was with him and made him very powerful." The Lord had clearly blessed his life and confirmed him as king. As he begins his reign, he gathers all of Israel together at the city of Gibeon. Even though David had previously taken the Ark of the Covenant to Jerusalem and placed it in a tent for safekeeping until the Temple was complete, Gibeon was still the sight of the tabernacle constructed by Moses that served the people as a place of worship from the time of the giving of the law at Sinai to this moment in history. With great diligence and reverence, Solomon seeks the Lord's instruction for the construction of the Temple and the movement of Worship to Jerusalem. In this passage, he asks God for wisdom. He acknowledges that what his father has said of him was true… that he was young and inexperienced. He wants to be skilled in leadership and so he asks for wisdom and God pours out blessings.

Application
Some of you might remember the "C" dorms located on the backside of Samford University's Campus back in the 1970s and 1980s. As the new campus quickly grew both in land and enrollment, additional dorm space was needed. The "C" dorms were built as temporary housing units. But you know how those things go… For at least 20 years they housed students on campus.

    I wonder if Moses had any idea how long the people of God would worship in the "temporary tent" called the tabernacle that he helped to construct during the wilderness experience. According to our focus verse, as Solomon leads the people in worship, they gather in front of the tabernacle where the bronze altar was still erected. By this point in history, the tabernacle had to be approximately 450 years old. That's a long time for a canvas tent and few wooden poles to last! I am reminded of the way in which we are called to "house" the Holy Spirit. "Do you not know that your bodies are temples of the Holy Spirit, who is in you, whom you have received from God?" (1 Cor. 6:19 NIV). We, too, are temporary in nature, are we not? This tabernacle of human flesh will only last a century at best. We serve as the temporary dwelling place of God until God's Kingdom comes. But in the fullness of time, that which is temporary will become permanent, that which is finite will become eternal.

Prayer
God, thank you for the promise of our eternal life and your continual presence. Amen.

Day 369 — 2 Chronicles 2: Creating Space

> "This must be a magnificent Temple because our God is greater than all other gods. But who can really build him a worthy home? Not even the highest heavens can contain him! So who am I to consider building a Temple for him, except as a place to burn sacrifices to him?"
>
> 2 Chronicles 2:5-6 (NLT)

Observation

It is evident by reading these accounts that the chronicler's focus, in terms of describing Solomon's reign, will be upon the construction of the Temple. This chapter is devoted to the collection of both men and materials to build the structure. King Solomon reaches out to King Hiram of Tyre for cedar logs to be used in the construction process. The logs will be felled in Lebanon and shipped down the coast to Joppa. In exchange for the logs, Solomon will send huge amounts of wheat, barley, wine, and olive oil to the king. Solomon also begins to focus on the workforce. Because there are many foreigners living in the land, Solomon will use them to manage the project. The text mentions that 70,000 laborers and 80,000 stone masons will be included in the project. Solomon sets forth plans to build not only the Temple, but his palace as well.

Application

In his conversation with Hiram of Tyre, Solomon declares that the Temple must be a "magnificent Temple" to reflect the greatness of God. Understanding that God is too vast to ever be contained within the walls of stone and mortar, Solomon's desire is that of building a structure that at least points to His greatness. Therefore, no expense is too great, nor material too extravagant.

Over the course of my life, I have had the opportunity of visiting some of the most impressive places of worship on the planet. I have stood in those places where architects and builders, like that of Solomon, have attempted to build glorious cathedrals that reflect the greatness of God and hush the worshipper to silence. I have stood in places like St. Peter's in Rome, St. Paul's in London, or the great cathedrals like those found in Salzburg, Munich, Florence, or Washington. Though I am cognizant of the fact that God does not permanently dwell in such places, surely God's presence can be felt as the faithful go to such places to worship. He inhabits the space as well as the hearts of those who seek God in those moments of worship. Most of us will never be called to build a cathedral to God, although like many of you, I have helped to build a few churches on mission projects around the world. What we are called to build, is a "magnificent Temple" within the confines of our own hearts. Have you created a space for God? Have you given God preeminence? Do you honor God daily?

Prayer

God, may we create a magnificent space deeply within us that honors you. Amen.

Day 370 — 2 Chronicles 3: For the Eyes of God

> "He made the Most Holy Place 30 feet wide, corresponding to the width of the Temple, and 30 feet deep. He overlaid its interior with 23 tons of fine gold." 2 Chronicles 3:8 (NLT)

Observation

This chapter marks the beginning of the Temple construction. It was begun in the early Spring of the fourth year of Solomon's reign. The description of the process is rather brief, much shorter than the account in 1 Kings 6. The emphasis seems to be more on the dedication of the Temple (ch. 5-7) than on its construction. The writer is emphasizing the purpose of the Temple more than its impressive size or ornate furnishings. The reader might ask why the chronicler downplays the splendor of the Temple in this passage. Remember that he is writing at a much later period in the history of Israel when the Jewish population was returning from exile in Babylon. They will lack the means to construct a new Temple in the splendor and scale of Solomon's Temple which had been destroyed in 587 B.C. He wants to emphasize that though it will be less in splendor, it is still just as important. Also notice in this passage, that the Temple will be located on Mount Moriah, on the very spot where Abraham once offered his son Isaac as a sacrifice. The location is the spot of two very important covenants offered by God… the covenant with Abraham and the covenant with David. And with the coming life and ministry of Jesus, it becomes the place (Jerusalem) where God's ultimate covenant of Grace will be extended to us.

Application

Our focus verse describes the interior of the most sacred place in the Temple… the Holy of Holies where the Ark of the Covenant will be placed and where the Spirit of God will rest on the Mercy Seat just above the Ark. The 30-foot-wide room is completely covered with 23 tons of gold… every inch overlaid. Can you imagine the glory and splendor of that room? Here's what's fascinating to me. Because of the extremely sacred and holy nature of that room, only one person was allowed to go into the room, for only one day each year. The high priest would visit with the presence of God in that place on Yom Kippur, the Day of Atonement. No one else was allowed inside at any time. So, except for that one day, only God would see the splendor of that room.

Let me pair that thought with these words of Paul, "And whatever you do or say, do it as a representative of the Lord Jesus, giving thanks through him to God the Father" (Colossians 3:17 NLT). I am reminded that many of our acts of grace, kindness, and charity will only be seen by God. Some of the splendor that we create will only be seen by God. And that should be enough. Our purpose is to glorify God in all that we do, not elevate ourselves.

Prayer

God, may we honor you in both the public and private moments of our lives. Amen.

Day 371   2 Chronicles 4: The Importance of Worship

> "Solomon also made a bronze altar 30 feet long, 30 feet wide, and 15 feet high." 2 Chronicles 4:1 (NLT)

Observation

This chapter indicates that Solomon went to great lengths to follow meticulously the details and plans outlined by his father David for the Temple furnishings. Two key features are described that were vital to the practice of worship. One was the bronze altar, used to make atonement for sin, and the other was the bronze sea (basin) used for cleansing/purification purposes. The account also describes 10 basins to be placed within the Temple, a feature not included in the tabernacle. Ten lampstands replaced the single lampstand in the tabernacle. And again, 10 tables to hold the showbread replaced the single table that had once been in place in the tabernacle. The increase in the number of these items, along with the increased size of the Temple, pointed to both the majesty of God and the increasing size of the Jewish nation. As the absolute focal point of worship, the Temple had to be large enough, grand enough, and beautiful enough to bring honor and glory to God.

Application

As I read this passage, I was struck by the sheer size of the altar that sat in front of the Temple as described in our focus verse. Notice the dimensions... 30 feet long, 30 feet wide, and 15 feet high. This huge, bronze platform was the instrument used by the priests to offer sacrifices to God on behalf of the people. This altar facilitated the atonement required to bring redemption and forgiveness for the sins of Israel. It was not a small, insignificant detail easily overlooked by anyone coming to worship at the Temple. It was prominent. It was important. It was vital.

Atonement is still a big deal. Nothing has changed about our sin problem since the creation of the world. What has changed is how we find forgiveness and restoration in the eyes of God. Because blood represents life, in the days of the Old Testament a "blood sacrifice" was offered on an altar to atone for the sins of the people. The taking of an animal's life restored the life of a sinner. Sacrifices were made to remove the stain of one's disgrace before God. But things have changed. Our churches no longer have an altar in front of the building where animals are slain on our behalf. Instead, we celebrate a perfect sacrifice that has been made that forever takes away the guilt of our transgressions. When Jesus Christ offered his life as a sacrifice on our behalf, his spilt blood became our hope. He died so that we don't have to. He offered his life so that we could know the joy of real, abundant, eternal life. How well we worship him is an indication of how much we value his sacrifice.

Prayer

God, may we be forever grateful of the Savior's sacrifice on our behalf. Amen.

Day 372 — 2 Chronicles 5: Evidence of God

> "At that moment a thick cloud filled the Temple of the Lord. The priests could not continue their service because of the cloud, for the glorious presence of the Lord filled the Temple of God."
> 2 Chronicles 5:13b-14 (NLT)

Observation
As the scene opens in Chapter 5, the Temple construction is complete. King Solomon moves all the silver, gold, and various objects collected by David into the Temple treasuries. The final step is to bring the Ark of the Covenant into the Temple. With Levites carefully placing the Ark on poles, carried on their shoulders, the Ark is taken from the temporary tent that David had provided, and moved into the Temple. This huge moment is celebrated by a remarkable moment of worship. Countless sacrifices are made, the priests purify themselves, musicians play, and the singers sing. And at the culminating moment, the glorious presence of God visibly fills the Temple. God, present in the form of a cloud, enters the Temple. So complete and dominate is God's presence that the priests must cease their duties until the cloud subsides.

Application
What a moment to experience, right? To stand in Jerusalem as the Temple is dedicated and to see the presence of God fill the building must have been a mind-blowing, life-changing, conversation-starting event. Oh, how we long to see something like that in our day. What if we could see the "invisible God," in a very visible way? Now I know what you're thinking, and I agree… God is revealed in many ways in our world. We can catch a glimpse of God in a lot of places. We see God revealed in nature. We see God revealed in the lives of followers. We see God revealed in acts of kindness, mercy, and justice. Whenever the people of God gather, isn't God's presence felt and God's Spirit evident? Of course. But let's go a little deeper. What if we could see a manifestation of God like those moments in the Old Testament when God appeared as a pillar of fire or as a pillar of cloud, or as in this moment, a thick cloud that filled the Temple?

Notice how this event unfolded. In a place dedicated to house the indwelling Spirit, in a moment devoted to worship, in a room considered so holy that no mere human could stand in that place, God blew into the Temple with power, force, and majesty. When we dedicate our hearts as a place of absolute reverence and respect for God's indwelling Spirit, when we devote ourselves fully and passionately to God's purposes, and when we disallow the influence of impurity in our minds, then the Spirit will blow into us like a mighty wind. No… we may not see a white cloud, but what we will see, is the evidence of God's presence.

Prayer
God, we welcome your presence in our lives this day. Make us as a holy temple. Amen.

Day 373 — 2 Chronicles 6: The God Who Always Hears

> "May you hear the humble and earnest requests from me and your people Israel when we pray toward this place. Yes, hear us from heaven where you live, and when you hear, forgive." 2 Chronicles 6:21 (NLT)

Observation
The first section of this chapter is a speech made by Solomon as he dedicates the Temple. He stands on a huge bronze platform in front of the Temple as he speaks to all the people. In both his speech, and in the prayer that will follow, Solomon speaks with deeply felt emotions and dedication. There is a depth of respect and solemnity on this occasion. In the second half of the chapter, Solomon lifts his hands toward God in a posture of humble and obedient worship and offers a prayer for the nation. This prayer has been called by some commentators "one of the great prayers of the Bible." In it, Solomon asks that God would always hear the prayers that are offered at this place and those that are directed, with humility, before God who lives in heaven. He voices the various circumstances that could arise within the community of Israel and asks that God would always hear and heal through God's forgiving spirit.

Application
Our prayers are never a waste of time. Those moments spent in the presence of God always yield results because they are always heard. Solomon locked into that truth. He prayed that whenever God heard the people's prayers, that God would forgive. Let me offer you some assurance this morning. Every time you pray, God listens. Every time. Your prayers are not offered in vain. Though we might sometimes think that God has not heard because our prayers are not answered in the way we think they should be answered or with the speed with which we desire, let us know with certainty, that they are always heard. Our needs, our thoughts, our concerns, our fears… are all heard by our heavenly Father. I say that, not just out of some pious hope, but out of the assurances that God has placed in the Word.

Here are a few verses to mull over this morning. "He will be gracious if you ask for help. He will surely respond to the sound of your cries" (Isaiah 30:19 NLT). "The eyes of the Lord are toward the righteous, and His ears are open to their cry" (Psalm 34:15 NASB). "And this is the confidence which we have before Him, that, if we ask anything according to His will, He hears us" (1 John 5:14 NASB). "You always hear me…" (John 11:42 NASB). Sometimes, in our distress, sorrow, confusion, and pain, it helps to know that someone is listening. As children of God, we can walk through this day and every day with the assurance that God is always listening to every prayer we make. Every single prayer. No matter how great or small.

Prayer
God, thank you for always listening to every prayer we offer. Amen.

Day 374 — 2 Chronicles 7: The Promise of Restoration

> "Then if my people who are called by my name will humble themselves and pray and seek my face and turn from their wicked ways, I will hear from heaven and will forgive their sins and restore their land."
>
> 2 Chronicles 7:14 (NLT)

Observation

This chapter contains one of the most familiar and often quoted verses in the Old Testament. Allow me for a moment to set its context. As soon as Solomon had offered his prayer (previous chapter), the fire from heaven fell to the earth. The offerings and sacrifices made on the altar were consumed and then for the second time, the glory of the Lord filled the Temple in a visible, tangible way. It was confirmation that the Lord had accepted this structure as God's home among the people. The people bowed in worship and praise. All of this takes place during the Festival of Booths, which was one of the three large festivals celebrated each year. Solomon had intentionally delayed the dedication of the Temple several months so that the dedication would happen when the city was filled-to-overflowing with worshippers. At some later point, after the Temple and palace had been completed, the Lord spoke to Solomon in the night. He reiterated the proper attitude and actions of the people needed to receive God's continued blessing. Our focus verse was a promise of restoration when the people wandered away from God and suffered as a result. This verse is not meant to be a set of prescriptive steps to take in a process, but rather the tangible, on-going expressions that should be a part of an active relationship with God.

Application

My dad owned a lot of cars when I was a kid... I mean, a LOT of cars. It was his hobby and obsession. For a few years, he owned a 1950 4-door Packard Super 8 Sedan. It was a thing of beauty. It was dark blue with lots of chrome, white-wall tires, and a huge swan hood-ornament resting on the front of the hood, which must have been eight feet long. It was pristine. It only had about 10,000 total miles on the odometer. The tires were original, the jack in the trunk was still in the cardboard box, and the upholstered seats were immaculate. The only thing not original was the exterior paint. Apparently, the older woman who had owned the car previously, was a little meticulous herself. Each time it had a small scratch, she had the entire car repainted. It had a deep luster and shine like you wouldn't believe.

When things are well-kept, they don't need a lot of restoration. But when things are not maintained, a lot of help is needed. None of us have done a good job in maintaining our relationship with God. We sin. We disobey. We make mistakes. Yet God is full of grace and is willing to make all things new. Confess your sins this morning. Seek forgiveness. Become restored.

Prayer

Dear Father, thank you making us new again... and again. Amen.

Day 375   2 Chronicles 8: When You Know Something Is Wrong

> "Solomon moved his wife, Pharaoh's daughter, from the City of David to the new palace he had built for her. He said, 'My wife must not live in King David's palace, for the Ark of the Lord has been there, and it is holy ground.'" 2 Chronicles 8:11 (NLT)

Observation

Chapter 8 picks up the story of Solomon's reign about 20 years into the narrative. By this point, Solomon had completed the building of the Temple and the building of his palace. He now turns to some of the challenges and duties of governing his kingdom. In his wisdom, he builds cities for defense in some of the outlying areas. He also stabilizes the security walls for some of the cities he will use for storage and for the keeping of his chariots and horses. He also continues to extend his networks, alliances, and influences among the surrounding nations. Our focus verse indicates that Solomon built a new palace for his wife, who is the daughter of Pharaoh. He is wise enough to know that it would be inappropriate for her to live in David's palace because of the connection to the Ark of the Covenant. This sacred space could not be inhabited by someone who worshipped a pagan deity. God had warned him that his relationships and marriages to foreign women would lead his heart astray. At least in this passage, he seems to understand the dangers that such marriages pose, and yet he continues in the relationship and even builds a palace in which she might live. It's as if he sees the warning flags but chooses to ignore them.

Application

Sometimes, we tragically ignore warning signs that we should carefully heed. Several years ago, my wife and I spent a few days relaxing down on the Georgia coast on St. Simons Island. While we were there, a terribly tragic event took place. A young family was vacationing in the area. They wanted to play in the surf with their children. The beach warning flags indicated that the surf was potentially dangerous and contained a strong rip tide. They ignored the warning and waded out into the surf several hundred feet where they could stand knee-deep on a sandbar and play. A rogue wave suddenly washed across the sandbar, knocking everyone off their feet. The mother was able to grab the hand of her youngest child, but the older boy was swept away in an instant. Rescuers searched frantically for several days but never found him. The warnings had been posted… unfortunately, they were ignored.

What warning signs are waving in your life this morning? Where do you sense a little trouble on the horizon? Is there a relationship that is fragile? Is there a health concern you continue to ignore? Is there financial pressure that you need to address? Is there some sin that needs to be confessed and resolved? Don't ignore the warnings. They might just save your life.

Prayer

Dear Father, grant us the wisdom to heed the warning signs in our lives. Amen.

Day 376   2 Chronicles 9: Some Things You Have to See to Believe

> "She exclaimed to the king, 'Everything I heard in my country about your achievements and wisdom is true! I didn't believe what was said until I arrived here and saw it with my own eyes. In fact, I had not heard the half of your great wisdom! It is far beyond what I was told.'"
>
> 2 Chronicles 9:5-6 (NLT)

Observation

This chapter records the visit of the queen of Sheba to Solomon's palace. That a major world leader would visit Solomon and seek his wisdom is a significant sign of Solomon's power, wealth, and influence. She had heard of his wisdom and longed to test it for herself, not to trip him up, but to discover for herself what great ability he possessed. As our focus verses indicate, his wealth, wisdom, and influence are more than she could have even imagined. As the chapter continues, verse 22 indicates that "King Solomon became richer and wiser than any other king on earth." The final verses of the chapter give a very quick summation of his reign and death. There is no mention whatsoever of his failures involving his foreign wives. The chronicler's point was not to emphasize his shortcomings, but to highlight the complete fulfillment of God's promises in his life.

Application

There are some things in this world that a person just has to see to believe. In our focus passage, the queen of Sheba had to make the trek to Jerusalem to see the splendor of Solomon's wealth with her own eyes. We understand the sentiment. There are sights and sounds that we can read about, view in photographs, and listen as others describe them, but until that experience becomes our own, something is missing. For example, I can't fully describe for you the experience of seeing the Blue Angels perform at an airshow, or watching the stadium erupt when the Crimson Tide takes the field, or standing on the shore as the ocean waves crash onto the sand (a few of my favorite things...). Recently my son and daughter-in-law visited the Grand Canyon. He just wanted to see it with his own eyes. Some things have to be seen, felt, heard, and experienced.

Faith is the same way. It is not a second-hand kind of experience. You can hear someone offer a testimony. You can watch a life changed by the grace of God. You can surround yourself with a thousand worshippers all giving voice through a song of praise. But until *you* experience faith in your own heart and mind, something is missing. It is when faith becomes personal that it becomes the life-altering, comfort-giving, hope-inspiring entity that God intends for it to be in your life. You cannot borrow the faith experience of another. So, go and see. Pray. Search the scriptures. Listen for the Spirit's voice. Be open to the experience.

Prayer

Dear Father, may we allow faith to become a personal experience this day. Amen.

Day 377 — 2 Chronicles 10: When It All Unravels

> "The older counselors replied, 'If you are good to these people and do your best to please them and give them a favorable answer, they will always be your loyal subjects.' But Rehoboam rejected the advice of the older men and instead asked the opinion of the young men who had grown up with him and were now his advisers." 2 Chronicles 10:7-8 (NLT)

Observation

Chapter 10 describes the tipping point at which the northern tribes revolt because of the unpopular leadership of Rehoboam, son of Solomon. The story opens with Rehoboam going to Shechem to be crowned king over all of Israel. (Shechem had already become a major political center for the northern tribes and would eventually become the capital.) Jeroboam, who had been previously exiled by Solomon (1 Kings 11:26-40), returns as the leader and spokesman for the 10 northern tribes who felt that the hard labor demands and heavy taxes imposed by Solomon needed to be reduced. Rather than ask God for wisdom like his father would have done, Rehoboam seeks the counsel of men. The older men advise a little mediation and relaxation of the demands. The younger men advise for an even greater burden. Rehoboam listens to the unwise counsel of the younger men. As a result, the northern tribes revolt and the unity of the kingdom is forever shattered.

Application

Have you ever noticed that one bad decision tends to cascade into another bad decision and then into another? Young King Rehoboam made several key mistakes. First, he sought counsel in the wrong places. Rather than seek the wisdom of God, he welcomed the thoughts and opinions of men. And once he sought the counsel of others, he failed to listen to sound reason, but only listened to those around him who agreed with his opinion. The fabric of the kingdom began to unravel as soon as Rehoboam imposed self-will and wisdom, over the direction of godly counsel. This same scenario is often played out in our lives. One bad choice soon leads to a second and then to a third. At some moment, we reach a tipping point at which our foolish choices can no longer be reversed or corrected and so we suffer the consequences. The problem lies in the meantime. Often, we fail to see the consequences of our mistakes in the present moment. It is only as we look back on the trail of our poor choices that we understand how we should have responded differently. So how can we live differently? How can we make better choices? First, learn from previous mistakes. Some bridges only need to be crossed but once. Second, pay attention to the source of wisdom in your life. Have you sought the direction and will of God or are you listening more to your own whims and opinions?

Prayer

God, forgive our foolish ways and grant us wisdom in each hour to pursue what is right. Amen.

Day 378 — 2 Chronicles 11: The Strong Call of God

> "The Levites even abandoned their pasturelands and property and moved to Judah and Jerusalem, because Jeroboam and his sons would not allow them to serve the Lord as priests." 2 Chronicles 11:14 (NLT)

Observation
This chapter highlights much of the reign of King Rehoboam (Solomon's son), who ruled over the tribes of Benjamin and Judah that will become known as the southern kingdom of Judah. As the chapter opens, Rehoboam mobilizes his troops for battle against the 10 tribes to the north who have rebelled. But God speaks to him through the prophet Shemaiah telling him not to fight against his relatives. God says, "What has happened is of my doing!" The assumption is that God is punishing the sins of Solomon and the hubris of Rehoboam. So, Rehoboam relents and does not plunge the nation into civil war. He does take on the challenge of fortifying several strategic cities to provide a strong defense of the southern kingdom. The priests and Levites living in the north will migrate to the south to continue their practice of worship and service in the Temple. The chapter ends with an accounting of all of Rehoboam's wives and children. He has apparently followed in his father's misguided ways. He has 18 wives, 60 concubines, 28 sons, and 60 daughters.

Application
The call of God is a powerful thing. Whether God is calling us to professional ministry, missionary service, faithful witness in the workplace, or to responsible and faithful marriage and family responsibilities, those of us who take God's authority seriously understand the importance of being in the right place and doing the right things. Because of God's lordship over us, we live our lives and conduct our affairs all at the prompting of the Spirit. Notice what the priests and Levites did to stay true to their calling. They abandoned pasturelands and property, uprooting and moving to Jerusalem, because it was in Jerusalem where they could most carefully live out God's calling and purpose for their lives.

So, here's my question for you this morning… What do you need to do today to pursue the call of God in your life? What steps do you need to take? What barriers do you need to remove? What relationships need to end and which other ones need to begin? Is it time to uproot and move? Do you need to intentionally prepare yourself to be God's instrument? Are there issues with others that need to be resolved? Can you honestly pray this prayer… "God help me to do your will, nothing more, nothing less, nothing else?" Whenever God calls, our response must be decisive and obedient. There is no greater joy than that of being in the center of God's will and purpose, and no greater sense of bewilderment when we are not.

Prayer
God, thank you for your call in our lives. Make us faithful and obedient servants. Amen.

Day 379   2 Chronicles 12: The Cost of Disobedience

> "The prophet Shemaiah then met with Rehoboam and Judah's leaders, who had all fled to Jerusalem because of Shishak. Shemaiah told them, 'This is what the Lord says: You have abandoned me, so I am abandoning you to Shishak.'" 2 Chronicles 12:5 (NLT)

Observation

Once firmly established, King Rehoboam began to abandon the law of God and all of Israel followed him in his sin. (As a side note… the northern kingdom was named Israel and the southern kingdom was named Judah. However, as the chronicler writes his narrative, he refers to the southern kingdom as the "true Israel" because the Temple and Jerusalem were contained within its domain.) Because of the unfaithful nature of the nation, God allows King Shishak of Egypt to attack Jerusalem during the fifth year of Rehoboam's rule. He brings a huge fighting force that includes 1,200 chariots and 60,000 horses. The people humble themselves before God and so God does not allow the complete destruction of Jerusalem, but all the objects contained in the Temple treasuries and in the king's palace are taken. Rehoboam will continue to rule in Jerusalem over a very limited kingdom. His reign is summed up with these words, "But he was an evil king, for he did not seek the Lord with all his heart" (vs. 14 NLT).

Application

Most any car owner knows it is vital to check the oil level in the engine. (If you haven't checked your engine's dipstick lately, you should go do that right now!) I have a neighbor whose daughter didn't pay much attention to such things. She went for months without checking the oil, even after the little engine "oil light" became illumined on her dashboard. And then one day it happened. As she was driving along the interstate, suddenly the engine made a horrible sound as it completely seized-up. The entire engine had to be replaced at an exorbitant cost. Her father had warned her about checking the oil. The owner's manual clearly reminded her to do so. But her lack of attention to this important detail cost dearly.

There is a price to be paid for disobedience. We all know enough Bible to understand that God has expectations and demands of each of us. This is God's world, and we are God's creation. God expects our obedience to God's commandments and to God's authority. Whenever we make choices that place ourselves over and above God's directions for our lives, there will be a price to pay. No, we may not be attacked by the king of Egypt, but we will be attacked by the circumstances and results of our poor choices. We have to live with the conviction that God matters. We have to pledge a fidelity to God's constraints in our lives. God wills what is best for us. We discover meaningful life through a commitment to obedience.

Prayer

Father, forgive us when we willfully choose disobedience… we should know better. Amen.

Day 380   2 Chronicles 13: Trust in the Proven Source

> "So Judah defeated Israel on that occasion because they trusted in the Lord, the God of their ancestors." 2 Chronicles 13:18 (NLT)

Observation
As this chapter opens, Abijah, son of Rehoboam, becomes the king of Judah. In the third year of his reign, war breaks out between Israel in the north and Judah in the south. Abijah will march out against Jeroboam with 400,000 soldiers. Jeroboam rallies an army of more than 800,000. As the battle lines are drawn, Abijah shouts to all of Israel from the top of Mount Zemaraim. As he yells at Jeroboam and his army, he points out the rebellious action of Israel and their continuing sins of idolatry. He also points out their lack of respect and recognition for the Davidic line of leadership when Jeroboam earlier rebelled against Rehoboam. Abijah warns Rehoboam against going to war saying that God is on the side of Judah because of the nation's continued allegiance to God. When Abijah discovers that his troops are caught in an ambush, his soldiers cry out to God and God intervenes in the battle. As a result, 500,000 soldiers from the northern kingdom of Israel are killed. The loss is so devastating that Jeroboam will never regain all his power. Abijah, on the other hand, will continue to gain power and influence.

Application
A few weeks ago, Belmont's Campus came to a complete standstill. A cable company employee was working down the street, not far from campus. The worker accidentally cut the fiber-optic cable that supplies internet service to the entire campus. No one on campus had internet capabilities. No one could access the web, their working files, or their email. There was no WIFI, no file sharing, no Facebook! People roamed the halls like zombies not knowing what to do because they were unable to connect to their electronic world. After several hours, the service was restored, and everyone breathed a sigh of relief.

It made me think for a moment how dependent we have become on our electronic devices, our machines, our inventions, and our smartphones. We trust that we will always have cell service, a dependable car, electricity in our homes, and running water in our pipes. How unnerving it is when any of those "trusted sources" fail. Surely our lives must be dependent on something that promises greater certainty, assurance, and hope. Maybe our lives should be dependent on the greater things… like a God who promises omnipotent presence, a Savior who removes every sin, and a Kingdom that will surely come. We will find success and claim victory over our enemies when our trust is placed in God and nowhere else.

Prayer
Father, in a world of great peril and uncertainty, thank you for your abiding presence. Amen.

Day 381   2 Chronicles 14: Living in the Good Times

> "During those peaceful years, he was able to build up the fortified towns throughout Judah. No one tried to make war against him at this time, for the Lord was giving him rest from his enemies." 2 Chronicles 14:6 (NLT)

Observation

When Abijah dies, his son, Asa, becomes the king of Judah. This chapter details some of the early events of his reign when things were going well. The chronicler is careful to tell the reader that things are going well because of faithfulness and obedience to God. For the first 10 years of his reign, Asa enjoyed peace because he did what was pleasing and good in the eyes of God and commanded the nation to follow his example. During the time of peace, he tore down pagan altars and worship sites, fortified several cities, and built up an army of 580,000 men. Once, during this period, Judah was attacked by Zerah of Ethiopia, who brought an army of 1,000,000 men to Judah. Asa cried out to the Lord for help, and because of his faithfulness, God responded, and the army of the Ethiopians was defeated and Asa gained much spoil from the battle.

Application

You read a lot of devotional thoughts about living in the "meantime," how to respond when the world seems like a difficult place to be, and daily life is filled with setbacks. Many say things like, "Trust in God," "All things work together for good…," or "The Lord is always with you." Nothing wrong with those words of counsel. We *do* need to cling to our faith when the foundations of our lives seem to be resting on shifting sand. The storms of life should call us to cling ever more tightly to our faith, rather than tempt us to abandon our "life anchor." My thought this morning is a little different… How are we to live amid peace and prosperity? How should we live when life is going well and blessings seem endless?

First, acknowledge that all you have, any success you achieve, and any peace you experience, is all a result of God's gracious actions towards you and your family. In other words, you must live with an attitude of gratefulness. Each day, you should spend as much time thanking God for blessings as you do asking God for help when things go poorly. Second, you must look for a way to infuse peace and stability in the lives of those around you who are not currently enjoying such a life experience. You must ask, "How can I share? How can I ease the burdens of another? How can I pass along the blessing of God in my life to those around me?" Third, look for ways to "give yourself away." There are all kinds of ministries, initiatives, and volunteer opportunities that need your time, energy, and resources. While you are able to help, you must do it. Live a life of gratitude that finds expression.

Prayer

Father, thank you for times of peace and prosperity. Grant us a generous spirit. Amen.

Day 382   2 Chronicles 15: God's Broken Rule of Relationship

> "Then the Spirit of God came upon Azariah son of Oded, and he went out to meet King Asa as he was returning from the battle. 'Listen to me, Asa!' he shouted. 'Listen, all you people of Judah and Benjamin! The Lord will stay with you as long as you stay with him! Whenever you seek him, you will find him. But if you abandon him, he will abandon you.'"
>
> 2 Chronicles 15:1-2 (NLT)

Observation
This chapter describes a moment in the reign of King Asa when a prophet of God named Azariah offered a prophetic word to the king and to the nation. He called them to seek the Lord continually. The assurance offered by the prophet said that the Lord would stay with all those who stayed with the Lord… meaning that anyone who continually lived in a relationship with God would find God's presence and leadership in their lives. The prophet further encouraged the nation by saying that if they stayed strong and courageous, that their work would be rewarded. Asa received the prophet's message and removed all the detestable idols from the lands that he and his army had captured. He also repaired the altar of the Lord in front of the Temple. With a huge ceremony, the people of Judah and Benjamin, (the two tribes that comprised the southern kingdom), renewed their covenant relationship with the Lord and the Lord gave them rest from their enemies for many years. In fact, the kingdom would not be attacked until the 35th year of Asa's reign.

Application
The kind of relationship with God that is described in this passage is *not* the kind of relationship or covenant that we want to have with God. In this passage, the prophet declares that the "Lord will stay with you as long as you stay with him… but if you abandon him, he will abandon you." We really don't want that two-way relationship, do we? We want God to watch over us, bless us, answer our prayers, and protect our families, even when we are out of fellowship with God. We want God to be faithful even when we are unfaithful. And the Good News is that God's faithfulness always continues towards us, even when we are far from following God. "If we are unfaithful, he remains faithful, for he cannot deny who he is" (2 Timothy 2:13 NLT). We should be very, very grateful that the rules of relationships don't apply to our Heavenly Father. It is quite true, that when we fall out of fellowship and ignore God's leadership in our lives, that we miss out on the full blessings and benefits that could be ours as God's children. We could realize more peace, more hope, more comfort, if we invested in the relationship. But because God loves us completely, wholly, and unconditionally, we can never sever the relationship… even if it remains one-sided at times. Through the atoning death of Christ, we have been brought into God's family… forever.

Prayer
Father, may we know the joy of being in relationship with you. Amen.

Day 383 — 2 Chronicles 16: Misplaced Trust

> "At that time Hanani the seer came to King Asa and told him, 'Because you have put your trust in the king of Aram instead of in the Lord your God, you missed your chance to destroy the army of the king of Aram.'"
> 2 Chronicles 16:7 (NLT)

Observation
During the 36th year of King Asa's reign as king of Judah, King Baasha, who was leading the northern kingdom of Israel, attacked Judah. King Asa responded by reaching out to King Ben-hadad of Aram to form an alliance. Asa took the gold and silver from the Temple treasuries and from his palace and gave them to Ben-hadad as payment for the protection the alliance would provide. Ben-hadad sent an army and the northern kingdom abandoned its assault and left Judah. A seer named Hanani appeared with a word from the Lord. He told Asa of the mess he created by trusting in King Ben-hadad rather than in the Lord. God would have given him full victory had he trusted in God alone. Several years later, Asa begins to suffer from a foot disease that would eventually take his life. Again, rather than trusting God to bring healing in his life, he reached out to some physicians who could not heal him. He died in the 41st year of his reign having trusted in self-reliance rather than in God-dependency.

Application
I think there are some folks that never quite get this point... Life is better, richer, fuller, more joyful, and filled with much greater peace when ultimate trust is placed in our All-Powerful, All-Knowing, Able-to-provide-for-all-our-needs God. However, for a lot of crazy reasons, we tend to put our trust in a lot of other places. We trust the advice of friends. We rely on our experience and knowledge. We "Google" an answer on the web. We trust in the people who service our accounts and manage our lives. The truth is that we can certainly live our lives placing trust in those often flawed and temporary things. And... we may enjoy some success. But at the end of the day, our greatest life is found through a trusting relationship with our Heavenly Father. Look again at the life of King Asa. According to Hanani, he could have destroyed the king of Aram had he trusted in the Lord. By placing his trust elsewhere, he gained some victory but no lasting peace and certainly no lasting resolve. Or again, when he suffered from a foot disease, he could have sought the Lord's healing, but instead he trusted only in men. The last several years of life must have been filled with needless suffering. So, here's the point. You can live without trusting in God, but when you choose that path, you are choosing a lesser life. When we place our lives in God's hands, looking to God for wisdom, direction, and insight, God pours abundant blessings into our hearts. So, choose well as you plot the course of your life. Where you place your trust matters.

Prayer
Father, help us to experience the peace and grace of trusting fully in you. Amen.

Day 384   2 Chronicles 17: Jumpin' Jehoshaphat!

> "Then the fear of the Lord fell over all the surrounding kingdoms so that none of them wanted to declare war on Jehoshaphat."
> 2 Chronicles 17:10 (NLT)

Observation

At the death of Asa, his son Jehoshaphat becomes king of Judah. According to the writings of the chronicler, Jehoshaphat enjoyed a very successful reign. He strengthened Judah against any attack by Israel by stationing troops in all the fortified towns of Judah as well assigning several garrisons to various strategic locations. He found favor in the eyes of the Lord because he followed the example of the early years of his father's reign. He continually sought the Lord and followed the Lord's commands. He sent religious leaders to all the towns of Judah to teach the Book of the Law of the Lord to everyone in his kingdom. Because of the Lord's favor, he became wealthy and highly esteemed. The fear of the Lord fell on all the surrounding kingdoms. No one wanted to declare war on Judah. Even the Philistines brought tribute to Jehoshaphat in the form of silver.

Application

I'm interested in the expression, "Jumpin' Jehoshaphat!" Ever heard it? No one really knows its origin, although several searches indicate that it was first found in print in 1866 in Mayne Reid's book, *Headless Horseman*. (Nowhere in scripture does Jehoshaphat jump over anything.) Most agree that it's a slang expression… a euphemism for "Jehovah," or even "Jesus." It is one of many phrases sometimes used as an alliterative euphemism—a phrase to replace profane swearing or cussing. Instead of crying out, "Jesus!" or "Jesus Christ!," different words are substituted that have the same initial consonants. So, for "Jesus!," folks might shout out "Jeepers!" or, for "Jesus Christ," "Jiminy Cricket!" The list is endless. So, many agree that "Jumpin' Jehoshaphat" is a way of cussing without using the Lord's name in vain.

However, there is also a suggestion of an origin for the phrase from a Jewish scholar, who seems to think that its origin is based on Midrashic commentary. According to Midrash, most of the kings of Judea and Israel were rotten and evil. Jehoshaphat was an exception and is praised as being one of the few kings of Judah who was close to God. One of the ways this was illustrated was (according to Midrash) when he would see or encounter a great Torah scholar or sage he would "jump" off his throne to greet and honor the wise man… thus the phrase, "Jumpin' Jehoshaphat!" Let's go with that possibility. I like the image of someone who was so excited about God and God's messengers that he would jump to his feet to greet them. How excited are you today to encounter the Lord? Are you grateful for those who bring you God's message? Maybe it's time to jump up and praise the Lord!

Prayer

Father, may we live this day with the exciting joy of knowing Jesus. Amen.

Day 385 — 2 Chronicles 18: First Things, First

> "Then Jehoshaphat added, 'But first let's find out what the Lord says.'"
> 2 Chronicles 18:4 (NLT)

Observation
Chapter 18 opens with Jehoshaphat doing well in his role as king of Judah. But for whatever reason, he forms an alliance with Ahab, king of Israel. Perhaps he thought good relations with the northern kingdom would continue to bring peace to the land. So, his son marries Ahab's daughter. A bit later, Ahab asks Jehoshaphat to join him in his effort to reclaim Ramoth-gilead from the Arameans. Jehoshaphat agrees to help with the endeavor but insists that they should seek the Lord's counsel first. Ahab gathers 400 prophets, who wanted to gain favor with the king by affirming his decision. They say, "yes," the battle should be undertaken. Jehoshaphat asks if there is a prophet of the Lord who can be enlisted to help with the decision, and Micaiah is suggested. Ahab protests because Micaiah has never given Ahab the answer he wants, and he won't do so in this matter. Micaiah prophesies that destruction will come to Ahab. One of the other prophets even slaps him for his opposing prediction! The battle is foolishly undertaken, and Ahab will die from his wounds.

Application
What if we had the wisdom, the patience, the insight, and the spiritual maturity to seek the counsel of God in whatever important decisions we must make? Can you imagine how much wiser our choices would be and how much greater they would honor the Lord? What would that even look like? Let me give you a couple of thoughts. Let's say that you have to decide about a bank loan, or about a car to purchase, or about a job offer. What if your first thought was to seek the Lord's direction prior to making the decision, rather than asking for blessing after you already made your choice? The key question becomes, "How do we seek the counsel of God?" Because God is revealed to us primarily in three ways… voice, word, and messenger… then we should explore those ways of hearing from God. First, we pray. We seek discernment and clarity as we communicate with the Father, asking that the Spirit will prompt our minds into making the correct choice. Second, we dig into scripture. We ask, "What does God's Word have to say about this situation?" If we seek God's wisdom, there are passages that will bring clarity. We need to get into the habit of consulting the Bible. Third, we should seek godly counsel through a conversation with a Christ-follower. Having a second or even third perspective on a situation is far better than making decisions on our own.

Prayer
Father, teach us to always think, "Let's find out what the Lord says." Amen.

Day 386 2 Chronicles 19: Listening to Criticism

> "Jehu son of Hanani the seer went out to meet him. 'Why should you help the wicked and love those who hate the Lord?' he asked the king. 'Because of what you have done, the Lord is very angry with you.'"
> 2 Chronicles 19:2 (NLT)

Observation

As this chapter begins, Jehoshaphat and his army are just returning to Jerusalem after battle with the Arameans. Remember that in the previous chapter, Jehoshaphat had been talked into an alliance with King Ahab of the northern kingdom. Even though the kings had been warned about going into battle, they pursued the endeavor. King Ahab was killed in the battle. But as Jehoshaphat returns, he is met by a prophet of God named Jehu. Jehu is sent to rebuke him for his foolish actions. He tells him that God is angry because he had chosen to align himself with wicked King Ahab. The point of his rebuke is simple: "Faithfulness to God is not an option." To his credit, Jehoshaphat receives the prophet's rebuke and responds by taking actions to strengthen his kingdom and point the people in more godly behavior. He appoints judges throughout the land to help with civil matters and he appoints Levites and priests throughout the land to deal with spiritual questions and practices.

Application

We are all familiar with the term "Constructive Criticism." We just don't like receiving it. None of us wants to be criticized for the work we are doing. We long to be praised and patted on the back. We want to be affirmed, not criticized. When the boss comes in with a critique, we cringe. When the supervisor comes in with a complaint, we wince. It's hard to hear that something we have done is less than good and acceptable. But the truth is we sometimes need the outside voice and opinion. If the only standard of judgment we raise is that of our own opinion, our judgements will be a little biased and cloudy at best.

There is the old argument that says there is no such thing as constructive criticism… that criticism is always a negative force in our lives that forces us to feel poorly about our work and lower our self-esteem. And certainly, all of us have felt the sting of being criticized for something we have done. It's hard to listen and learn, but sometimes that's the point. Sometimes we need a mid-course correction. We need to see the areas in which we can improve. And sometimes, it is only the outside voice that can speak clarity into our hearts and minds. So, the next time you receive a little criticism, ask yourself, "Is there any truth in what was said? Is the person who offered the criticism offering it in my best interest?" And, if after some reflection, you realize that some things need to be improved, ask yourself, "What are the positive steps that I need to take so that I will no longer be criticized for my actions?"

Prayer

Father, may we see our imperfections and work redemptively to correct them. Amen.

Day 387   2 Chronicles 20: What's Your Battle Strategy?

> "After consulting the people, the king appointed singers to walk ahead of the army, singing to the Lord and praising him for his holy splendor. This is what they sang: 'Give thanks to the Lord; his faithful love endures forever!'"
> 2 Chronicles 20:21 (NLT)

Observation
There is a lot to unpack in this chapter. It begins with a surprise invasion of Judah by three armies from the south... the Moabites, the Ammonites, and the Meunites. These three armies had banded together to declare war on Jehoshaphat. Because of the size of their army and because of the surprise nature of their attack, Jehoshaphat had little time to prepare and was thus "fearful." He begs the Lord for guidance and orders all of Judah to fast as a way of seeking discernment about God's intervention. He also gathers the people together at the Temple and offers a very public prayer in which he speaks of God's sovereignty, God's covenantal relationship, and God's faithfulness. Jahaziel, a prophet, tells the nation that the battle is not theirs, but the Lord's, and that God will give them the victory. The army of Judah goes out to fight with a group of singers leading the battle array. They sing songs of praise to the Lord. The opposing army is set in such disarray that they begin to fight each other. All that is left for the army of Judah to do is to collect the spoils.

Application
Chances are that you have a few battles on the horizon... maybe you have a few to fight even today. Let me guess that some of you have financial battles to face, or broken relationships to mend, or difficult conversations to host, or problems to solve at work. We all have our battles to face and how we approach them makes all the difference. We fret and worry, then we plan a strategy, we rehearse our conversations, and we head off into the battle with our knees shaking and our hearts pounding. Jehoshaphat and his army tried something a little different... something a little better. First, they carefully sought out the Lord for comfort, for peace of mind, for leadership. They prayed and fasted rather than run to the war room to plan a strategy. And once they heard from the Lord, they believed what they heard. So confident were they in God's deliverance that they went into battle with musicians leading the way, singing songs of praise.

    So, what's your battle strategy today? Does it involve serious, reflective prayer? Does it involve discerning and listening to the Lord's direction? Does it involve praising God for God's strength, deliverance, and faithfulness? If not, then you need a different strategy. Most of us try to plot, plan, and prepare for our battles with our own strength and initiative. We quickly find that we are ill-prepared to face our foes. Maybe it's time to pray and then to sing.

Prayer
Father, teach us to trust in you for all the battles we face. Amen.

Day 388 — 2 Chronicles 21: A Horrible Death

> "Jehoram was thirty-two years old when he became king, and he reigned in Jerusalem eight years. No one was sorry when he died. They buried him in the City of David, but not in the royal cemetery."
> 2 Chronicles 21:20 (NLT)

Observation

After a time of peace and prosperity under the leadership of King Jehoshaphat, his son, Jehoram, becomes king at the time of his death. Jehoram is the oldest of seven sons. Not long after he is established as king, Jehoram kills all his brothers along with several other key leaders in the land. It would be a foolish attempt to rid the land of all political rivals. He then began to follow the example of the wicked kings of Israel (northern kingdom). It was said that he was as wicked as King Ahab. (Remember that he had earlier married one of his daughters.) He built pagan shrines and worshipped pagan deities. Soon his power and influence began to erode. Edom and the town of Libnah were able to break away and become independent. The Philistines and the Arabs from the south attacked and plundered Jerusalem. Elijah, the great prophet of God, visited him and told him that his lack of obedience to God would bring severe punishment. Elijah correctly predicted that he would suffer and die from a severe intestinal disease.

Application

It is evident from the text that King Jehoram died a horrible death. According to the account, he suffered for two years from this intestinal disease, likely some form of dysentery, until his bowels gushed out of his body. But perhaps even more horrible than his painful death, was the reminder that "no one was sorry when he died." Notice that he was not even given a proper burial normally reserved for a king. What a horrible legacy and reputation to have earned, that no one grieved at all at the moment of his death.

Recently, my wife and I were discussing several news items that each of us had read. I made the comment that some musician had passed away. I said to her, "I didn't know that so-and-so had died." Not knowing the name at all, she responded, "I didn't know that he had lived." Let's talk about legacy for a moment. Will we be missed when we are gone? Will people even know that we have lived… that we walked the planet and lived a life? The goal is not so much about success, but significance. What's the difference? Success is typically measured by the things that we have accomplished, the money we have earned, the trophies we have collected. Significance is all about the lives we have changed, the hearts we have mended, and the attitudes we have altered. Where are you investing your life's energies? Success will be forgotten within a few years. Significance will be felt for generations to come.

Prayer

Heavenly Father, may we find our worth as we build value in the lives of others. Amen.

Day 389   2 Chronicles 22: Courage in the Face of Chaos

> "But Ahaziah's sister Jehosheba, the daughter of King Jehoram, took Ahaziah's infant son, Joash, and stole him away from among the rest of the king's children, who were about to be killed. She put Joash and his nurse in a bedroom. In this way, Jehosheba, wife of Jehoiada the priest and sister of Ahaziah, hid the child so that Athaliah could not murder him."
>
> 2 Chronicles 22:11 (NLT)

Observation

After the death of Jehoram, the people made his youngest son, Ahaziah, the king of Judah. (He was the only surviving son of Jehoram after an Arab raid murdered all the older brothers.) Ahaziah would rule for a single year. He did evil in the eyes of the Lord. His mother had encouraged him to do wrong. She followed in the footsteps of her family who were descendants of King Ahab. Ahaziah struck an alliance with King Joram of Israel to battle the Arameans. When Joram was injured, Ahaziah went to visit him but was assassinated by Jehu. This power vacuum caused Ahaziah's mother (Athaliah) to go on a campaign to kill all the remaining descendants of King David's line. But Ahaziah's sister, Jehosheba, took Ahaziah's infant son and protected him by hiding him in the Temple for six years. His name was Joash.

Application

I must admit that this chapter is a challenging read. It contains a lot of similar names, coupled with a quick succession of events. It's a little hard to keep all the events straight. But I wanted to zero in on our focus verse in which one character named Jehosheba shows remarkable courage. In the face of a very chaotic and dark moment of history, at the risk of personal threat and exposure, she hid the young son of Ahaziah. I am reminded by her story that there are moments in which a courageous heart must rise above the chaos of culture.

I was reminded recently about an event that happened in my former church. We wanted to do something significant for the city of Nashville as a Christmas gift one year. We decided to build a huge 28-foot-tall Christmas tree made of canned goods. At the end of the season we were going to give all 18,000 cans to local food banks. No sooner did we give vision to the plan that the nay-sayers got involved. "What if the cans freeze? What if the sidewalk collapses under the weight? What if someone steals them? What if the wind blows them over? What if… what if… what if?" Finally, one man stood up in the middle of the doubting crowd and said, "But what if it works?" His courage changed the course of the conversation and the church successfully carried out the project. I want to challenge you this morning to become a person of courage… a person who will stand against doubts, fears, and misguided attitudes and proclaim a word of hope amid chaos. You can make a huge difference!

Prayer

Heavenly Father, may we have the courage to act well in the midst of chaos. Amen.

Day 390 2 Chronicles 23: A Royal Escort

> "Then the commanders, nobles, rulers, and all the people of the land escorted the king from the Temple of the Lord. They went through the upper gate and into the palace, and they seated the king on the royal throne." 2 Chronicles 23:20 (NLT)

Observation
When King Ahaziah was killed, his mother, whose name was Athaliah, claimed authority and seized control of the nation. She was ruthless and cruel. It was during the seventh year of her reign that the priest Jehoiada decided that it was time to take young Joash out of hiding and anoint him as king. This was a dangerous step to take and Jehoiada went to great lengths to ensure things would unfold correctly. He made a pact with five key army commanders and summoned all the Levites and family clan leaders to Jerusalem. In very dramatic fashion they surrounded the Temple so that Joash could be safely brought to steps of the Temple where they anointed him as the new king. When Athaliah heard the noise of celebration she went to see what was taking place. She was captured and led away to be executed. The new king was escorted to the palace where he was seated on the throne as the new king of Judah.

Application
Have you ever been escorted from one place to another by a group of officials because of the importance of the company in which you found yourself? I have. Years ago, when Jimmy Carter was serving as governor of Georgia, long before his service as president, he was a guest in my childhood home. He and my father had been friends and when he visited Rome in some official capacity, he came to our home for a few minutes. When it became time for him to be escorted to the local airport, I was invited to ride along. I got to ride in the backseat with the governor. It was a pretty cool experience for a kid. We had police on motorcycles in front of us and a squad car or two behind us as we raced our way through town. We didn't have to stop for red lights or obey the speed limits. We were "escorting" the governor.

Maybe you have never been a part of some motorcade or been escorted through town like you were the most important person within miles. But let me tell you about a moment you will one day get to experience. The day will come when you stand in the presence of God. Who do you think will escort you to the throne? Who's going to walk with you and declare to God, "This one is with me. He stands here before you without sin because I have chosen to take all those sins away"? Jesus. Talk about a Royal Escort. Can you just image the joy, the exhilaration, and the wonder of such an experience? That moment is being planned for your life. It is by your faith in Jesus Christ that you will get to experience it.

Prayer
Heavenly Father, thank you again for all that Christ has done for us. Amen.

Day 391 — 2 Chronicles 24: Who's Keeping You Grounded?

> "Joash did what was pleasing in the Lord's sight throughout the lifetime of Jehoiada the priest." 2 Chronicles 24:2 (NLT)

Observation
Joash was seven years old when he began his 40-year rule over Judah. There was a very close alliance between the king and Jehoiada, the priest. Under the influence of this powerful and righteous priest, Joash flourished as a leader. He did "what was right in the sight of the Lord." He took on a project of repairing and restoring the Temple. To finance the project, he sent priests and Levites all throughout the land to collect the Temple tax required by the Law of Moses. A large chest was built and placed in front of the Temple to hold the tax money. It was filled repeatedly so that masons and carpenters could be hired to repair the Temple to its original splendor. The text then mentions that Jehoiada died at the age of 130. He was buried in Bethlehem with the kings of Judah because he had done so much good for the nation. But when he died, Joash turned away from the Lord and abandoned the Temple and its Law. Zechariah, the prophet, was sent to warn him of his sins, but Joash had him killed for his words. As the chapter ends, Joash, himself, is assassinated by his own officials.

Application
Years ago I went fishing with a good buddy named Chuck. Chuck owned a small bass boat and was so proud of the new trolling motor that his wife had given him as a present. We had planned to take the boat, along with the new tolling motor, out for its first day of fishing. (For those of you who are ignorant of such things, a trolling motor is a small electric motor that attaches to the boat to help maneuver the boat while fishing along a shoreline.) We tried it out before we left the dock and all seemed well. But as soon as we powered up the main engine and headed out for the deeper water, the small trolling motor slipped off the boat and plunged into the lake. We spent the rest of our trip diving into the lake trying to find the motor in the murky water. By the way… we finally retrieved it and after a few days of drying out, it worked!

The point of that story is to illustrate the importance of being well grounded. If we had been more careful to securely attach the small motor, we would not have had the same experience. Notice what happened to King Joash when he failed to ground his life. As soon as his connection to Johaida was broken, his life fell into ruin. Apparently, there was no one else around to offer him wise counsel. So, who's keeping you grounded these days? Who's holding you accountable? Who's giving you solid advice? Who's making sure you make good decisions? It is vital to surround yourself with wise friends and associates who will tell you what you need to hear and not just what you want to hear. Seek out those who will help.

Prayer
Heavenly Father, may our lives be filled with wise counselors. Amen.

Day 392 — 2 Chronicles 25: It's All or Nothing

> "Amaziah did what was pleasing in the Lord's sight, but not wholeheartedly." 2 Chronicles 25:2 (NLT)

Observation
After the death of Joash, his son, Amaziah, becomes king at the age of 25. Verse 2 is a critically important description of his reign. Notice the ending phrase, "But not wholeheartedly." Here was a man who, in some situations, listened to and submitted to God, but at other times made rash decisions and poor choices out of self-serving pride. Over the course of time, he set out to do battle with the Edomites. Feeling that his army was not quite large enough, he hired 100,000 mercenaries from the northern kingdom of Israel. A prophet was sent to deliver the message that God was not "with the people of Israel." The king was warned not to take the mercenaries into battle. He sent them home but was angered by the waste of money he had to pay them. He went on to defeat the Edomites in battle but made the tragic mistake of bringing home their pagan idols to Judah. He set them up and worshiped them. The anger of God became focused on Amaziah because of his sinfulness. Yet, empowered by his win against the Edomites, he took on a battle against Israel. Judah was defeated, but not destroyed. However, Amaziah's fate was sealed as he was killed by assassins.

Application
If I were to ask you to evaluate your allegiance to faith and your fidelity to the Word of God, how would you respond? I know what each of us would like to say that we are doing that which is pleasing in the Lord's sight. But, the phrase, "but not wholeheartedly," should probably get tagged onto the end of the descriptive words about our commitment to God and God's Kingdom. To be sure, for the most part we attempt to do the right thing. We long to be faithful. We strive to be obedient. We work at active discipleship. But sometimes we fail. Sometimes we are not wholehearted in our pursuit. Why? Maybe we suffer from the same sin of King Amaziah. Maybe we make rash decisions and poor choices because of our self-serving pride. We mistakenly bow down to the idol of self rather than offer our full allegiance to God. We momentarily forget that we were created to glorify God and not ourselves. So, let me offer you some good news. It's called grace. When we stumble… when we fail… when we let our attention be drawn in the wrong direction, God carefully, lovingly, and faithfully, calls us back into relationship. So, just in case you have missed the mark lately and have been less than wholehearted in your pursuit of God, know that God waits to welcome you home and offer you a second chance, and a third…

Prayer
Heavenly Father, thank you for your patience when our discipleship is erratic. Amen.

Day 393   2 Chronicles 26: Too Big for Your Britches

> "But when he had become powerful, he also became proud, which led to his downfall. He sinned against the Lord his God by entering the sanctuary of the Lord's Temple and personally burning incense on the incense altar."
> 2 Chronicles 26:16 (NLT)

Observation
The story of King Uzziah could have been so wonderfully told and his reign so beautifully executed except for one small thing… pride. Arrogant pride. He was placed on the throne at the age of 16 when his father Amaziah died. He reigned over Judah for 52 years and did extraordinary things because he sought the Lord in all things. (Zechariah was the prophet who gave counsel and wisdom to the king during this time.) He defeated the Philistines and others in critical battles. He reclaimed land and cities. He fortified towns and built forts in the wilderness. He promoted successful farms and vineyards. But then, he entered the Temple and personally burned incense on the altar—the exclusive duty of the priests. The high priest and 80 other priests tried to stop his poor behavior. Suddenly, God struck him with leprosy, and he was forced to live excluded from the palace for the rest of his life. When he died, he was buried near the kings of Judah but not with them because of his leprosy.

Application
I have to admit that when I was in college, I was a little cocky. Hard to believe, right? I was in a fraternity, and we thought that we owned the world. We always claimed to be the best at everything. When people told me I was too cocky or conceited, I would reply, "I'm not conceited, I'm convinced!" You learn a few things over the course of life, sometimes lessons taught on the heels of a tough experience or difficult time. And if you will allow life to teach you, you will soon discover that you are not the center of the universe, and the world doesn't revolve around you. Somewhere along the way, hopefully, we all learn a little humility and kindness. Notice King Uzziah's mistake. When he had become powerful, he became proud. He's not the first or the last to make that mistake. Maybe your success, your wealth, your influence, or your position has made you a little proud. Not proud in the sense of "taking pride in what you do," but arrogance. What most of us need are a few gentle reminders that teach us that all that we have, all that we are, and all that we shall ever become are the results of God's grace in our lives and not the result of anything that we have done. We are to be the recipients of grace, not the producers of arrogance. Your blessings have not been given to make you special, they have been given to make you generous. If you should become powerful, become thankful, not proud.

Prayer
Heavenly Father, teach us humility and gratitude, even this day. Amen.

Day 394   2 Chronicles 27: The Difficult Task of Erasing Evil

> "Jotham did what was pleasing in the Lord's sight. He did everything his father, Uzziah, had done, except that Jotham did not sin by entering the Temple of the Lord. But the people continued in their corrupt ways."
> 2 Chronicles 27:2 (NLT)

Observation
Beginning with this chapter and extending through the next nine chapters, the chronicler describes the reign of the final six kings of Judah. He alternates between good kings and bad kings. Some trusted in the Lord to guide them, while the others did not. The ultimate lack of blessing will be the Babylonian captivity described a bit later in the text. The first of these final six kings is Jotham, son of Uzziah. He was 25 years old when he took the throne and would reign for 16 years. Like his father, Jotham did right in the eyes of the Lord, but he did not act unfaithfully as his father, Uzziah, had done when he burned the incense in the Temple. Although he was a good and faithful leader, the people continued to act unfaithfully, still influenced by pagan cultures that had been introduced during the reign of earlier kings. Jotham is noted for fortifying and refurbishing some of the areas surrounding the Temple as well as building outpost cities in the wilderness of Judah. He also was victorious in battle against the Ammonites who were required to pay a great deal of tribute in silver and agricultural produce to the people of Judah.

Application
Our focus verse today, reminds us that even though Jotham was a good and effective leader, the nation continued in her corrupt ways. The story illustrates how difficult it is to erase deep-seeded evil from the heart of a nation. Qualities like greed, anger, prejudice, and hatred become deeply embedded and the task of removing such demonic forces from the hearts of people is a slow and difficult struggle. I remember the days of my childhood and adolescence, lived in the heart of the deep south where Bible ethics were well-taught, but where racial prejudice and hatred were also a part of the landscape. My hometown went through the race riots and the deconstruction of segregation that many southern towns had to endure during that time. And many of us came to believe that things were better. We felt that we had made progress... that racial reconciliation was taking hold and tensions were easing. And yet the progress made in those years was not a final and lasting answer. Recent events and demonstrations across the nation remind us all, that we still have a long way to go. But as people of faith we cannot give up, nor lose hope, nor remain on the sidelines. We are called to change the world and sometimes that takes courage, great resolve, and much patience. And of course, it takes much grace, extended towards those who oppose our efforts.

Prayer
Heavenly Father, if not us, then who? If not now, then when? Amen.

Day 395 — 2 Chronicles 28: A Stumbling Block

> "The king took the various articles from the Temple of God and broke them into pieces. He shut the doors of the Lord's Temple so that no one could worship there, and he set up altars to pagan gods in every corner of Jerusalem." 2 Chronicles 28:24 (NLT)

Observation
In contrast to the positive and effective leadership of Jotham, the new king, Ahaz, was one of the most wicked and corrupt of all the 20 kings who once ruled Judah. He began a blatant practice of Baal worship, the fertility god of the Canaanites. Part of his worship included child sacrifice that resulted in the death of his own sons. Because of his wickedness, the Lord was against him. The king of Aram and the king of Israel both attacked Judah successfully. So devastating was the defeat that many from Judah were led away into captivity to the northern kingdom of Israel. Things were so bad that a prophet spoke to the leaders in Israel telling them not to hold their fellow Israelites from the southern kingdom in captivity. They were released and allowed to return home. In another dangerous move, King Ahaz established an alliance with the Assyrians to help with some of the border conflicts he was experiencing. As our focus verse indicates, so wicked was the heart of King Ahaz, that he shut the doors of the Temple and would no longer allow God's people to worship in that place.

Application
Can you just imagine the heartache, grief, and despair experienced by the faithful God-followers of Judah when the king closed the doors of the Temple? What must it have been like to see the Temple become a deteriorating relic while altars to pagan gods were erected in every corner of Jerusalem? How wicked was the heart of Ahaz to close off the Temple and deny the people an opportunity to worship God? We shake our heads and wonder how such a thing could happen... and then we are forced to consider our own actions.

Most of us, in fact, I pray that all of us reading this thought would never be party to such action. Surely, we would never board up the front door of a church or stretch a chain across the door handles. We would never dream of denying anyone access to the church, nor to the worship of God. But then again, maybe we have already done it, and maybe more than once. Whenever we claim the name of Christ but don't let our faith become evident in our thoughts, attitudes, and interactions with others, we have begun the process of sending folks away. Whenever we pledge fidelity to the Bible but then disobey its demands, again, we are shutting the doors of the church to those who are searching, seeking, and asking. Whenever talk with an exclusionary tone, a racist mindset, or a judgmental attitude, then surely, we are closing the door on the invitation to grace that so many need to discover.

Prayer
Dear God, may our actions invite and never repel others from the faith. Amen.

Day 396   2 Chronicles 29: Taking Out the Trash

> "The priests went into the sanctuary of the Temple of the Lord to cleanse it, and they took out to the Temple courtyard all the defiled things they found. From there the Levites carted it all out to the Kidron Valley."
> 2 Chronicles 29:16 (NLT)

Observation
The reign of King Ahaz is remembered as the lowest point in the line of Davidic kings that led the nation of Judah. There was little hope in the land that things could be reversed. But his son, Hezekiah, became a high point in the history of Judah. In fact, many suggest that his leadership closely paralleled that of David and Solomon. The chronicler will spend four chapters describing his rule and reign, which lasted 29 years. Under Hezekiah's leadership, true revival broke out in the land. On the first day of the first month of his reign, Hezekiah began the process of reopening and restoring the Temple. The doors of the Temple were repaired, and all the pagan influences were removed. The people responded enthusiastically to his leadership and within 16 days, the Temple was ready to serve the nation again. Sacrifices were offered and the people sang songs of praise and joy. Repentance, renewal, and restoration had begun.

Application
When the priests began to reclaim and cleanse the Temple, they took all the pagan deities, altars, and influences and carted them off to the Kidron Valley. Not only did they want to remove them far away from the Temple itself, but they chose the Kidron Valley, which was the lowest spot geographically on the outskirts of the city. It was as if they symbolically wanted to cast away the pagan things to the lowest and most insignificant place they could find. There is something to be said for taking out the trash.

Trash day at our house is Wednesday. Every Tuesday night, I go through the house collecting all the trash. And of course, we have to separate everything into two containers… one for the landfill and the other for recycling. I take it all out to the street and early Wednesday morning the trucks roll through the neighborhood, making it all disappear. There is something cathartic in that process. I can't fully explain it, but it feels good to declutter, and rid the house of all the garbage that has collected.

We need to do the same thing with our lives. We need to throw out the trash. Our life experiences, our poor choices, our regrets and mistakes, all have a way of piling up. They squeeze the joy out of our lives. They lead to guilt and shame. They destroy our self-esteem and make us feel less than what God created us to be. So how do we take out the trash? It's called confession. We admit the mistakes, we pray for forgiveness, and we lean into grace.

Prayer
Dear God, may we experience and know the joy of being cleansed. Amen.

Day 397 — 2 Chronicles 30: State of Readiness

> "They were unable to celebrate it at the prescribed time because not enough priests could be purified by then, and the people had not yet assembled at Jerusalem." 2 Chronicles 30:3 (NLT)

Observation
Part of the reform that King Hezekiah brought to Judah was a renewal and reinstatement of the Celebration of Passover. Apparently, through the years, the practice had been abandoned. Hezekiah desired to invite and welcome all of Israel to Jerusalem to participate in the celebration. He sent messengers, not only all throughout Judah, but to those living east of the Jordan, and to those remnants in the north who remained after the Assyrian captivity in 722 B.C. It was a call to unity and worship for all the people of God. Though some rejected the messengers and their invitation, a huge assembly gathered in Jerusalem to celebrate Passover. The date of celebration had to be deferred by a month for two reasons. First, people needed time to travel to Jerusalem from distant places, and second, there was an insufficient number of priests ready to offer the sacrifices and prayers of the people. It took time to consecrate one's life to be used by God in the Passover celebration and the month delay allowed more priests to be ready for the moment. The zeal and excitement of the celebration was so great that it was extended for an additional seven days.

Application
Like many of you, I like being prepared for the things that come my way. Take preaching for an example. Now that I am no longer pastoring a church, I don't speak with the regularity that I once did. For 32 years, I spent a portion of every week, praying, preparing, and practicing my way through a sermon. As those who share this occupation can attest, you get into a rhythm of preparing for each Sunday. Some of that pressure and pleasure stays with me still. I continue to get invitations to speak to different groups, gatherings, and churches and welcome every opportunity. And though my weekly routine has changed a little, I keep a sermon always "cooking on the stove." I continue to pore over a passage, write a few notes, and collect a few illustrations to have something "fresh" prepared whenever I am called upon to speak. I want to be ready, even at a moment's notice, to fill the pulpit.

Being prepared to share a word from the Lord, is not an activity reserved for the professional clergy. It's a responsibility that should be felt by every believer. Peter writes, "Instead, you must worship Christ as Lord of your life. And if someone asks about your Christian hope, always be ready to explain it. But do this in a gentle and respectful way" (1 Peter 3:15-16a NLT). All of us should have a little "something" prepared. We should be ready if a moment presents itself to say a word of hope and promise. Get ready now.

Prayer
Dear God, give us opportunities to share a word of hope with others. Amen.

Day 398 2 Chronicles 31: When Faith Prompts You to Action

> "When the festival ended, the Israelites who attended went to all the towns of Judah, Benjamin, Ephraim, and Manasseh, and they smashed all the sacred pillars, cut down the Asherah poles, and removed the pagan shrines and altars. After this, the Israelites returned to their own towns and homes."
> 2 Chronicles 31:1 (NLT)

Observation
This chapter continues the story of Hezekiah and all the reforms brought to Judah under his leadership. The narrative continues the action from the previous chapter. As soon as the Feast of Passover was complete, the people, caught up in a sense of religious fervor, went to all the towns of Judah and destroyed all the pagan shrines, temples, and altars. Hezekiah then busied himself with organizing the priests and Levites by divisions to insure the on-going work of the Temple. Additionally, he offered a personal contribution of animals to be used in the sacrifices at the Temple. The people responded to his example and began bringing tithes and offerings to the Temple to honor God and to provide for the needs of the priests and Levites. The out-pouring of contributions was so great that storehouses had to be constructed. Hezekiah also made provision to insure the fair distribution of gifts and land to the priests. The final verse of the chapter reminds the reader that Hezekiah "sought his God wholeheartedly."

Application
It is quite true that faith, when actively lived out, should not only govern one's inner thoughts, but one's outward actions as well. In the time of Hezekiah, the people had such a sense of renewal about their faith, that they were led to do several things. First, they went throughout the land, cleansing the land from all pagan influences. Second, they brought tithes and offerings to the storehouses of God and offered the gift of land to take care of the needs of the priests. You get the idea. Their faith produced action. Out of a sense of joyful obedience and dedication, they responded to the prompting of God in their lives.

So, here's the question to ponder this morning… "What will your faith prompt you to do this day?" How will your belief in, allegiance to, and love for God be expressed in your actions over the course of this day? At the end of the day, there should be evidence that you are a Christ follower. Maybe today you will speak with kindness to the person who has not acted kindly towards you. Maybe you will share a little time with someone who is hurting that needs a compassionate person to whom they might speak. Maybe your faith will cause you to make a financial contribution to a noble cause. Perhaps your faith will change your attitude or convict you about a change you must make. What will faith prompt you to do even this day?

Prayer
Dear God, may our faith be active, alive, and life changing. Amen.

Day 399   2 Chronicles 32: Finding Strength in the Struggle

> "Then King Hezekiah and the prophet Isaiah son of Amoz cried out in prayer to God in heaven." 2 Chronicles 32:20 (NLT)

Observation
As the chronicler continues the story of Hezekiah, a sudden foe brings trouble to his doorstep. The Assyrian army, led by King Sennacherib, had already vanquished the northern kingdom of Israel, and was now moving to the south to conquer Judah. As soon as Hezekiah hears of the impending assault, he takes steps to protect Jerusalem. He repaired walls and built new fortifications. He manufactured large weapons and shields. He called the people together and told them to take courage, that God would battle for them. And then he did something very important. He brought the prophet Isaiah to his side and together they prayed for God's intervention. Hezekiah realized that it would take more than human intellect and military power to defeat the Assyrians. God heard the prayers of the king and Prophet and sent an angel to destroy the enemy. King Sennacherib was forced to return home in disgrace where his own sons assassinated him. The chapter then tells of a deathly illness that struck Hezekiah, but he was healed because he had taken the matter to God through prayer.

Application
There is a thread that winds its way through this narrative, connecting the stories that are told in this chapter. It's the thread of God dependency and the prayerful seeking of God's mercy and might. Hezekiah knew that to defeat his enemies, both those of military might and physical illness, that he needed to declare his dependency upon God alone and plead for God's intervention. It seems like a simple lesson to learn and to put into practice. And yet, for many of us, it is not the first step that we take whenever we encounter a huge enemy in our lives. Often, we look to our own resources and abilities and seek a way out of our troubles. When things start to trend in a negative way, only then do we become desperate enough to plead with God for mercy and help. What a dumb way to live our lives. We are loved fiercely by God, who longs to shower us with blessings, mercy, and answers to the problems we face. Why is it that we wait so long before we invite God into our daily struggles? Do we lack a confidence in God's ability to help? Do we think that God is powerless in the face of our struggles?

Rest assured that life is going to throw you a few curve balls. There are going to be problems to solve, questions to answer, and crisis moments to engage. You can struggle, worry, and fret your way through life… or you can immediately cry out to the almighty, all-powerful, all-knowing God who loves you beyond comprehension. The choice is yours.

Prayer
Dear God, give us the wisdom to place our trust in you, first and foremost. Amen.

Day 400 — 2 Chronicles 33: Never Too Late

> "But while in deep distress, Manasseh sought the Lord his God and sincerely humbled himself before the God of his ancestors."
> 2 Chronicles 33:12 (NLT)

Observation
Chapter 33 tells of the interesting reign of King Manasseh, son of Hezekiah. He was 12 years old when he took the throne and would reign for 55 years. Unlike his father, he did evil in the eyes of the Lord. He rebuilt the pagan shrines that his father had destroyed. He created altars to worship the image of Baal. As verse 3 states, "He bowed down to all the powers of the heavens and worshipped them." He even sacrificed some of his own sons in the valley of Ben-Hinnom. And maybe worst of all, he took a carved idol and placed it within the Temple. In anger, the Lord sent the commanders of the armies of Assyria to Jerusalem. They took him prisoner, leading him away to Babylon with a ring in his nose and chains on his feet. It was in a moment of deep distress and remorse that he cried out to God with a prayer of repentance. God heard his prayer and restored him to Jerusalem and to power. He tore down the pagan altars that he had created. When he died, his son, Amon, became king. Amon was also exceedingly wicked. He was assassinated by his own men after only two years of reigning as king.

Application
Most of us are familiar with the concept of repentance. Repentance before the Lord indicates a complete change of directions. It is a 180-degree turnaround. Repentance causes us to step away from sin and move in the direction of God's plan for our lives. Fortunately for King Manasseh, his realization of his sinfulness led him to a point of repentance and regret. He sought the Lord and God responded to his prayer.

Maybe we need to take a moment to consider the intersection of forgiveness and repentance. Both are needed as we long to make our hearts right before the Father. By His grace, God offers us forgiveness… complete, amazing, wonderful grace that erases our sins and restores our relationship with God. Repentance on our part, is the action we take to prevent ourselves from further sin. It is what keeps us from abusing the grace that God offers. With a sincerity of heart, we must seek God's forgiveness as we pledge that we will change the steps in our lives that lead us away. In other words, grace is God's gift to us… repentance is our pledge to God. It is our pledge to walk a different path, to choose better options, and to listen to a better voice. Repentance takes willful and deliberate resolve. And here's the really good news. Whenever we take a step towards God and away from our sinfulness, we will always find God's warm embrace and compassionate heart. Take a moment this morning to consider the role of repentance in your life. What paths need new direction?

Prayer
Father God, may we see our sins and courageously walk away from them. Amen.

Day 401 — 2 Chronicles 34: Fidelity to the Word

> "Go to the Temple and speak to the Lord for me and for all the remnant of Israel and Judah. Inquire about the words written in the scroll that has been found. For the Lord's great anger has been poured out on us because our ancestors have not obeyed the word of the Lord. We have not been doing everything this scroll says we must do." 2 Chronicles 34:21 (NLT)

Observation

After the reign of two very wicked kings, the Lord raised up Josiah as a king who would bring bright revival to the nation. From an early age, Josiah showed spiritual maturity and did what was pleasing in the eyes of the Lord. By age 20 he began to purge the nation of the idolatry that plagued it. He destroyed the altars and idols dedicated to pagan deities. At age 26, Josiah ordered the restoration of the Temple, which had fallen into severe ruin. While doing the restoration work, Hilkiah, the priest, discovered a scroll that turned out to be the Law of Moses (probably the Pentateuch). As the words of the scroll were read to the king, he tore his clothing as a sign of remorse and shame at what the nation had become. He took the scroll to the prophet Huldah to receive a word from the Lord. She told him that God was going to destroy the nation along with Jerusalem for all the wickedness that had been lived out among the people. She told Josiah that this destruction would not come during his lifetime because of his faithfulness to God. As the king read it to the people, renewal began.

Application

As I read this narrative, I am struck with the accidental discovery of the scroll of Moses. Surely this scroll had once been an extremely valuable and important document for the people of God. How it could have been neglected and even forgotten shows the extent to which idolatry had overcome the nation. My guess is that some priest, in an attempt to protect the scroll, had hidden it years earlier. Surely Hilkiah must have trembled as he held this ancient parchment in his hands. I am also struck with the serious nature of the king's response. He immediately recognized its authority over the life of the nation. He knew that the people had not practiced obedience to what God had written in the Law. It was a fidelity to the Law that began a sense of revival across the land.

Chances are that you are not going to discover an ancient parchment, tucked away in some dark corner of your house that will change both your heart and the direction of your life. But hopefully, you will discover the leather-bound treasure you hold in your hand that contains the Word of God. The scriptures are "living and active" and have been preserved for each of us in order that we might know God's will and purpose for our lives. I hope that you will let it surprise you today, let it convict you today, and let it change the direction of your life.

Prayer

Father God, give us a love for and a fidelity to, your written Word. Amen.

Day 402   2 Chronicles 35: Go Big or Go Home

> "Never since the time of the prophet Samuel had there been such a Passover. None of the kings of Israel had ever kept a Passover as Josiah did, involving all the priests and Levites, all the people of Jerusalem, and people from all over Judah and Israel." 2 Chronicles 35:18 (NLT)

Observation
Part of the renewal/revival that King Josiah brought to the nation was a return to a proper celebration of Passover. Apparently, the celebration had been all but neglected through the years. Josiah ordered that it be observed on the fourteenth day of the first month… all according to the Law of Moses. To prepare, he set all the priests in their duties and offices and encouraged them in their work. He also returned the Ark of the Covenant to the Temple. Had it been hidden during the reign of Manasseh and Amon to protect it? Or had it been removed during the restoration of the Temple and was now being set back in its place? Either way, the preparations were complete, and the celebration undertaken. It was a huge national observance with every detail addressed. The king himself had given 30,000 lambs and 3,000 cattle to be used in the sacrifices and celebrations. As our focus verse indicates, it was a celebration like the nation hadn't seen in centuries. The chapter ends with the death of the king. The chronicler mentions it as almost a side note to the story. It is apparent that he wants to emphasize the king's good works rather than his death after being wounded in a battle involving the armies of Egypt.

Application
No doubt you are familiar with the expression, "Go big or go home." It can be applied to a lot of situations. It's really another way of saying, "If you are going to do something, do it right! Do it with all of your heart and strength!" I doubt King Josiah was familiar with the phrase, but obviously, he was familiar with the intent, especially when it came to observing the Passover celebration. He made sure that it would be big and bold. He made sure that everything was done well. He made sure that the people worshipped God to the best of their abilities.

Perhaps some of us need to be challenged about the way we approach worship week in and week out. (I'm not talking so much about those who lead the services… I'm talking about all of us who are participants.) Do we give it our best? Do we anticipate the joyful moments of being in God's presence? Do we sing with fervor, pray with passion, and listen with intensity? Do we go into a sanctuary believing that it is the most important hour of our week? Do we echo the psalmist who writes, "I was glad when they said unto me, let us go into the house of the Lord" (Psalm 122:1 KJV)? When next Sunday rolls around, go big or go home.

Prayer
Father God, give us a passion for worship. May we value its importance. Amen.

Day 403   2 Chronicles 36: The Exhaustion of Grace

> "But the people mocked these messengers of God and despised their words. They scoffed at the prophets until the Lord's anger could no longer be restrained and nothing could be done." 2 Chronicles 36:16 (NLT)

Observation

This final chapter of the book of 2 Chronicles describes the quick succession of four kings, the rise of Babylon, and the ultimate destruction of Jerusalem and the Temple. (In terms of the way the Old Testament is organized, the books of the prophets who spoke to both the northern and southern kingdoms during the time of the Monarchies, will be recorded next.) The son of Josiah was named Jehoahaz. He was deported to Egypt by King Necco. His son Jehoiakim became the next king. He ruled for 11 years but did evil in the sight of the Lord. King Nebuchadnezzar captured Jerusalem and took Jehoiakim as a captive to Babylon. His son took over the throne, but for only three months and 10 days. Nebuchadnezzar then installed Zedekiah as king, who reigned for 11 years, but as his ancestors did, he did not follow the ways of the Lord and rejected the counsel of the prophets whom God sent to warn the people. Finally, Babylon brings all its strength against Jerusalem and it falls in 587 B.C. The city and the Temple are destroyed, and the remaining people are taken to Babylon as captives.

Application

Obviously, the people of Judah had reached a tipping point in their relationship with God. After having been warned by the prophets repeatedly, and, after having suffered hardship because of disobedience through the years, God's anger is no longer "restrained," and God allows the people to experience punishment for their sins. The city is destroyed, the Temple is obliterated, and the people are taking into captivity. In God's mercy, a remnant is allowed to survive the period of the exile and will eventually return to Israel.

Is it possible for us to exhaust the patience and grace of God? Is there a limit to God's forgiveness, God's love, and God's mercy towards us? At least in this passage you get a sense that God's growing anger at the nation's disobedience causes a fearful result. God allows for the destruction of the Temple and the city of Jerusalem. Yet it is important to note, that even in anger, God refuses to destroy a relationship with God's people. God continues to love them, relate to them, and will eventually restore them. So, let me answer the question this way, "We can certainly exhaust God's patience, but we can never extinguish God's love for us." That means that we may well suffer the consequences of our actions. Our disobedience may be met with hardship and punishment. But nothing that we do can separate us from God's love and God's ability to reconcile with us.

Prayer

Father God, forgive our sins, restore us, and dwell among us. Amen.

Day 404 — Ezra 1: Effective and Forgotten Leadership

> "Cyrus directed Mithredath, the treasurer of Persia, to count these items and present them to Sheshbazzar, the leader of the exiles returning to Judah." Ezra 1:8 (NLT)

Observation
The book of Ezra tells the story of the end of the exilic period and the return of the captives to Jerusalem. In 538 B.C., God put it in the mind of King Cyrus of Persia (during the first year of his reign) to allow the displaced Israelites to return to their homeland. (The Persians became the dominant world power for the moment and conquered the Babylonians.) Not only does God give permission for their return, but also provides for a freewill offering to be collected to aid them in their journey and in the task of rebuilding the Temple. Many of the items taken by King Nebuchadnezzar are given to the Israelites to be used once again in the Temple, once completed. A man named Sheshbazzar is appointed by King Cyrus to lead the first of the group back to Judah. He was a Babylonian Jew, sometimes referred to as the Prince of Judah, who led the people in this four-month long journey.

Application
Sometimes, good, effective leadership is carried out in anonymity. How many times is something great accomplished, but those responsible for initiating the action are unknown or soon forgotten? Sometimes those who have a great idea are barely noticed when the dream becomes a reality. I was recently in a board meeting when a suggestion was made to implement a new idea. By the time the discussion was over, the person making the original motion was forgotten and the chairman later took credit for the idea! The key to leadership is not in the notoriety that it brings, but rather in the results that are accomplished. Take as an example this man mentioned in our focus verse named, Sheshbazzar. He led a group of worn, weary, and worried Israelites on a four-month journey back to Jerusalem. Such a journey would have been arduous and riddled with setbacks. And yet, under his leadership, the return to the homeland was begun. But if I had asked you before you read this devotion, "Who led the Israelites back to Jerusalem," would you have known the answer? Of course not. His name is never mentioned and barely even recorded in scripture.

Great leaders are called to lead, regardless of the status or notoriety it brings. You may not ever receive a pat on the back for a job well done. You may not ever get the credit you deserve for giving key leadership at a critical time. What you will get is the satisfaction that you answered the call to lead, and that success was claimed. Jesus says about such things, "Your Father who sees what is done in secret will reward you" (Matthew 6:4 NASB). Today, you may be called upon to lead a group in a task or decision. Don't worry if you never get credit. Your Father knows.

Prayer
Father God, forge us into humble leadership that honors you in all decisions. Amen.

Day 405 — Ezra 2: Disqualified to Serve

> "Three families of priests—Hobaiah, Hakkoz, and Barzillai—also returned. (This Barzillai had married a woman who was a descendant of Barzillai of Gilead, and he had taken her family name.) They searched for their names in the genealogical records, but they were not found, so they were disqualified from serving as priests." Ezra 2:61-62 (NLT)

Observation
This chapter lists the names and numbers of Jewish exiles from various tribes and clans that were a part of the original group returning from Babylon. Because their return marked the beginning of God's restorative work, it was important to verify everyone's lineage and qualifications for roles of service. It would be vital to re-establish purity within bloodlines and within the genealogies of those who served as priests. The chapter lists numerous tribes along with those who were to serve as priests, singers, gatekeepers, and Temple servants. The chapter also includes a recognition of the offerings given by the people as they returned to help begin the Temple building project.

Application
There are some interesting historical details surrounding three priestly families who returned to Judah. Listed in our focus text, the families of Hobaiah, Hakkoz, and Barzillai are disqualified to serve as priests because there were no genealogical records found that traced their lineage back to the priestly tribe of Aaron. Because the records were not intact, these families were not able to serve. There was such an emphasis on purity and strict adherence to the Law of Moses that these families had to abandon their roles as priests. In other words, they lacked the proper credentials to serve, even though these families may well have been in the right tribe. The lack of documentation was a real problem.

Having the right credentials is always important. You can't enter the country without a valid passport. You can't buy a new tag without the proper registration. You can't drive a car without a valid license. In my county of residence, you can't even haul trash to the dump without some proof of residency! Credentials matter.

What credentials do we hold that allow us to gain access to the eternal Kingdom of Heaven? There are no documents to safeguard, no fees to pay, no papers to have signed. The one and only credential we need is our faith in Jesus Christ. Several places in scripture, the text speaks of the Lamb's Book of Life and how those who have demonstrated faith in Christ, have their names recorded in that book. "Nevertheless do not rejoice in this, that the spirits are subject to you, but rejoice that your names are recorded in heaven" (Luke 10:20 NASB). Your assurance is found in your faith. You are included.

Prayer
God, we thank you that through our faith in Christ, that our names are recorded. Amen.

Day 406 — Ezra 3: The Praise of God's People

> "The joyful shouting and weeping mingled together in a loud noise that could be heard far in the distance." Ezra 3:13 (NLT)

Observation
Chapter 3 of Ezra describes the rebuilding of the altar in Jerusalem, along with the construction of the foundation for the Temple. As the Israelites began the process of building the altar and offering sacrifices, their actions were met with opposition by some of the pagan population who continued to inhabit Jerusalem during this time. Yet even in the face of this unpopular action in the eyes of the community, the altar was built on the exact spot of the previous altar and sacrifices were made each morning and evening according to the Law of Moses. It is interesting to note that the altar was completed and in use before the foundation of the Temple was even begun. There was a priority of worship that motivated the people. The construction of the Temple began during the second year of the return (probably 536 B.C.). When the foundations were complete, a huge celebration took place. Trumpets were blown, cymbals rang, and praise songs filled the air. The people sang a song anticipating the glory and greatness of God from Psalm 100. There was a mixture of emotion on that day. The old priests wailed with lament as they remembered the former glory of the old Temple, while the younger men shouted with joy at the hope of what was yet to come.

Application
About a decade ago, the University of Alabama expanded the capacity of Bryant-Denny Stadium so that it could hold more than 100,000 people. Pulitzer-prize winning author, Rick Bragg, wrote an article for *Sports Illustrated* when it was completed. In his article, he wrote about an old man who lived a couple of miles away from the stadium. On the day when the huge crowd gathered at the stadium for the first time, the old man walked out onto his back porch, which faced the stadium. He wanted to hear the sound of 100,000 people all shouting together on a beautiful autumn afternoon. I too, have heard the sound on many occasions. It's pretty impressive.

My attention was caught by the final verse of the chapter in which the author states that the loud noise of shouting and weeping, "could be heard far in the distance." I like the image of the sound of God's people being heard throughout the land. Maybe it's time for such a sound to be heard again… not one long shout from a group of excited priests, but a long, sustained echo of God's presence and grace spoken over and over again throughout the land by God's faithful people. Let's raise God's praise among the nation.

Prayer
God, may we never tire or grow weary of echoing your praise. Amen.

Day 407 — Ezra 4: Bumps Along the Way

> "When this letter from King Artaxerxes was read to Rehum, Shimshai, and their colleagues, they hurried to Jerusalem. Then, with a show of strength, they forced the Jews to stop building." Ezra 4:23 (NLT)

Observation
The return of the Jewish nation back to Judah was not a smooth and easy process. It's not like the exiles were welcomed with open arms by those groups who had spent the past 50 to 60 years living in the land. In fact, these various groups would express unrelenting hostility for decades as the Jews attempted to rebuild both Jerusalem and the Temple. At first, the opposition was rather subtle. Some of these groups tried to infiltrate the population by saying they wanted to help build the Temple with the Jews. But out of concern for purity of worship and blood lines, they were denied. As the narrative rolls on, groups wrote to the king of Persia telling him that the Jews could not be trusted, and that they would stop paying taxes and tributes to the king. The king was persuaded by their rhetoric and sent a letter back to Jerusalem insisting that construction on the Temple and the wall of Jerusalem be halted.

Application
It is foolish to believe that when we are called by God to pursue God's purposes that there will be no opposition. In fact, sometimes just the opposite is true. The forces of evil, often embodied in the hearts and attitudes of men, can sometimes present roadblocks to the work of the Kingdom. People will provide a little fear mongering, some negative attitudes, and even some poor excuses in their attempts to thwart the work of God. And some of those people can even be found in the local church! Even Christ himself, on the way to beginning his public ministry, was led out into the wilderness to be tempted by Satan, who would eventually leave him, only to look for more opportune times to attack.

If you are a ministry leader in the life of your church, organization, or group and you feel the strong prompting of God to move in a certain direction, let me encourage you not to become defeated when opposition begins to surface. In fact, in some ways you should be encouraged knowing that when great things are attempted for God, that opposition is a normal by-product. Recorded in Matthew 16, Jesus once said to Peter, that the "gates of hell" could not prevent the ever-forward march of the Kingdom. Can you wrap your mind around that? Even the greatest strongholds imaginable, the nastiest negativity, and the strongest opposition, will not defeat the work of God. You and I may experience some bumps along the road that challenge our resolve and slow our progress. But take heart. The things of God, the ministries ordained by God's Spirit and moved forward by God's strength, will prevail.

Prayer
God, even in the face of opposition, may we find the courage to do your will. Amen.

Day 408 — Ezra 5: Safeguarded by the Written Word

> "Therefore, if it pleases the king, we request that a search be made in the royal archives of Babylon to discover whether King Cyrus ever issued a decree to rebuild God's Temple in Jerusalem. And then let the king send us his decision in this matter." Ezra 5:17 (NLT)

Observation

For a period of 10 years, work on the Temple had ceased because of local opposition. At that time, God raised up two prophets, Haggai and Zechariah, to call the Israelites to action. Their unified voice directed the Jews to continue with plans to build the Temple. The Temple was more than a structure of wood and stone. It represented the presence of God in the midst of the people. Its construction would give security and protection to the people. As they continued to build, they were challenged by local and regional leaders who wondered by what authority they were carrying out their work. They agreed to send a letter to King Darius to see if the work was properly sanctioned. They wanted to search the archives of the king to see if King Cyrus had indeed ordered such a project. As the narrative bleeds over into the next chapter, a record of the king's decree is found.

Application

Sometimes it helps to write things down. I have discovered through the years that taking notes during important conversations and meetings is an important discipline. It is vital, at times, to remember key facts and conversations. Whenever I go to Kroger to "pick-up a few things," my wife always insists that I take along a list. It keeps me from bringing home a whole bunch of crazy things and ensures that I actually return with the items needed. In similar fashion, when I make a promise to pray for people, I am always careful to record their names on my prayer list, lest I forget to remember them as I had promised.

Ever wonder why God has gone to such great lengths to preserve scripture through the ages? It is not so *God* will remember God's dealings with humankind… it is so *we* will remember. God inspired Biblical writers to carefully record God's laws, God's stories, and God's history with humanity so that we will never forget the important details of God's history and future plan for all of us. How important it is to have that record! When we have doubts, when our lives swirl with uncertainty, when we need solutions to relationship problems, when we worry our lives away, when we fear the road ahead, all we have to do is open the Bible and start reading. God is revealed over and over again. The writer of Hebrews reminds us, "For the Word of God is living and active…" (Hebrews 4:12 NASB). It speaks to our uncertainty and encourages our fearful steps. God has safeguarded God's word by insisting on the written form. I hope you will become a life-long student of the written Word.

Prayer

Father God, thank you for giving each of us your written and lasting Word. Amen.

Day 409 — Ezra 6: The Joy of Celebration

> "The Temple of God was then dedicated with great joy by the people of Israel, the priests, the Levites, and the rest of the people who had returned from exile." Ezra 6:16 (NLT)

Observation

In response to the inquiry by his governors, King Darius has his officials search for the original document, signed by King Cyrus, which allowed the Jews to return to Israel. A scroll was found in the fortress at Echatana. After reading the document, King Darius affirms the order and calls for the leaders of Israel to complete the work. He tells his officials that they are to allow them to do so without any interference. In fact, the king goes a step further and orders that the finances needed to fund the restoration be paid out of the royal treasuries. It is to be built on the original site, staying as true as possible to the instructions outlined in the Law of Moses. The Temple was completed in the sixth year of Darius' reign. One month later the people returned to celebrate Passover. I was struck by the wording of our focus verse… the people celebrated "with great joy."

Application

I wonder if we take the time to celebrate often enough. As the ancient Israelites discovered, there is joy found in celebration, particularly when we celebrate the actions of God in our midst. It is my experience, in my daily interaction with co-workers, friends, and acquaintances, that there seems to be a scarcity of joy. Many find it hard to infuse joy into the routines of their lives. I know a lot of people who get caught up in the drudgery of everyday life. The monotony, the routine, and the lack of excitement cause many to live dull and insipid lives. Maybe it's time to look for the moments that bring joy and take the time to celebrate those moments more deliberately.

For example, yesterday I was going through the mail after I arrived home at the end a long day. I was tired. I was ready to be out of traffic and out of my "dress-up clothes." As I thumbed through the mail, I saw an envelope that looked as though it might contain a check. And sure enough, it seems that I had overpaid a medical bill and was being refunded $50. I know that's not a lot of cash… it's not like I won the lottery… but it was a nice greeting at the end of a long day. I shared the news with my wife, and we celebrated with a fist-bump.

It doesn't take a lot of celebration to refill the tank. A little joy can go a long way. So do this… look for something in your routine today that brings you a little joy. And when it does, celebrate the moment. Offer a prayer of thanks. Share with a friend. Laugh for a moment. Look for the actions of God in your life today and celebrate them with a little joy.

Prayer

Father God, may we see beyond the drudgery of today to claim a moment of joy. Amen.

Day 410 — Ezra 7: The Wisdom to Study

> "...for the gracious hand of his God was on him. This was because Ezra had determined to study and obey the Law of the Lord and to teach those decrees and regulations to the people of Israel." Ezra 7:9b-10 (NLT)

Observation
If you have ever taken an Old Testament survey class, you will know of the importance of the work performed by Ezra. He is known as the great law giver, second only to Moses in the importance of teaching God's law to the Israelites. (His lineage is traced all the way back to Aaron.) Much of what is recorded throughout the remainder of the book are personal memoirs of the prophet. (The reader will notice that much of the narrative switches to a first-person pronoun account.) The events described in this chapter take place 80 years after the first wave of exiles returned to Judah and 58 years after the completion of the Temple. Ezra will take on the task of leading the Jews to practice purity in their faith practices. He will usher in a time of reformation and renewal. Sent with King Artaxerxes blessings and resources, Ezra will faithfully teach the Law and will appoint magistrates and judges throughout the land to ensure that the people are living in obedience to the commands of God.

Application
If you read the focus verses carefully, you will notice that one of the reasons that God's gracious hands were upon Ezra was because he had "determined" to study and obey the Law of the Lord. Ezra had made a conscious, deliberate, important decision to be a student of God's Word and that discipline brought success in his life. Our experience will be no different. Because there is power, truth, wisdom, and insight in God's Word, the more deliberate our discipline of study, the greater the reward. The more that we invest in the Word, the more it speaks truth to our lives and gives direction to our days. It's a choice, right? In order to find the time to spend with the scriptures, we have to take that time away from things that are less important in our lives.

I read recently that the average adult, checks the content of his or her phone about 160 times a day. We all do it. We check the email messages. We look at Twitter. We scroll through Facebook and Instagram. And so, if we are honest, we must confess that social media has more of an influence over our lives than the Bible does, because that is where we have chosen to invest our time and energy. How foolish and short-sighted we have become. We have let the unimportant take prominence in our lives. The wisdom and insight needed to live as God's people is not being planted in our lives… but cat videos, cooking recipes, and hate-filled rants are. Isn't it time to understand the wisdom that comes through careful study of God's Word?

Prayer
Father God, help us to have a longing for the knowledge of your Word. Amen.

Day 411 — Ezra 8: Standing on Your Faith

> "For I was ashamed to ask the king for soldiers and horsemen to accompany us and protect us from enemies along the way. After all, we had told the king, 'Our God's hand of protection is on all who worship him, but his fierce anger rages against those who abandon him.' So we fasted and earnestly prayed that our God would take care of us, and he heard our prayer." Ezra 8:22-23 (NLT)

Observation
This chapter shares more of the narrative of Ezra's return to Jerusalem and those who traveled with him. There is a listing of 15 families, totaling 1,500 people, who will make the 900-mile journey with Ezra. As the people gather, Ezra notices that there are no Levites who volunteered for the journey and so he has to recruit several to staff the Temple. As the people assemble prior to the journey, Ezra leads them in a time of prayer and fasting, seeking the protection of God for their journey. Once they arrive safely in Jerusalem, a huge worship service is planned with several sacrifices offered to the Lord.

Application
Notice from our focus passage that Ezra's declaration of faith in God governs his actions and even his conversation with the king of Persia. Obviously, the journey was long, and Ezra and his followers were going to take with them, a lot of gold and other precious objects for the work being done in Jerusalem. It would not have been unusual to ask the king to dispatch soldiers to protect the travelers. However, Ezra had boldly and correctly proclaimed that God's hand of protection would be on those who worship the Lord. And so, standing on his faith, he chooses not to call on the king but to call on God for protection. The people fasted and prayed, and God listened. Their prayers were answered, and their journey was safe.

Does your faith govern your action? Does your faith factor into the decisions you make, the conversations you have, and the relationships that you build? Do you stand daily on the promises of your faith, or is your faith something that you hold in reserve and only examine when times get tough? Either we are followers of Christ or we are not. Because we seek to pattern our lives after Jesus, every facet of our lives should reflect an obedience to him. Our pursuit of Jesus should affect our language, our relationships, our ethics, our attitudes, and even our priorities. And yes, sometimes, because we have made our faith declarations, we choose the path of uncertainty, unknown destination, and dogged reliance upon God, to demonstrate that we walk by faith and not by sight, nor even human intellect.

Prayer
Father God, may our faith be real, powerful, and manipulative of our actions. Amen.

Day 412 — Ezra 9: The Posture of Repentant Prayer

> "At the time of the sacrifice, I stood up from where I had sat in mourning with my clothes torn. I fell to my knees and lifted my hands to the Lord my God." Ezra 9:5 (NLT)

Observation

One of the key themes in the book of Ezra is an insistence upon purity… the purity of worship, religious practices, and bloodlines. Ezra is particularly concerned over mixed marriages. He saw the intermingling of Jews with non-Jews as a threat to the covenantal identity of the people of Israel. As the chapter begins, the Jewish leaders bring the matter to his attention. The problem is not just with intermarriage, but the pull towards idolatry that occurs as households are pulled in multiple directions religiously. Ezra expresses his outrage through mourning. He tears his clothing and pulls hair from his beard and head. At the time of the evening sacrifice he falls to his knees and lifts his hands toward the heavens in a prayer of confession. Even though the sins are corporate in nature, Ezra takes personal responsibility for the actions of the nation. As he describes the situation, however, he notes that God has allowed a remnant to survive the exile, which is an indication of God's mercy.

Application

I want you to notice in this passage the posture of prayer that Ezra assumes as he confesses the sinfulness of the people. First, he falls on his knees as a sign of humility. Second, he lifts his hands towards the heavens, acknowledging that his only hope is found in the mercy of God. And so, he both confesses the sin and pleads for mercy.

I wonder if physical posture is important as we pray? I hope you have a time and place where you consistently go to the Father each day. It's that prayer closet, that quiet place, that moment in your day when you can think clearly and pray intentionally. It may be in the morning, or at the end of day. It may be at your bedside, or at your desk, or at the kitchen table as you drink that cup of morning coffee. But if you are like me, there is very little physical action in your prayers. Sure, I bow my head and close my eyes, but for the most part, nothing about my posture changes. Maybe it should. Maybe there are times we need to fall on our knees as we honestly and deliberately confess our sins before God. And maybe there are times we need to lift our hands towards heaven to remind ourselves from whom all blessings flow. Maybe there are times we need to kneel beside the bed or at the altar of our church. Maybe we need to clasp our hands and bow our heads. I don't think there is any special formula or position that gets the most results, but I do think our physical posture can sometimes remind us how we need to focus our prayers, carefully and deliberately.

Prayer

Father God, teach us to pray, fervently, faithfully, and even more concisely. Amen.

Day 413 — Ezra 10: The Driving Priority

> "Let us now make a covenant with our God to divorce our pagan wives and to send them away with their children. We will follow the advice given by you and by the others who respect the commands of our God. Let it be done according to the Law of God." Ezra 10:3 (NLT)

Observation

In this final chapter of the book of Ezra, the community of Israel must come to terms with their infidelity of intermarriage with pagan wives. To follow the commands of God, tough choices must be made to bring renewal and reformation. It will require that all those who had married women from pagan backgrounds divorce their wives and, potentially, leave their children. According to the names listed in this chapter, there are 110 women who will be affected by this decision. Obviously, it is a gut-wrenching choice to make. The people wept bitterly both about their sins, and the separation from their loved ones. The community agrees that such action is the only choice to make to ensure obedience to the Law. As readers, we wonder at the emotional havoc that must have ensued when these marriages ended. In most cases, the wives had two choices. They could return to their original families, or they could convert to Judaism, which could bring about their inclusion in the community as proselytes. Either way, the divorces had to occur to pursue the holiness that God required.

Application

There are times when faith forces us to make difficult decisions. It is not always easy following the demands of God. (Please understand that this passage is not a proof-text giving sanction to divorce. Divorce is clearly not God's intention for human relationships and marriages.) In the context of re-establishing a chosen race, it was important for the people of God to rid themselves of the influence of paganism, expressed in this case through the divorces from pagan women. Our choices today are certainly not the same in content nor in context. But the point of the passage is well made. The driving priority of our lives must be obedience to God. We cannot willfully pursue passions, plans, or people that interrupt our fidelity to God's lordship. And so, our lives are governed by our faith. There are involvements that we cannot accept. There are attitudes that we cannot harbor. There are relationships that we cannot form. There are actions that we cannot allow. Faith will demand of us, deliberate, consistent, and important choices. One of the prevailing themes in this chapter is that of restoration. God certainly did not abandon those who lived with a history of poor choices. It is important to state that God will not abandon us as well. He is a forward-thinking Father who cares little for what we have been, and more about what we will one day become.

Prayer

Father God, teach us how to align our lives with your priorities. Amen.

Day 414 — Nehemiah 1: Build the Wall

> "They said to me, 'Those who survived the exile and are back in the province are in great trouble and disgrace. The wall of Jerusalem is broken down, and its gates have been burned with fire.'" Nehemiah 1:3 (NIV)

Observation

Nehemiah served as a cup bearer for the king of Persia whose name was Artaxerxes. Persia had defeated the Babylonians a century earlier and had allowed the Israelites to return to the promised land. Nehemiah had inquired from his brother, Hanani, about the state of things in Jerusalem. Our focus verse is the essence of that report. Though many had returned and had been occupying the land for almost 100 years, the city was still in great upheaval... morally, spiritually, and physically. Even the protective wall around the city had never been repaired and the city gates were in shambles. Nehemiah is distraught at the news he has received. He wept, fasted, and prayed to God for direction. He prays specifically that God would make him "favorable" to the king when he will go to the king to ask for his permission and protection to rebuild the wall.

Application

Just a few miles from where I live, along the main road to the south, there are a number beautiful, sprawling homes that sit on several acres of land. Some of them are surrounded by picturesque stone walls, some of which date back to the Civil War. I notice, however, that many of the walls are crumbling. In fact, the pastures they protect have no protection at all.

It's a dangerous thing to let walls fall into disrepair. When the walls are not strong and well-fortified, the enemy has a way of gaining easy access to the treasures inside. For the ancient Israelites, a failure to rebuild the walls of Jerusalem made them vulnerable to attack. Nehemiah would challenge the residents to rebuild the walls, which they did in just 52 days. We would do well to learn that lesson. My concern this morning is not about walls of brick and mortar that might protect our homes, or chain-link fences that might protect our borders, or even steel doors to guard our businesses. I'm thinking more in terms of the walls which surround our hearts and minds. How careful are you to build a strong defense against the forces that long to take control of the treasures inside? Do you guard your heart? Do you protect your mind? Or do you allow anything and everything to come marching in? It might not hurt to take stock of the shows you watch, the websites you visit, and the things you read. You may be allowing the enemies of your soul to slowly creep in. If you lose that battle, what's left? Pay attention. Build the wall.

Prayer

God, teach us carefully guard our hearts. May we learn to repel those influences that seek to destroy both our character and integrity. Amen.

Day 415 — Nehemiah 2: Pray First

> "The king said to me, 'What is it you want?' Then I prayed to the God of heaven, and I answered the king, 'If it pleases the king and if your servant has found favor in his sight, let him send me to the city in Judah where my ancestors are buried so that I can rebuild it.'" Nehemiah 2:4-5 (NIV)

Observation
Troubled by the poor condition of the walls of Jerusalem, Nehemiah feels led to go before the king and ask for permission to travel back to Israel and repair the city. He knows the request is both unusual and potentially upsetting to the king. Nehemiah was a favored servant of the king, but a servant none-the-less. It was a bit presumptuous for him to even petition the king in this manner. Not only would he ask the king for permission to travel to Judah, but he also wanted to ask the king for letter of protection to carry with him as he traveled through the various regions. Don't miss the small detail in the story... before Nehemiah approaches the king, he first approaches an even greater king. He prays to God first. The king not only grants his requests, but even sends along military support to protect him along his journey. After arriving in Judah, Nehemiah makes a careful assessment of the wall and begins to rally the people in support of his plans.

Application
We would do well to follow Nehemiah's example. Whenever there are choices to make, plans to discuss, or dreams to chase, does it not make sense to first invite both the presence and wisdom of God in all our decisions? Nehemiah needed several things before speaking to the king. He needed courage. He needed wisdom. He needed God to be at work in the heart of the king. The story reminds me of our need to bathe all of life in a sea of prayer. If we truly learned the value and importance of daily connection with the Lord, how much less would be the struggles in our lives? What if we sought God's wisdom before every big decision? What if we prayed for wisdom before every important conversation? What if we asked God to work in the hearts of others long before we began to dialogue with them? Sometimes we get the order of things all wrong. We speak before we think, we act without reason, we force a decision before careful consideration and so we find ourselves saying, "What have I done?" We cry out to God to rescue us from our bad decisions rather than seeking God's counsel before those decisions are made. Figure it out. The time to involve God in our lives, decisions, and thoughts, is at the genesis of an idea and not at the recovery stage.

Prayer
God, forgive our foolish attempts at self-sufficiency. May we be reminded this day to seek your counsel, your wisdom, and your grace. Amen.

Day 416 — Nehemiah 3: Working Together

> "Eliashib the high priest and his fellow priests went to work and rebuilt the Sheep Gate. They dedicated it and set its doors in place, building as far as the Tower of the Hundred, which they dedicated, and as far as the Tower of Hananel." Nehemiah 3:1 (NIV)

Observation

This entire chapter reads just like the opening verse listed above. Verse after verse lists the various sections of the wall being rebuilt and those who did the work. Nehemiah is careful to record the contributions that each tribe, family, or group was careful to complete. Why is that important? Why take the time to list all those who labored on the wall? Is it not to illustrate the power of unity that manifests itself when people labor together for a common cause? Nehemiah did not bring with him from Babylon, a group of workers to rebuild the wall. He brought a vision with him. And it was through the casting of the vision that the people rallied to do the work. We are always stronger, better, and wiser when we work together.

Application

Could you pick up and carry a car on your shoulders? Of course not. But what if you had help? What if 15 of your friends joined with you in your attempt? Just maybe you could carry a Volkswagen Beetle up a flight of stairs as a prank... not that I am confessing anything...

More than 2,000 years ago, Christ told his followers to go and change the world, to preach, teach, and live the Gospel. Surely the task overwhelmed them, challenged them, and frightened them. But before their fears could slow their steps or temper their zeal, Christ reminded them that his presence would be with them, and the Holy Spirit would empower them. In other words, the task became doable with the promises of Jesus undergirding their labor. We continue to share in that same sense of calling. Christ has challenged us to change the world... to preach, teach, and live the Gospel. It is still a very daunting task. In fact, it's an overwhelming task. But again, we are not alone. Not only do we have the promises of Christ undergirding our work, but we also have each other. Remember that we are stronger, better, and wiser when we work together. There is amazing strength when we unite around a task. The community of Christ reminds us to use the right pronouns. It's not about what "I" can do, it's about what "we" can do. When we join hands and labor together to share the hope of the Gospel, not even the gates of hell can stand against us. Don't become a lone-ranger Christian. The battle is too big for just you to undertake. Join with the believers at your church and see what great things can result.

Prayer

God, we thank you for the creation of the church. Thank you for calling us to a common task. Preserve our unity and grant us both wisdom and power. Amen.

Day 417 — Nehemiah 4: Do Your Thing

> "From that day on, half of my men did the work, while the other half were equipped with spears, shields, bows and armor. The officers posted themselves behind all the people of Judah." Nehemiah 4:16 (NIV)

Observation

As the wall of Jerusalem began to take form and strength again, the enemies of Israel began to take notice. Several, in fact, began to plan attacks against the city hoping to keep the Israelites from accomplishing their task. To thwart those efforts, Nehemiah developed a strategy of having half the men do the work while the other half provided protection. They were equipped with weapons. Families of those working on the wall were encouraged to live inside of the city to prevent them from falling into the hands of any enemy. Additionally, Nehemiah stationed trumpeters at strategic points around the city. In the event of an attack, everyone was to rally to the place where the trumpet was being sounded. The strategy of using half the men to work and half of the men to stand guard allowed the work to progress very quickly.

Application

Sometimes the work of the church is best accomplished when various people are called to take on various tasks. It is when each person takes his or her duty seriously that great things begin to happen. Consider for a moment the variety of tasks required for a "successful" Sunday to unfold. Greeters are needed at the door. Sunday school teachers are needed in the classes. Childcare workers are needed in the nursery. Choir members are needed in the loft. Ushers are needed to take up the offering. Deacons are needed to pray. Maintenance workers are needed to heat and cool the building. Television and sound personnel are needed to broadcast the service. I once calculated that it took about 70 people each week for my former church to function properly on a Sunday morning. Just as in the days of Nehemiah, every person had a role to play. Understand that no single role is of any greater or lesser importance than any other in the life and ministry of the local church. All are essential for the church to move forward. What I want you to appreciate this morning is your importance in the work of your congregation. Some build while others protect. Some teach while others serve. Some pray while others preach. Take that talent that you possess, that passion that burns within you, and find a place in the church to give expression to that gift. Be faithful. Be present. Be excited. Be used. When all of us serve in whatever ways God has called us to serve, the church will move forward. Find your spot and do your thing.

Prayer

Dear Father, help us to see with great clarity, the place you wish for us to serve. May we then serve to bring you glory. Amen

Day 418 — Nehemiah 5: Occupy Jerusalem

> "I also shook out the folds of my robe and said, 'In this way may God shake out of their house and possessions anyone who does not keep this promise. So may such a person be shaken out and emptied!' At this the whole assembly said, 'Amen,' and praised the Lord. And the people did as they had promised." Nehemiah 5:13 (NIV)

Observation

In this passage, Nehemiah is addressing the economic downturn that affected many of the Jews living in Jerusalem. Because of famine and poverty, many of the Jews had become vulnerable to extortion by the rich and powerful. Many had been forced to sell their farms. Others were paying exorbitant interest on loans. Still others had to sell their children into slavery to avoid losing all they had. Nehemiah gathered the leaders, both the wealthy and the politically powerful, and challenged them to honor God by refusing to participate any longer in such a system of greed and exploitation. The leaders agreed. In a prophetic act, Nehemiah then shook out his robe declaring that God would shake out those who refused to keep their promise. The threat was that God would leave them shaken and emptied if they failed to keep their word.

Application

Does our "need for greed," our obsession to have more and more, become exploitative in the lives of others? While most of us would never consider ourselves to be a part of the global problems of poverty and sweat-shop slavery, our actions might contribute more than we think. The truth is that most of us live in excess. We buy more than we need. We possess more than our fair share. Think about it... how many of us have closets stuffed to overflowing because we always have to have the latest and greatest styles? How many of us have canned goods in our pantries or leftovers in our refrigerators that we have to throw out because they get outdated because we didn't really need them? How many of us have more than one computer, more than one TV, more than one phone, etc.? We have conditioned ourselves to live at levels of excess that force us to ignore the needs of the poor around us. Add up your credit card debt or the amounts of your loans that you are paying when you just "had to buy something you wanted on credit." (Not something you needed, but something you wanted.) The more we encumber ourselves with the obligations of excess, the less we are able to share with those in need. When the next Christmas shopping season hits full stride, let me challenge you to think a little less selfishly. Your simple restraint while shopping could allow you to be more generous toward the needy. It's not all about you. Some of your blessings from God were meant to find their way into the hands of others.

Prayer

Father, forgive our excesses and create in us, hearts of generosity and compassion.

Day 419 — Nehemiah 6: It's a God Thing

> "When all our enemies heard about this, all the surrounding nations were afraid and lost their self-confidence, because they realized that this work had been done with the help of our God." Nehemiah 6:16 (NIV)

Observation
In this Chapter, Nehemiah tells of the opposition that he encountered from neighboring nations and kings concerning the rebuilding of the wall. These enemies were attempting to discourage the work and prevent the wall's completion. In fact, several even plotted ways to draw Nehemiah out of the city to do him harm. Nehemiah continues to be faithful both to his God and to his God-given vision. He prays for God's deliverance from his enemies. The second half of the chapter tells of the completion of the wall. According to verse 15, the wall was rebuilt in just 52 days. When the surrounding nations heard that report, they became fearful, realizing that the work had been accomplished through the miraculous help of God.

Application
We are not alone. We need to remember that whenever God gives us a vision or direction, that God will empower that plan. Not only does God call us to attempt great things in God's name, but the Spirit works through us to accomplish God's purpose. The ancient Israelites achieved an extraordinary feat... they rebuilt the entire wall of Jerusalem in just 52 days... a task that should have taken years to accomplish. The reason for their success was simple. God was with them. It was a "God-thing" toward which they were working.

Sometimes God asks us to be a part of something that is greater than ourselves. Sometimes God wants a building built, a heart remade, a church transformed, a family united, a mission team sent. Through the work of the Spirit, God begins to allow a vision to grow in the hearts and minds of God's people. As the vision begins to grow, so does the list of resources and people for accomplishing that work. Suddenly and miraculously things begin to fall into place, and we have the joy of watching the work of God unfold. Want to be a part of such a plan? Then pray this simple prayer... "Father may your will be accomplished in my life. Use me as you see fit. May I do your will... nothing more, nothing less, nothing else." Believe me, if you are bold enough to make yourself available before God, your life will be used in amazing ways. Open your heart fully to God and watch how God will move. Even now, God is up to something big... something that only God can accomplish. The only question that remains is whether you will allow God to work through your life.

Prayer
Father, make our lives fit for service this day. May we know the joy of complete surrender. Make us pliable, usable, and willing to serve. Amen.

Day 420 — Nehemiah 7: A Fearful Reputation

> "I put in charge of Jerusalem my brother Hanani, along with Hananiah the commander of the citadel, because he was a man of integrity and feared God more than most people do." Nehemiah 7:2 (NIV)

Observation
As the walls were completed, Nehemiah appointed two men to serve as guards over the city. One was his own brother Hanani, who had visited Jerusalem and brought back a bleak report to Nehemiah in Susa (1:2). The other guard was Hananiah. Nehemiah put him over the citadel (fortress that protected the city) because of his faithfulness and because of his impressive fear of God. The remainder of this chapter is an account of a registration of the people who had returned to Israel following the time of captivity. Nehemiah feels called of God to make this census of the people. According to all the records he can find, along with the reports he has received, Nehemiah is able to account for 42,360 exiles who have returned since the king of Persia made provision for their release.

Application
Let's talk for a moment about reputations. For what are you known? How do people view your life and reputation? Are you trustworthy? Honest? Dependable? Hard-working? Loyal? Obedient? Kind? Or are you the opposite of most of those attributes… lazy, dishonest, and crooked? We tend to build our reputations one day at a time, one decision at a time, one promise at a time. After a while, the patterns we have established tend to "stick." The reputation is either good or bad, positive or negative. Notice the reputation afforded the man named Hananiah in our focus verse. It was said of him that he "was a man of integrity and feared God more than most." Integrity is easy to explain. The word means that he was honest, trustworthy, principled, and consistent. But what does it mean for him "to have feared God more than most"? Think in terms of respect for God and for the Word of God. Think in terms of awe and reverence for the authority of God. Think in terms of making a serious commitment to worship God through obedience each day. I wonder if those who know us best would ever use such a phrase when describing us? Do we fear God, and does it show? Are we seriously committed to God each day and is it our chief aim to honor God in all that we do? Today, you will add or take away a small component of your reputation. You will continue to forge the perception that others have of you. How will you live? Will you fear God more than most, or will you disappoint God like many of the rest?

Prayer
Father, may our lives reveal such a commitment to you and to your Kingdom that when people hear our words, see our actions, and learn our thoughts, they will know that we hold a healthy fear and reverence for your authority. Amen.

Day 421 — Nehemiah 8: A Powerful Word

> "Then Nehemiah the governor, Ezra the priest and teacher of the Law, and the Levites who were instructing the people said to them all, 'This day is holy to the Lord your God. Do not mourn or weep.' For all the people had been weeping as they listened to the words of the Law."
> Nehemiah 8:9 (NIV)

Observation
When the rebuilding of the wall was completed, the people of God living in Jerusalem were called to assemble within the city gates. A wooden platform was built and Ezra, the lawgiver, began reading the Word of God to all the people. Ezra read from early morning until midday. As the people heard the reading of the Word, they felt an overwhelming sense of conviction about the ways of God contrasted against the way in which they had been living. With hearts broken, they began to weep over their sinfulness. The priest challenged them not to grieve over their past mistakes, but to rejoice in the ways God was revealed to them through the Law. As they continued to read God's Word, they realized they had failed to properly observe the Festival of Booths to honor their ancestors who lived in temporary dwellings during the wilderness experience. So, they observed the festival with great fanfare.

Application
"For the word of God is living and active and sharper than any two-edged sword, and piercing as far as the division of soul and spirit, of both joints and marrow, and able to judge the thoughts and intentions of the heart" (Hebrews 4:12 NASB). As I read of the experience of ancient Israel, I have to wonder about the seriousness with which we read the Word of God. It is powerful. It is convicting. It is sacred. It is life changing. It is all that and more, but only to the extent that we are willing to let it change us. It can only affect us as are willing to read it and be challenged by its teaching. Most of us approach the Bible with the hope of having a "feel good" experience. We want the words to offer comfort, but not conviction... joy, but not a jolt... peace but not punishment. Have we really allowed it to speak to us and to challenge our way of living and thinking? When the Israelites listened carefully enough, they were brought to tears. It was that convicting. When was the last time that your reading of the Word brought you to tears? When was the last time that you felt its conviction, calling you to change? We need to hear the Word of God... really hear it. We need to be willing for it to change us, challenge us, and convict us. I invite you to take it seriously and let it transform your heart. Spend some time with the Word and in so doing, you will spend time with The Father.

Prayer
Father, may we treat the Word of God with the same seriousness that you do. Let it transform us, break us, renew us, and challenge us. Amen.

Day 422 — Nehemiah 9: The Power of Confession

> "They stood where they were and read from the Book of the Law of the Lord their God for a quarter of the day, and spent another quarter in confession and in worshiping the Lord their God." Nehemiah 9:3 (NIV)

Observation

As the ancient inhabitants of Jerusalem gathered to worship God after the completion of the wall, their worship included two significant things. First, they spent a quarter of the day reading from the Book of the Law. Following that time of encouragement and instruction from God, they devoted another quarter of the day to confession. For up to six hours they confessed their sins before God. (Within the text is a brief overview of the history of the Israelites that includes the confession of those moments when they acted disobediently.) At the close of the narrative, the people make a solemn vow to the Lord, putting it in writing, to show the sincerity of their resolve to follow God. The document is sealed with the names of their priests and leaders.

Application

I get the impression from this passage that the people confessed their sins in corporate fashion. That together, they verbally expressed to God and to each other the sins of their hearts. In an atmosphere of worship, they took the time to speak of their sins and seek the forgiveness of God. Surely, they experienced a time of cleansing and renewal. For most of us, at least in Baptist life, confession is rarely offered in the context of corporate worship. It is a rarity when a service is planned around the theme of confession and the worshippers are asked to stand and speak publicly of their sins. Believing strongly in the doctrine of "the priesthood of the believer," most of us confess our sins directly to God and not to each other. We take comfort in the thought that we do not have to "broadcast" our sins, nor even confess them to a priest, but speak of them directly to God. What we may miss however, is the accountability that corporate confession could bring. My fear is that we simply fail to confess often enough, even in the intimacy of our private prayer moments with God. When was the last time that you poured out your heart in confession before God? When was the last time that you took the time to list your sins and seek forgiveness? Most of us are guilty of the blanket prayer that states, "Search my heart and forgive me of my sins." Sometimes we need to do more. We need to pray specifically, openly, sorrowfully, and confessionally. We need to know the cleansing power of Christ when each of our sins are named and then forgiven by his blood. So find a time to do a little real confession. It's good for the soul.

Prayer

Father, teach us the importance of confession. Give us quiet moments of prayerful reflection in which we might name our sins and claim your grace. Amen.

Day 423 — Nehemiah 10: Setting the Standard

> "When the neighboring peoples bring merchandise or grain to sell on the Sabbath, we will not buy from them on the Sabbath or on any holy day. Every seventh year we will forgo working the land and will cancel all debts."
> Nehemiah 10:31 (NIV)

Observation

In this chapter, all the key leaders—the governor, the priests, and the Levites—signed a binding oath in which they pledged themselves to a renewal of faithful living. They promised to observe all the commandments of God. They promised to observe feast days, collect offerings, and keep their bloodlines pure. In our focus verse, they swear out an allegiance concerning the Sabbath not to buy or sell even from neighboring nations. They even pledge to observe the law of Sabbath regarding their fields and to debts owed. Their promises also include appropriate giving to the Temple tax, offering the first fruits of their harvests, and providing for the Bread of Presence. To the best of their ability, they pledge to honor both God and the on-going work of the Temple.

Application

Growing up in a pastor's family, there were certain standards that governed family life. There were things that we did and didn't do, because of a sense of obedience to our faith. For example, Sabbath rules were important. We didn't cut the grass, go to movies, or work on cars on Sunday. It was important to live according to a standard.

The ancient inhabitants of Jerusalem desired to honor God in ways that had been neglected for many years. They called themselves to a renewal of faith and lifestyle that would honor God. Notice that regarding the Sabbath observance, they wanted to raise a standard of godly living that would bear testimony to the peoples living around them. Their insistence on not buying or selling grain on the Sabbath would send a clear message to all, that they were serious about their faith and its demands. They wanted to set a standard and send a message.

Part of our discipline of faith is the setting of standards for our lives. Faith demands that we draw boundaries, live within parameters, and set a standard. We are called to be distinct, different, holy, and distinguishable from the world around us. We choose a life of such obedience because we want to honor our God. As we observe such a life of disciplined living, we also send a message. The message is one of allegiance, faithfulness, and obedience to the God we claim. It is as our faith matters to us that it testifies to others. The more consistent our walk, the greater our testimony. I challenge you this day to live a life worthy of the Gospel. Be faithful. Be intentional. Be disciplined. Be contagious. Set a standard and send a message.

Prayer

Father, may we set high standards and seek to live according to them each day. Amen.

Day 424 — Nehemiah 11: In Praise of Volunteers

> "And the people commended everyone who volunteered to resettle in Jerusalem." Nehemiah 11:2 (NLT)

Observation
When the wall of Jerusalem had been completed, a special process was put into place to encourage people to move back into the city. Key leaders lived in the city, but more individuals were needed to build the population. A lottery of sorts was held and one out of every ten from the surrounding villages was selected to move to Jerusalem. A process known as "casting lots" was used. The casting of lots was to determine God's will in the process. One out of ten was needed to repopulate the city to the level deemed necessary for its strength and viability. To be selected was to be "chosen" by God. Those who volunteered to move were commended by all the people.

Application
Sometimes volunteering is the right thing to do, although burdensome at times. In the life of my former church, we relied heavily upon volunteers to do the work of the church. Volunteers taught our Sunday school classes. They kept our children in the nursery. They handed out the bulletins. They sang in the choir. They cooked our meals. The list goes on and on. We would have been less of a church without their help. Most of the positions for which people volunteered were "less than glorious." In fact, many of the positions were downright difficult and took a lot of effort to do well. I admire those who continued to give of themselves week after week simply because it was the right thing to do.

Let me encourage you to do two things. First, commend the volunteers. Take the time to thank those who serve in the life of your church. Your thankfulness could find expression in many ways... maybe a hand-written note, a gift card, a warm smile, or a hug around the neck. Make sure that the volunteers who serve you each week know of your appreciation. Second, become a volunteer. Find a place to quietly serve the Kingdom. Without fanfare or pretense, find a spot to plug in and invest your life. Think of something about which you are passionate. Think of something that brings you both joy and satisfaction and plant your life in that spot. You will discover the joy that serving others brings and your heart will be made glad. You may or may not get the commendation of your peers, but God is watching and will reward you. Each of us needs a place to serve and I hope that you will take the time and make the effort to discover your unique place. Become a faithful servant and don't forget to thank those who are already in place, ministering in special ways.

Prayer
Father, thank you for allowing us to have places of service in your Kingdom's work. Teach us to serve well as we are reminded that every task, great or small, is vital to your work. Amen.

Day 425 — Nehemiah 12: Ready for Worship?

> "When the priests and Levites had purified themselves ceremonially, they purified the people, the gates and the wall." Nehemiah 12:30 (NIV)

Observation
The completion of the wall of Jerusalem resulted in a huge celebration of dedication. All the priests from the region, as well as all the musicians, gathered to lead the city in worship. A mass choir assembled, and the people sang and rejoiced over what God had done in their midst. It was said that the joy in Jerusalem could be heard for miles away. Notice how the priests prepared for that day. Prior to their participation in the celebration, they first purified themselves. Following their own purification, they purified the people, the gates, and the wall. In other words, before they led in worship, they were careful to ensure that they had purified their own hearts and minds to lead. The worship procession must have been an impressive sight. The worship choir, musicians, and trumpeters split in half with each half marching in the opposite direction on the top of the wall. The two sides met together near the Temple where the worship celebration began.

Application
I wonder what most of us do to prepare for worship each week. We assume that those who preach or lead in worship have prayed over all their duties, asking God to bless their efforts in worship leadership. But what does it take on behalf of every congregant to ensure worship is all that it can be? I remember as a child, certain routines that were followed. One was the proverbial "Saturday night bath," when the dirt of a childhood Saturday had to be carefully scrubbed away. I also recall shining shoes and making sure that my "Sunday clothes" were ready to be worn. I also remember how important it was to read my Sunday school quarterly so I could participate in class the following morning. Remember those days? We took the time to ensure we were ready for the day. What about now, as adults… how do we prepare for worship? Do we anticipate the day and prepare for it? Do we cleanse our hearts and minds? Do we ready our clothes and our lives? I believe that worship should be a very active discipline for us all. Sure, the preacher will ready his/her sermon, the song-leader will prompt the choir, the musicians will be prepared. But what about all the others who come to worship? Is there forethought and preparation? Is there a confession of sin and a cleansing of heart? Is there growing anticipation as the moments with God draw near? I challenge you to get ready for your experience of worship this week. Pray about what God might reveal. Purify your heart. Have your lesson ready and your shoes shined. Remember that you will be entering into the presence of God.

Prayer
Father, may we remember the Sabbath day and keep it holy. Amen.

Day 426 — Nehemiah 13: The House of God

> "So I rebuked the officials and asked them, 'Why is the house of God neglected?' Then I called them together and stationed them at their posts."
> Nehemiah 13:11 (NIV)

Observation
One of the key themes in the book of Nehemiah is his rebuke of the people's neglect of the house of God. It is apparent that they had rebuilt their own homes as the city of Jerusalem began to repopulate but had neglected the upkeep of the Temple. In fact, Nehemiah discovered that one of the main storage areas for sacred things had been occupied by a foreigner who was using it as a dwelling place. When Nehemiah discovered this, he threw the man and his belongings out of the storage place and demanded that all the rooms be purified. He then returned the Temple supplies back to this space. As a part of his continued leadership, Nehemiah reclaimed the Temple, set the priests back in place, and challenged the people to obey the laws of God once again, being especially careful to challenge them about marrying foreign women.

Application
Nehemiah makes a valid point about the upkeep of the house of God. Is it ever right to settle for mediocrity in terms of how well we maintain the buildings in which we worship God? Will we allow things to deteriorate at church in ways we would never allow them to deteriorate in our own homes? Reflect for a moment on the sin of ancient Israel. The people were careful to build new homes and maintain them and yet the Temple remained in a state of disrepair for years. To provide for themselves while neglecting the house of God was understandably seen as a sin before God. Maybe we suffer from the same transgression. Do we focus on ourselves and our dwelling places while we let the dwelling place of God suffer neglect? How is God honored when little attention is paid to the church building? I understand the tension that necessarily exists between spending too much on internal needs at church with the possibility of neglecting external giving towards missions. Obviously, we need to do both and find a good balance. But my point is that God is to be honored in all that we do. And if that is right, then how well we maintain the building matters, and... even how well we maintain our own bodies as dwelling places of the Spirit matters. We are called to stewardship. We are called to maintain both the brick-and-mortar house of the Lord as well as the house of flesh in which God dwells. It's easy to practice "deferred maintenance," especially in terms of our own bodies. Do a quick health assessment and if needed, take steps to improve your own version of God's house. We are called to honor God and part of that needs to include proper maintenance.

Prayer
Father, teach us to honor you through all that we do. May we be good stewards of both the church and our lives. Amen.

Day 427 — Esther 1: The Timing of God

> "But Queen Vashti refused to come at the king's command delivered by the eunuchs. Then the king became very angry and his wrath burned within him." Esther 1:12 (NASB)

Observation

The book of Esther is unique in several ways. First, it is one of only two books in the Bible named for a woman. (Ruth is the other.) Second, God's name is never mentioned in the book. Third, the subject of prayer is also never mentioned. Despite those factors, the book tells the story of God's salvation of the Jews during the time of the Persian empire. The story itself centers around a disobedient queen (Vashti) who refuses the orders of the king (Ahasuerus) and in so doing, is removed from her position. The decision is made to create a nationwide beauty contest to replace her. Esther is chosen, though her Jewish heritage is not revealed until later in the story. Because of her role in the unfolding story, the Jews will be spared from slaughter. This opening chapter speaks of the king's wealth and influence demonstrated by an elaborate party that is thrown during his third year of reign. So vast is the empire that people from India to Ethiopia attend the gathering, at which Vashti disobeys an order from her husband the king.

Application

What I find interesting about the story is the way in which God orchestrates events to bring Esther into a position to one day save her people. As you read the story, you discover how God has been at work arranging the people, places, and events to God's glory. What might seem like coincidence to some is the careful moving of God in the lives of the people.

God is never removed from the events of our lives. God cares for us and the details of our lives. God carefully arranges the situations, people, and moments that govern our days. Often, it is only in hindsight that we can trace out the movements of God's hand. We look back with amazement to see the ways in which God moved through the complexity of our days to accomplish God's purpose in our lives. For example, have you ever experienced one of those "God moments" when suddenly the right person just happened to be in the right spot at just the right moment? Or maybe a certain word of encouragement came at the precise moment you needed it? Those moments are not the result of mere coincidence or dumb luck. They are the evidence of God's movement in your life. God sweats the details. Be amazed at God's provision and protection in your life and praise God whenever you discover one of those moments unfolding.

Prayer

Father, we thank you that nothing in our lives escapes your notice. May we live confidently this day, knowing that you are at work in our lives. Amen.

Day 428 — Esther 2: The Problem with Anger

> "After these things when the anger of King Ahasuerus had subsided, he remembered Vashti and what she had done and what had been decreed against her." Esther 2:1 (NASB)

Observation
As the story of Esther continues to unfold, a new queen is to be selected for King Ahasuerus to replace his former queen, Vashti. The decision is made to gather beautiful women from throughout the kingdom to let the king select his new queen. It is very much a beauty pageant. The women are brought to the palace, given food and cosmetics (I kid you not, that's what the scriptures say), and they are eventually presented to the king. In this process, Esther enters the picture. She is beautiful in "form and face" and quickly catches the king's eye. He declares her to be the new queen. But go back to our focus verse for a moment and ask what caused the problem in the first place. Was it not the king's anger? Because he was angered by his wife, Vashti, he made some rash decisions that he later regretted.

Application
Anger can be a destructive emotion. To be sure, there are different kinds of anger. One kind is "righteous" anger, when we become angry about the things that make God angry. We should become angry when we see the will of God not being accomplished in the world. We should be angered over poverty, injustice, abuse, hatred, prejudice, or a lack of forgiveness. Such things disturb God, and they should disturb us as well. But most of our anger is anything but righteous. Typically, we become angry over selfish things. When we don't get our way, we become angry. When we lose a game, we become angry. When we get cut off in traffic, we become angry. When someone has a different opinion, we become angry. Most of our anger is over the wrong stuff. We get all worked up over things that are not all that important. And the real problem is that our anger leads us into angry action. Stupid action. Damaging action. Regret-it-later action. In anger, we sometimes say things and do things that inflict a lot of pain and hurt, and it can become very difficult to undo that which we have done. My counsel to you this morning is to live with less anger. Slow down. Remove yourself from the moment. Think through your actions. James 1:20 reminds us "for the anger of man does not achieve the righteousness of God" (NASB). It's difficult to love, speak truth, and offer grace when you are filled with caustic anger. James is right; you are never your best when you are angry. Anger is a human emotion. It is embedded in each of our lives. There is no use pretending that it's not just below the surface waiting to erupt. The key is to acknowledge its destructive potential. Handle your anger with care.

Prayer
Father, teach us that self-control is possible if we are controlled by your Spirit. Amen.

Day 429 — Esther 3: Lending Out Your Good Name

> "Then the king took his signet ring from his hand and gave it to Haman, the son of Hammedatha the Agagite, the enemy of the Jews."
> Esther 3:10 (NASB)

Observation
There are a lot of twists and turns in the story of Esther. At this point in the narrative, Haman, a court official whose jealousy over Mordecai (Esther's cousin) becomes destructive, tricks the king into writing a decree declaring that all the Jews living throughout the kingdom should be put to death on a single day. The king, who has been duped into believing such an action would ensure safety in his kingdom, takes his signet ring and gives it to Haman to seal all the letters to be sent out to the various provinces, commanding the leaders of each province to slaughter the Jews. These letters would carry the authority of the king because his seal was affixed to them. When the king placed his royal seal upon a document, it meant that he was willing to put both his name and reputation behind it. The seal represented his authority.

Application
My grandfather Roebuck was a Ford man. My grandfather Blair loved Pontiacs. Both were very brand loyal. If a car bore the Ford logo, Fulton thought well of its construction. Any car branded with the Pontiac symbol caught the attention of Sam. I get that. When we see a certain brand or logo, we make certain judgments about quality and value. Think about companies like Nike, Apple, and Coca Cola and how much they protect their mark.

On what are we willing to place our mark? What are we willing to have bear our name? In other words, are we proud of the things that are connected to our identity? Are we pleased with the reputation that follows us? We need to be careful of those things with which we are willing to be associated. We need to examine our involvements, our interests, and our activities and ask whether they bring honor to our good name and especially whether they bring honor to our Lord. We should care how our names are used. We should care about the reputation that we forge each day. Because we have been called to represent Christ in all that we do, our deeds should be above reproach, our thoughts noble, and our words consistent with the mind of Christ. Whenever we attach our name to something, people should be able to count on our authenticity and integrity. It always makes a difference how we behave and for what we stand because our lives reflect on Christ. We either help or hurt the reputation of the Kingdom by our spoken and lived-out testimonies. So be careful with the things on which you are willing to place your name. You represent more than just yourself.

Prayer
Father, remind us that we are to bear the image of Christ before the world. May others see consistency and integrity in all that we do. Amen.

Day 430 — Esther 4: Living in the Moment

> "For if you remain silent at this time, relief and deliverance for the Jews will arise from another place, but you and your father's family will perish. And who knows but that you have come to your royal position for such a time as this?" Esther 4:14 (NIV)

Observation

At a pivotal moment in the story of Esther, Mordecai (Esther's cousin) reveals to Esther the news of Haman's plot to kill all the Jews. He even sends her a copy of the king's decree. At first, she is reluctant to enter the king's presence to reveal the evil plot, for to enter the king's presence when not summoned could be punishable by death. It is then that Mordecai offers the words of our focus verse. He reminds her that without her intervention she, along with all the other Jews, will be killed. He also reminds her that perhaps she has been placed in her royal position for this time. She is to fulfill her purpose and destiny and in so doing, to save the Jewish nation.

Application

God has a purpose for your life. God has a destiny for you to fulfill. God has a plan that requires your involvement. The key is knowing both the time and place to play your part. The discernment of God's will can be tricky. Perhaps all of us search life-long for the answer to this question of God's will. Maybe the point is not to long for the moment when we finally feel as though we have discovered our sweet spot of ministry and purpose, but to find it all along the way. It is my belief that to discover God's ultimate will for our lives, we must actively seek God's will in the day-to-day stuff. To be honest, we sometimes see God's will most clearly only in retrospect. We look back at the events and people of our lives and see the way in which God carefully orchestrated some moment. We occasionally stand in awe as we consider the careful arranging of our lives to be used in some impacting moment.

There is always a bigger picture to God's unfolding plan than we can ever imagine. Though we may sometimes doubt our ability to be used by God, the truth of the matter is that God is in the process right now of preparing our lives for a specific purpose. There is a life that needs to be touched, an encouraging word that needs to be said, a wrong that needs to be made right, and a truth that needs to be revealed. And God is planning on using each of us to do such a work. Truthfully, we may not sense exactly when that moment will occur. We don't get an email from God saying, "This is the day!" So, the key is to be always faithful and ready. It is as we live an authentic Christian life, in which we attempt to be faithful each day, that God may use us in a special way. Don't worry about trying to find the right moment. It will find you. Just live today in gratitude that God is appointing you.

Prayer

Father, may we be used this day for your purpose and glory. Amen.

Day 431 — Esther 5: Healthy Heart?

> "Haman went out that day happy and in high spirits. But when he saw Mordecai at the king's gate and observed that he neither rose nor showed fear in his presence, he was filled with rage against Mordecai."
> Esther 5:9 (NIV)

Observation
Haman had been invited by Queen Esther to a private banquet with just the king, herself, and Haman in attendance. (Her goal was to earn his trust so that a day or so later she could reveal his jealous behavior to the king.) Haman, thinking that he had attained special privilege with the royals, left the celebration in high spirits. On the way home, he observed Mordecai at the king's gate and Mordecai did not give him the respect he felt he should receive. He was suddenly filled with rage. The joy and merriment that he had experienced moments earlier was completely erased by his disdain for Mordecai. He so despised Mordecai that he ordered a 75-foot-tall pole to be erected and planned to get the king's permission to impale Mordecai upon it.

Application
Pretty simple lesson here... hatred in our hearts can steal our joy. Our hearts can only hold so much. If we fill our hearts with joy and laughter, emotions like hatred and envy will be rooted out. On the other hand, if we fill our hearts with hatred and jealousy, we soon crowd out any semblance of hope and joy. In fact, most of us who seem to have little joy and laughter in our lives have let the darker side of our personalities win out. We forfeit the abundant life that we could experience in exchange for a lesser life of selfishness and greed.

So how can we do better? How can we claim a more noble life, filled with greater joy and peace? First, understand the high cost of anger. Anger can become a cancer that eats away joy and destroys our very souls. Don't let it linger. Don't let it dominate your life. Second, learn to value that which is good in others rather than dwelling on their flaws. Every life has its imperfections. Christ teaches us to love beyond the mistakes, and to offer acceptance beyond the differences. Third, take responsibility for your own attitudes and emotions. It is always easy to place blame on others for your own bad behavior. You alone have the power over your emotions. Hatred is a choice. Acceptance and forgiveness are also choices. Take a moment this morning and x-ray your heart. What do you see? Does it harbor grace, gladness, and joy? Or is it filled with bitterness, anger, and resentment? Which heart do you really want beating in your chest? The choice is yours.

Prayer
Father, may we possess both the heart and mind of Christ. Remind us that those things we choose to have dwell within us, will become the emotions that will emanate from us. Amen.

Day 432 — Esther 6: Kind Words Go a Long Way

> "'What honor and recognition has Mordecai received for this?' the king asked. 'Nothing has been done for him,' his attendants answered."
> Esther 6:3 (NIV)

Observation
Late one night, while having difficulty sleeping, the king ordered his servants to read the chronicles of the events that had occurred during his reign. He was reminded of the way in which Mordecai had discovered an evil plot against the king that was thwarted by Mordecai's careful handling of the situation. And so, in our focus verse, the king asks whether Mordecai has been honored publicly for his actions. When the king was told that nothing had been done, he quickly made plans to honor Mordecai throughout the city of Susa. And to rub a little salt in the wound of Haman's jealousy, the king asks Haman to lead the procession around the city declaring the words that the king had told him to declare, "This is what the king does for someone he wishes to honor!"

Application
Recognition and expressions of thanks are always appropriate when people do kind or brave deeds. Who among us doesn't like a pat on the back? Who among us is not encouraged to do even more when words of praise are offered? Simply put, it's nice to be thanked. Though it costs nothing to say a word of thanks, it seems increasingly rare these days to hear people get the recognition they deserve. All around us each day, there are those who serve the greater needs of our city and state, but who rarely get recognition. There are police officers who risk life and limb each day to protect us. There are firemen who stand on guard 24/7 to respond to our emergency calls. There are utility workers who keep the power flowing and postal workers who bring the mail. To be sure, none of these people do their jobs in the hope that someone will thank them, but how encouraging would it be from time to time for a kind word of praise to come from our lips?

There are also a lot of people who work behind the scenes each week in the life of the church, making sure that needs are met and things run smoothly. There are nursery workers who keep our children safe, teachers who break the bread of life with us, ushers who wait to meet any need we might have, custodians who ensure the building is clean, and greeters who make you feel welcomed. No one volunteers in the hope someone will thank them. They serve because that is their nature and heart. But a little encouragement could go a long way. I encourage you to find ways to thank the people who serve all of us each week, consistently, unselfishly, and faithfully.

Prayer
Father, thank you for the faithful servants of the church and community who give of themselves each week. Give us opportunities to express our sincere thanks. Amen.

Day 433   Esther 7: Forgiven Sinners

> "So they impaled Haman on the pole he had set up for Mordecai. Then the king's fury subsided." Esther 7:10 (NIV)

Observation
At a climactic scene in the story of Esther, the king finally sees Haman for who he is. Haman's deceit and jealousy are revealed and in an ironic twist, the 75-foot pole that Haman had intended to use to impale Mordecai is used instead on Haman. The king orders a quick execution. Esther's brave efforts to save the Hebrews bear fruit and the horrific plot to annihilate the entire race is thwarted. Haman has brought justice on himself and the people rejoice as Haman gets exactly what he deserves.

Application
We like it when stories end this way. We rejoice when villains are brought to justice and when evildoers get exactly what they deserve. In fact, we even get a little angry when some trials end with the defendant getting released by some loophole in the law or mismanagement of the legal proceedings. There is something within us that longs for justice to be served. That is, unless we are the ones being put on trial. Go back and read the book of Romans. Paul reminds us "for all have sinned and fall short of the glory of God" (Romans 3:23 NASB). He goes further to remind us "for the wages of sin is death" (Romans 6:23 NASB). Those are frightening words and concepts. Biblical truth proclaims our guilt. Our disobedience and rebellion are clearly noted. Not only is our guilt exposed, but our punishment is pronounced... death.

Now who wants "the guilty" to get what they deserve? Not Christ. Jesus has come to offer us freedom from our past and forgiveness from our sins. Though we deserve all that we should get, Christ intercedes on our behalf and bears away the price of our sins. Now read this verse from Romans, "But God demonstrates His own love toward us, in that while we were yet sinners, Christ died for us" (Romans 5:8 NASB). Because of the love of God expressed through Jesus Christ, we are the recipients of a "stay of execution." We are not going to get what we deserve. We are going to receive mercy and know the joy of walking blamelessly in the presence of God. There is a loophole in the law and his name is Jesus. So, if we have found such hope and rescue in the midst of our guilt, should we not learn to extend grace toward the guilty among us? Christ even proclaimed in the Sermon on the Mount that only those who are willing to forgive others would find the forgiveness they seek from God (Matthew 6:15). Let's model the heart of Christ. Let's love extravagantly, forgive generously, and live graciously.

Prayer
Father, teach us that one of the ways we express our gratitude to you is by acting with mercy toward those around us who also need a little grace. Amen.

Day 434 — Esther 8: Sealed Orders

> "Now write another decree in the king's name in behalf of the Jews as seems best to you, and seal it with the king's signet ring—for no document written in the king's name and sealed with his ring can be revoked."
> Esther 8:8 (NIV)

Observation

At the insistence of Esther, the king demands that a new decree be written and sent to the entire empire... a decree that would spare the Jews destruction and give them legal protection against their enemies. The king asks Mordecai to write the actual document in his own words. Then, because the king had given Mordecai his own signet ring, Mordecai was to seal the document and have it distributed throughout the whole empire. Because of the king's name and seal, the decree would have to be enforced.

Application

If you are fortunate enough to have a wooden deck on the back of your house, you know the importance of protecting the wood by sealing it. There are many waterproofing products on the market, as well as deck paint that will do the job. Sealing the wood ensures the longevity and strength of the lumber. It preserves, protects, and strengthens.

You and I need to catch the truth of this focus verse. There is a very important Biblical promise contained in these words. It's the idea of being "sealed." In the world of ancient Persia, once the king had sealed a document, it became official and irrevocable. Whatever the king had signed became as law and could not be retracted. Now move to the language of the New Testament. At least twice in his writings, Paul speaks of being "sealed" by God. "And you also were included in Christ when you heard the message of truth, the gospel of your salvation. When you believed, you were marked in him with a seal, the promised Holy Spirit" (Ephesians 1:13 NIV). Also, "Who also sealed us and gave us the Spirit in our hearts as a pledge" (2 Corinthians 1:22 NASB). Do you hear the echoing refrain? In Christ, we have been "sealed." Our salvation has been granted and our destinies secured. Because the King of all kings has declared it, the decree is irrevocable. There is no force, no power, no enemy that can snatch us out of his hands. And... as a further reminder of that promise, God has given us the Holy Spirit to dwell within us. Each time the Spirit offers us a word of encouragement, or gives us a moment of protection, or offers us a morsel of wisdom, we should be reminded not only of the Spirit's work in our lives, but also of our inclusion in God's Kingdom. We are sealed. Protected. Saved. Spend a moment this morning thanking God that your name has been written forever in the Lamb's Book of Life.

Prayer

Father, we thank you that in Christ you have sealed us securely in your Kingdom. May we rejoice today, knowing that we are kept safe in your arms. Amen.

Day 435   Esther 9: Start a Tradition

> "The Jews took it on themselves to establish the custom that they and their descendants and all who join them should, without fail, observe these two days every year, in the way prescribed and at the time appointed."
> Esther 9:27 (NIV)

Observation
Our focus verse describes the establishment of the Feast of Purim, which the Jewish faithful still observe to this day. The feast is a celebration of all that Esther did to preserve the Jews by daring to make her petition before the king. It celebrates the great victory that the Jews achieved against their enemies throughout the kingdom. This chapter describes the very forceful defeat of all the key enemies of the Jews throughout the empire. In total, over 75,000 were slain across the span of the empire. (The name *Purim* is taken from the word *Pur*, which means "to cast the lots." Evil Haman had "cast the lot" against the Jews, but ultimately was defeated.)

Application
There are a lot of traditions that swirl across the deep south during college football season each year. Every program has traditions and celebrations that mark the high moments of that school's legacy. Traditions like tailgating, fight songs, and impressive marching bands are all a part of the pageantry of each fall weekend. Part of the reason such traditions are kept is because fans want to remember and celebrate the moment when their team one a big game or defeated a huge rival. Maybe in terms of our faith story, there are a few things we should remember and celebrate.

One of the things that I want to draw from this portion of the story is the establishment of a tradition used to celebrate the blessings of God. It's my thought that as families, we seldom take the time to really celebrate God's blessings, much less turn our celebrations into traditions. Most families have the occasional celebration... like Thanksgiving and Christmas. But do we take the time to remember and celebrate various "God moments" in our lives? I know one family that has a birthday party to recognize the anniversary of their child's profession of faith. Each year, as a family, they celebrate what God has done. That child will long remember the day he came to faith. Is there some faith moment that your family should learn to celebrate? Maybe we ought to develop traditions around baptisms, mission trip experiences, special blessings, and even answered prayers. Maybe we should be as careful to remember the moments when God intervened in our lives as the ancient Israelites once did. Here's the point... the ancient Israelites developed traditions so that they would never forget the things of God. It wouldn't hurt us to do the same. Let's celebrate, lest we dare to forget.

Prayer
Father, teach us to remember and celebrate your work in our lives. Amen.

Day 436 — Esther 10: Reputation

> "Mordecai the Jew was second in rank to King Xerxes, preeminent among the Jews, and held in high esteem by his many fellow Jews, because he worked for the good of his people and spoke up for the welfare of all the Jews." Esther 10:3 (NIV)

Observation
The story of Esther concludes with a last statement of tribute for Mordecai. Notice the reason that he is held in such high esteem by his fellow Jews. He worked for the good of his people and he spoke up for their welfare at the critical moments when their destinies were in doubt. Over a long period of time, Mordecai worked on their behalf. He had a consistent record of doing the right thing. He was recognized both by the Persians and the Jews for his efforts. Honor was not simply handed to him, it was forged on the anvil of hard work, dedication, and consistent effort.

Application
Everything seems to earn a reputation. People, places, businesses, universities, airline companies are all evaluated. Reputations are forged over time. People base their impressions on things like customer service, value of product, and durability of items sold. We develop a trust in those companies that consistently provide a good product at a good price while also providing good customer service. We also label people with a reputation. Are they trustworthy? Loyal? Dependable? So, let's talk for a moment about the reputation that you have earned. There can be any number of descriptive words that could be used to describe it. Try these… hardworking, lazy, faithful, inconsistent, caring, indifferent, compassionate, hateful, driven, apathetic, peaceful, angry… and so the list goes. Obviously, there are some words on that list that we would love to have said of us and other words we would not. Though we cannot always control what others think or say, we can certainly work on building irrefutable evidence in terms of our character and reputation. It's all about consistency and courage. It's about doing the right thing over and over and over. Sometimes doing the right thing can put you in a very lonely place. Sometimes the flow of culture's stream may attempt to push you in the wrong direction and offer you false motivation. But remember, we are not called to be popular. We are called to be faithful. Your name and the history of your actions will probably never be recorded in the pages of some leather-bound book. But they will be noted by your family and friends, and in their lives your influence will be great. So, work on the reputation. Be faithful. Be consistent. Be godly. Be noble.

Prayer
Father, thank you for placing us in areas of influence. May our reputations and our actions bring honor and glory to Christ, and may they inspire others to follow Christ with greater consistency. Amen.

www.ingramcontent.com/pod-product-compliance
Lightning Source LLC
Chambersburg PA
CBHW070843160426
43192CB00012B/2289